Care and Capitalism

Care and Capitalism
Why Affective Equality Matters for Social Justice

Kathleen Lynch

polity

First published in 2022 by Polity Press
Reprinted 2022

Polity Press
65 Bridge Street
Cambridge CB2 1UR, UK

Polity Press
101 Station Landing
Suite 300
Medford, MA 02155, USA

ISBN-13: 978-1-5095-4383-0
ISBN-13: 978-1-5095-4384-7 (pb)

A catalogue record for this book is available from the British Library.

Library of Congress Control Number: 2021939042

Typeset in 10.5 on 12 pt Plantin
by Fakenham Prepress Solutions, Fakenham, Norfolk NR21 8NL
Printed and bound in Great Britain by CPI Group (UK) Ltd, Croydon

The publisher has used its best endeavours to ensure that the URLs for external websites referred to in this book are correct and active at the time of going to press. However, the publisher has no responsibility for the websites and can make no guarantee that a site will remain live or that the content is or will remain appropriate.

Every effort has been made to trace all copyright holders, but if any have been overlooked the publisher will be pleased to include any necessary credits in any subsequent reprint or edition.
For further information on Polity, visit our website:

politybooks.com

Care and Capitalism is dedicated to all those who work and struggle to promote a more loving, caring and socially just world, and to the memory of my mother, Molly Neylon-Lynch, who loved and cared for so many throughout her long life of 104 years.

Contents

Acknowledgements

Financial support from the Irish Research Council (IRC) Advanced Research Project Grant (Advanced RPG) (RPG2013-2) to research *Equality of Opportunity in Practice: Studies in Working, Learning and Caring* provided me with the opportunity to write this book. I am deeply grateful to the IRC for what Bourdieu termed 'the freedom from necessity to write'.

I also want to express my appreciation to the many universities that invited me to speak on affective equality and social justice in recent years, as these visits both enriched and challenged my thinking: the Autonomous University of Barcelona, City University of New York, Glasgow Caledonian University, the WISE Centre for Economic Justice, the Havens-Wright Center, University of Wisconsin Madison, Jagiellonian University, Krakow, Universities of Linköping and Örebro, Sweden, University of Melbourne, University of Macedonia in Thessaloniki, Greece, University of Oulu, Finland, University of Oxford, UK, Peking University, Beijing, and University of Siegen, Germany.

The deep concern and frustration that I have seen, felt and documented through research on classed/raced/ableist and other inequalities in education over several decades (in *The Hidden Curriculum*, 1989, *Equality in Education*, 1999, and with Anne Lodge in *Equality and Power in Schools*, 2002), and on the gendering of injustices under neoliberalism (with Bernie Grummell and Dympna Devine in *New Managerialism in Education: Commercialization, Carelessness and Gender,* 2012), demanded that I write about the injustices and carelessness of neoliberalism in greater depth, and in ways that not only examined its harms but identified ways of challenging them.

The book builds on earlier work with John Baker, Sara Cantillon and Judy Walsh in *Equality: From Theory to Action* (2004) and particularly in *Affective Equality* (2009). When *Affective Equality: Love, Care and Injustice* was published first in English in 2009, it generated an unexpected level of interest. It was translated into Spanish in 2014, and into Korean by Prof. Dr Soon-Won Kang of Hanshin University in 2017. It seemed to speak to people's need to talk and read about things that mattered to them in their everyday lives, and how institutions and structures often impeded them in their love, care and solidarity work. I wanted to re-engage with the many issues that *Affective Equality* raised, in terms of understanding inequality and social injustice, and the politics of social change.

The encouragement and support I received from several colleagues in University College Dublin were also very important to me. I would like to thank the staff in the UCD School of Education, and especially Dympna Devine, for their ongoing support. I am really appreciative of the support of recent doctoral colleagues, Luciana Lolich, Majella Mulkeen, Meabh Savage and Dorothy Conaghan, who were pursuing studies in related fields, and of inspiring postdoctoral fellows with whom I worked when writing, John Bissett, Maria Ivancheva, Manolis Kalaitzake and Monica O'Connor. Thank you all for engaging conversations and comments at seminars, and chats over coffee and tea.

Sara Cantillon, Professor of Gender and Economics at the GCU Glasgow School for Business and Society and Director of the Centre for Economic Justice, was one of the first people who encouraged me to write a book on care and capitalism. I am deeply grateful for her support throughout. Mags Crean, UCD postdoctoral scholar, social justice activist, and sociologist in the School of Education, offered ongoing guidance, inspiration and critical feedback while I was writing the book; during the isolation of Covid-19 lockdown her support was invaluable. So indeed was that of other activist-scholars, especially John Bissett, Cathleen O'Neill and Ebun Joseph.

I could not have written the book without the belief and support of John, my beloved; as always, his hands-on love and care, his wit and sense of humour kept me going during hard times. The engagement, kindness and thoughtfulness of our children, Nóra and John, and their partners, Stephen and Rose, were of greater importance than they may have known. I also appreciated the quiet encouragement of my many friends, and of my sisters and brother throughout. I am especially grateful to my sister Ann for the time and attention she gave to proofing the text at the pre-submission stage.

Many thanks too to the staff at Polity Press, and especially to Jonathan Skerrett, Senior Commissioning Editor in Sociology, Health and Social Care, for believing in the concept of the book. His courtesy, encouragement and professionalism throughout were more than I could have hoped for. I also greatly appreciated the time and attention Karina Jákupsdóttir, Assistant Editor, gave to the work during different phases of writing and planning. The copy-editing undertaken by Fiona Sewell was invaluable. I am extremely grateful for her meticulous work, and the amount of time and consideration she devoted to the text.

Although written in my name, this book is owned by the many people who have contributed to it, the scholars from different disciplines from whom I learned so much, the many people who contributed to the empirical research that underpins it, the people whose names I do not know whom I met at so many different public lectures and conferences who challenged and encouraged me, and last but by no means least, the community groups and students, inside and outside the university, from whom I learned so much.

Introduction

Capitalism is the dominant political-economic system of the twenty-first century (Streeck 2016): profit-oriented companies own and control most of the world's productive resources and capacities (Block 2018). The human cost of the concentration of wealth among so few is unsustainable (Oxfam 2021),[1] something that became even more evident during the Covid-19 pandemic that took hold in 2020.[2]

Although capitalism has varied in character over time and place, from merchant to industrial to neoliberal, the fundamental principles governing its operation remain constant (Patel and Moore 2018). It institutionalizes and legitimates class-based economic inequalities, frequently in deeply racialized and gendered ways. It builds on and consolidates pre-existing hierarchical, patriarchal and racial divisions of wealth and power, thereby producing and reproducing eliminable forms of human suffering. Capitalism also contributes to a corrosion of democracy and community, the encouragement of environmentally destructive patterns of consumption, and, in a world of nation states, a fuelling of militarism and imperialism (Wright 2010: 37).

As neoliberal capitalism is the dominant form of capitalism in the twenty-first century (Harvey 2005; Streeck 2016), and although it can vary in form between nation states, depending on the politics and institutional structures in place (Hall and Soskice 2001; Hall and Gingerich 2009), its fundamental operational principles and ethics remain the same. This book will focus on its multiple implications for caring.

Neoliberal Capitalism

As with all forms of capitalism, neoliberal capitalism promotes the protection of private property and the privatization of assets. In addition, neoliberalism promotes state endorsement of free market economic systems across national and global settings, and the institutionalization of market-based cultural logics and values throughout public and private organizations. The state is defined as an agent of capital by providing it with legal protections to enforce contracts, protect property rights, and protect markets in times of economic crisis (Friedman 1948; Hayek 1960, 1994). As a corollary to this, neoliberalism prescribes limited investment in public services, based on its ideal of a small, 'cheap' state in welfare terms. The primary purpose of education and welfare institutions is seen as conditioning and training individuals to be self-reliant, individually responsible and entrepreneurial. In this self-reliant society, the need for public services will be greatly reduced if not eliminated. To ensure the restructuring of public services, neoliberals advocate for new managerial policies and corporate-style accountability metrics and performance indicators. These are regarded as mechanisms for eliminating wastefulness, monitoring and improving performances, and maximizing 'customer' satisfaction (Chubb and Moe 1990; Friedman 2002).

Neoliberalism also builds on the idealization of choice in classical liberalism, prioritizing freedom over equality. In cultural terms, it is assumed that the market can replace the state as the primary producer of cultural logic and cultural value. The citizen mutates from a person with rights vis-à-vis the state to a market actor, a consumer, an economic maximizer, a free chooser. As neoliberal capitalism endorses a form of entrepreneurial individualism that is highly competitive and self-referential (Harvey 2005; Bröckling 2015; Mau 2015), and as it regards these traits as natural and desirable (Friedman 2002), it is antithetical to caring and affective justice in deep and profound ways (Federici 2012; Fraser 2016; Oksala 2016).

To create a new narrative to challenge the ethics of capitalism in its current mutation, it is necessary to move beyond the non-relational, self-referential ontology that underpins neoliberalism's culture and politics. This means building a care-centric, relational concept of the individual person and of the wider economic, socio-political and legal order (Folbre 1994; Tronto 1993, 2013; Fineman 1995, 2004; Herring 2020).

While it would be foolhardy not to recognize the power of markets and the economy in determining the dynamics of social life, it is equally important not to place 'capital at the gravitational centre' of all 'meaning making' (Gibson-Graham, Cameron and Healy 2016: 194). A new paradigm is required, one that moves beyond the narrow capitalocentrism[3] of current thinking about social change (Gibson-Graham 1996). People have a care consciousness (Crean 2018) that gives purpose and meaning to everyday life. Their relationalities are central to their identities, impacting on their ambitions and priorities (Lynch, Baker and Lyons 2009) in ways that could and should be harnessed intellectually and politically to drive egalitarian and care-led social change (Care Collective 2020).

Creating a Care-Centric Narrative

Because neoliberalism provides not only an *analytical* but also a *normative* framework for understanding the world, explaining it and prescribing how it should be, it has an ideological power that is deeply embedded culturally and politically (Boltanski and Chiapello 2005). One of the aims of this book is to help create a counter-narrative to neoliberalism, one that does not simply critique its harms but helps challenge capitalocentric modes of thought that have crowded out narratives of care and social justice in thinking about social change.

As the atomistic vision of the self is closely aligned with neoliberal capitalism, one of the first tasks is to put the relational self at the centre of meaning-making, to move beyond the idea of the separated, bounded and self-contained self. The goal is to develop a political and cultural appreciation of how the self is co-created, through struggles and negotiations in relationships, for better or worse, both collectively and individually (Herring 2020).

People are not only economic and political agents, but cultural and relational actors; they are involved in nurturing, loving, hating, fighting, relating and co-creating each other. The selves they become 'can only exist in definite relationships to other selves' (Mead 1934: 164).[4] Recognizing relationality and interdependency helps reclaim the language and logics of care that make people up in nurturing terms. It helps enhance an appreciation of affective relations in giving meaning and purpose to everyday life, and it enables an appreciation of the interdependencies of humans, not only on each other, but also on non-human animals, other living species and the Earth itself.

The affective care domain of life gives people direction and purpose in their daily lives and is central to how they define themselves. The primary love relations within families/households are what first create people in their humanness. This primary nurturing and co-creating work (what I have called *love labour*: Lynch 1989a, 2007) is complemented by the *secondary caring* relations of schools and local communities that are created, in turn, by adults caring for each other as friends, neighbours, colleagues and, ultimately, as strangers at the political level, through showing solidarity for the unknown other (Lynch and Kalaitzake 2018). A society that is not caring cannot create people who are flourishing, as 'citizens are produced and reproduced through care' (Tronto 2013: 26), and individuals cannot flourish without love, as it is fundamental to their 'subjective and objective well-being' (Gheaus 2017: 743).[5] Although the nurturing values that underpin care relations are generally politically domesticated and silenced, naming and claiming them can help reinvigorate resistance to neoliberalism. It can create a new language and a new set of values and priorities for politics.

As became evident during the Covid-19 pandemic, even in a capitalist society people are often moved by motives arising directly from consideration of the claims of others. Because relationality feeds into morality within people, this enables them to identify morally appropriate behaviour in themselves and others that orients and regulates their actions (Vandenberghe 2017: 410). They act from a sense of justice, from concern, friendship, loyalty, compassion, gratitude, generosity, sympathy, family affection and other such relational considerations (Midgley 1991: 5). Though these latter motives are not necessarily dominant at a given time (Sayer 2011: 172), they are living, and there to be named and claimed politically and intellectually.

While humans are replete with contradictions, having the capacity to be altruistic and self-interested, kind and cruel, thoughtful and thoughtless, which dispositions are encouraged, developed and prioritized is contingent not only on their personal circumstances but also on the cultural and political values of their time. As Folbre (1994: 250) observes, 'altruism does not emanate from our genes or fall from the sky. It is socially and culturally constructed, economically and politically reinforced.' Research by epidemiologists Wilkinson and Pickett (2009, 2018) has demonstrated the truth of this claim: the more caring societies are in terms of re/distributing wealth more equally, the lower the rate of poverty and violence, the fewer the status distinctions, and the more likely people are to enjoy better physical and mental health. If people are to thrive, they need to thrive not only as individuals, but as members of communities, and as political persons. Because of this we 'need to pay attention to the conditions that foster people's capacity to form caring, responsible and intimate relationships with each other – as family members, friends, members of a community, and citizens of a state'(Nedelsky 1993: 355).[6]

To bring *homo curans* ('the caring human'; Tronto 2017) to life politically, however, it must also be brought to life intellectually. This requires extending the narrative about equality and social justice 'outside the master's house' of mainstream thinking about social change, and about politics and sociology, and recognizing the salience of affective justice (Lynch 2014; Lynch, Kalaitzake and Crean 2021).

While economic and political self-interest play a key role in determining people's political priorities, focusing on these alone fails to do justice to the ties and commitments that bind people to one another relationally. As Mauss (1954) observed, the 'gift economy' exists and underpins much of social and political life; it contests the logic of the 'invisible hand' of the market. It incentivizes people to collaborate to help, care for and support each other in a reciprocal manner. But the morality that drives reciprocity extends beyond it as even the gift giver knows that some gifts cannot and will not be reciprocated at the individual level. There are many affiliations, affections and commitments that bind people to one another 'in defiance of self-interested calculation' (Nussbaum 1995a: 380). Care, in its multiple manifestations, matters not only for intimate relations but also for community and political relations; it is a public and political matter and a personal one. Resistance to the ethics of carelessness that is endemic in neoliberal capitalism matters because the 'brutish pursuit of individual ends is harmful to the ends and the peace of all, to the rhythm of their work and joys – and rebounds on the individual himself' (Mauss 1954: 98).

Building on the Work of Mothers and Others

As I was working as a sociologist in a school of education in the 1980s, my academic interest in relationality is long-standing. It was informed initially by the philosophical work of Noddings (1984) on the cultivation of caring in education, and the ground-breaking psychological research of Carol Gilligan (1982) and that of Howard Gardner (1983). Not only did Gilligan provide a missing feminist perspective on moral development, but her work laid the foundations for a more generalized care-based theory of moral behaviour, thereby paving the way for the recognition of relationality and caring. In a very different context, Gardner's pioneering work on multiple intelligences, and especially his recognition of personal intelligences (both inter- and intra-personal), helped move mainstream educational thinking outside its Cartesian straitjacket and a narrow cognitive understanding of rationality.[7] I saw his work, and that of Gilligan, as having revolutionary potential for a reawakening of educationalists to the importance of relationality in social, political, personal and economic life.

As love was not an accepted concept in sociology, something I learned when publishing on this subject in 1989,[8] Eva Kittay's *Love's Labor* (1999) was a reassuring publication. Her critique of Rawls' theory of justice, and her connection-based concept of equality 'grounded in our understanding of ourselves as inherently related to others' (ibid.: 70), resonated not only with empirical research I was undertaking, but also with my personal experience of living with children and young women in residential care, and my personal family-care experience. The capabilities approach of Nussbaum (1995a, 1995b) also informed my thinking, especially Nussbaum's validation of the rationality of emotions, and her appreciation of the importance of affiliations for human life and well-being.

While Gilligan, Gardner, Nussbaum and Kittay inspired me to pursue my interest in love, care and solidarity, their analysis did not address the impact of wider political and economic structures on the operationalization of care institutions and practices. Their work did not engage with capitalism or neoliberal capitalism in any overt way. Those who did engage, and inspired me to write this book, were care theorists and feminist across different disciplines, who were implicit if not in all cases explicit critics of capitalism (Held 1993, 2006; Nelson 1993, 1997, 2013, 2018; Stanley and Wise 1993; Tronto 1993, 2013; Folbre 1994, 2001, 2020; Sevenhuijsen 1998; Kittay 1999; Fineman 2004; Puig de la Bellacasa 2011, 2017; Mies 2014). I was also encouraged by the work of sociologists, such as Archer (2000) and Sayer (2011), who have demonstrated the importance of meaning-making outside of market relations, and by that of critical political theorists, especially Nancy Fraser (1997, 2008), whose work has explored at length the intersectionality of injustices within capitalism and how gendered and raced care-related social injustices are in practice (Fraser 2016).

Given the depth and range of the work of the 'founding mothers'[9] of care theory and research, it is a challenge to identify what this book can contribute that is new. Working at the interface of political theory, ethics and feminist theory, Tronto (1993) was among the first to develop the political argument for an ethic of care, demonstrating the moral significance of human relationships, dependencies and interdependencies. Along with Gilligan (1982) and educationalists such as Noddings (1984), Tronto's work (and that of Ruddick 1989, Held 1993 and Kittay 1999) played a major role in challenging traditional care-indifferent approaches to morality; in particular, she challenged the universalistic claims of Neo-Kantian theorists of justice within liberal political theory. I owe a huge debt to all of these scholars but especially to Tronto in terms of normative political theory.

Having spent a few years living in residential care settings, with children and young women who were not only poor but also seriously deprived of care, I always felt there was something missing in conventional Marxism's analysis of social injustice. As the lyrics of John Denver's song professed, 'Hearts starve as well as bodies'; people need bread, but they also need roses. Tronto's early work (1993) on the ethics of care provided the moral foundation for this argument, highlighting how all people are needy at some time in life. This book hopes to build on her work, and especially on her latest ground-breaking book, *Caring Democracy* (2013), by illustrating sociological challenges that must be addressed.

Like Tronto, I too want to put care rather than the economy at the centre of political concerns. I see the urgency of replacing the ethics of capitalism with the ethics of care. However, while the purpose of Tronto's book is to define what 'caring with' means within a democracy, *Care and Capitalism* is focused more directly on how the dynamics of neoliberal capitalism preclude caring, not only institutionally but also ideologically. One of the contributions of the book is its close examination of the complex relationship between liberalism, individualism and neoliberalism at an intellectual and cultural level. It demonstrates how creating a care-centric society requires a radical ideological shift from the deep-rooted individualism of liberal thinking, intellectually, culturally and politically. It also explains why contesting care-harming ideologies of neoliberalism, especially meritocracy, competitiveness and metricization, is vital for creating a cultural shift in political thinking about care.

The book also wants to build on the work of feminist economist Nancy Folbre; my contribution is not as an economist of care, but as a sociologist and scholar who shares Folbre's deep commitment to equality and social justice. Her ground-breaking analysis of how patriarchal thinking and institutions preclude an economic appreciation of the value of care work (Folbre 1994) was something that encouraged me, as I had seen first-hand the impact of that devaluation on women.[10] Not only did Folbre identify the economic value of caring as (mostly) women's work, she also identified the importance of care as a social good (Folbre 2008), making a strong economic case for paying carers well (Folbre 2006). Her critique (and that of Julie Nelson 1997) of individualistic models of thinking about human preferences in economics, especially in relation to the use of time (Folbre and Bittman 2004), and her related identification of the importance of structures and institutions in determining choices and patterns of injustice, are something that has informed the analysis in this book.

I share Folbre's recognition of the vital importance of care as a public value. As she rightly observed in *The Invisible Heart* (2001), women know they can benefit economically by becoming achievers rather than caregivers. But they also know that if all of humanity, and especially women, adopt this strategy, society as a whole will become oriented further towards more and more achievement and less and less care.

While Tronto (2013) has made a compelling case in *Caring Democracy* for placing care, not economics, at the centre of democratic politics, and Folbre, in *The Rise and Decline of Patriarchal Systems* (2020), identifies the reasons why care rather than the market should be central to economic thought, this book examines the many challenges that have to be addressed intellectually and culturally in a neoliberal capitalist era to create a more care-centric society and, equally importantly, a more care-centric academy. It examines some of the major changes in cultural and intellectual practice that are required to replace the ethics of capitalism with the ethics of care.

The book underscores the primacy of affective care relations in social life, exploring why equality in the doing and receipt of care is a central matter of equality and social justice. It explains why education, both culturally and more formally, is potentially a powerful site of resistance to neoliberal capitalism, and to the racism, sexism, ableism, speciesism and many other injustices on which capitalism thrives. The book investigates reasons why a capitalist-oriented education is a threat to affective equality and social justice more generally. It claims that creating a socially just and caring global order demands challenging not only the economics and politics of capitalism but also its core affective, cultural and intellectual values.

Care and Capitalism focuses attention on creating an ideological platform for change, by mobilizing new languages and narratives around care, social justice and affective equality in cultural and political discourse, especially by educating people about care and social justice across all levels of society. In Gramsci's (1971) terms, there is a 'war of position' that must be fought at an ideological level. Winning the ideological battle with neoliberalism will not happen by accident. Research and teaching priorities that are driven by academic capitalism (Slaughter and Leslie 2001; O'Hagan, O'Connor, Myers, Baisner, Apostolov et al. 2019), and an educational system that does not educate about love, care and solidarity or social justice, and that undermines respect for care in daily practice under its new managerialist rules of engagement (Lynch 2010; Lynch, Grummell and Devine 2012), cannot enable or resource people to think with care, or to think how to create an egalitarian and caring society. To develop *care-centric* thinking there is a need to rethink the epistemology underpinning academic scholarship (Medina 2013; Puig de la Bellacasa 2012), because how we come to know impacts on what we know. Creating knowledge is a relational practice (Harding 1991), and how we do it impacts not only on what we come to know, but on the known other. There is a need to move beyond the idea of science and research as a means of controlling nature (and other peoples), to the idea of science as a site of learning through cooperation, not only with other scholars, but with nature and non-human animals with a view to arriving at a mutual understanding, driven by concerns for social, species and environmental justice, and an ethic of care.

To date, care theory and research has focused strongly on human relations, and while this book is within this tradition, it tries to move beyond it by extending the discussion about care to the environment, focusing especially on the care and suffering of non-human animals. If we are to have a rich and inclusive concept of care, then care of the Earth itself and all living species are all part of the relational world that must be considered. The book argues that one cannot fully understand care without exploring its nemesis, violence. Human capacities to show love, care and solidarity are always shadowed by their opposites: the capacities to be care-indifferent, neglectful, abusive, hateful and even violent. Which capacities are called out and lived personally and politically is not accidental; it depends on what values and capacities are nurtured and enabled culturally and economically. While violence is not the preserve of capitalism, it is frequently exacerbated by it, as is evident in sexual violence, the violences of war and trade, the passive violences of letting people die through neglect and indifference, and the many violences humans inflict on non-human animals in the interests of profit and pleasure.

It is a call to action in terms of bringing care talk out into the public spheres of formal and informal education, cultural practices, and community, professional and party politics. As Raymond Williams observed, there are always residual sites of resistance because of the fact 'that no mode of production, and therefore no dominant society or order of society, and therefore no dominant culture, in reality exhausts human practice, human energy, human intention' (1973: 12). While recognizing the realpolitik of capitalist economic and political power, *Care and Capitalism* suggests that there are strong residual values of care in most cultures that could be ignited politically and intellectually, especially given what humanity has learned about the primacy of care during the Covid-19 pandemic. While making political culture care conscious is a major struggle, even within democracies with strong care traditions, we must start building resistance to the hegemony of economic-centrism under capitalism (Gibson-Graham 2006; Engster 2010; Tronto 2013; Alcock 2020; Folbre 2020). The book takes Iris Marion Young's (1990) critique of liberal political egalitarian thinking seriously, highlighting the primacy of structures, including ideological structures and institutions, that must be contested if there is to be a reframing of contemporary intellectual and political thinking based on social justice.

One of the reasons for writing this book was to draw attention to the importance of relational justice and affective equality (Lynch, Baker and Lyons 2009; Lynch, Ivancheva, O'Flynn, Keating and O'Connor 2020; Lynch, Kalaitzake and Crean 2021). It not only explores why affective equality matters, but, building on the work of Fraser (2008, 2010) and many others, it investigates how relational justice is deeply embedded with re/distributive justice, recognition-led justice and representational justice arising from the intersectionality of group-based identities, and the continuity of structural injustices institutionally through time. My long-standing commitment to teaching and researching about equality and social justice (Lynch 1995, 1999), and my previous theoretical and empirical research with colleagues (Baker, Lynch, Cantillon and Walsh 2004; Lynch, Baker and Lyons 2009; Lynch, Grummell and Devine 2012), inform the analysis throughout.

The Text

The book opens in chapter 1 examining ways in which the failure to substantively engage with the politics of affective relations, including the political economy of domestic *non-care* work in which care relations are embedded in classed and racialized ways (Duffy 2005), has contributed to misrecognition of their pivotal role in generating social injustices in the production of people in their humanness (Federici 2012; Oksala 2016). It explores how focusing on affective (care-related) inequalities would facilitate the politicization of care relations (Tironi and Rodríguez-Giralt 2017) and provide an intellectual frame for challenging the care-indifferent immoralities of capitalism (Müller 2019).

The first part of the book is devoted to examining care matters inside and outside capitalism. Because being vulnerable and needy is defined as a sign of weakness in pre-market (Nussbaum 1995a) as well as market societies (Fraser and Gordon 1997), the work of caring for needy and dependent others is not regarded as citizenship-defining (Sevenhuijsen 1998; Lister 2003). It is lowly work undertaken with lowly people. Chapter 2 explores how women, as society's default carers (and carers generally), are made abject by association. The devaluation of care, especially hands-on care and the hands-on manual labour that is intrinsic to it, and the devaluation of women are not just inextricably linked; the devaluation of care is a major *generative* reason why women are disrespected and undervalued within and without capitalism.

As the production and reproduction of social classes require care labour, both the care of people, and of those parts of nature that are available for exploitation and commodity production (Patel and Moore 2018), to get this work completed, capitalism builds on and exacerbates pre-existing gendered care exploitations (Dalla Costa and James 1972; Folbre 1994, 2020; Federici 2012), in classed and racialized ways (Duffy 2005, 2011).

As women are strongly socialized and morally impelled to do hands-on care (Bubeck 1995) in a way that men are not (Hanlon 2012), women live at the point of convergence between care and capital, the point where the conflicts between doing caring and serving capitalist values are felt most acutely, especially if they are poor. Given this structural positioning, carers and those for whom they care go on co-producing each other relationally, often in the face of adversity. They experience the conflicts and contradictions between the instrumental, exploitative, *homo economicus* logic of capitalism (Brown 2005) and the cooperative, nurturing and non-exploitative values that are intrinsic to caring labour (Tronto 1993; Robinson 2011; Puig de la Bellacasa 2017). They undertake necessary nurturing, relational work, labour that has no assigned market value and a very low voice politically. The ethics and values underpinning their work are not political incidentals, however, but cultural residuals (Williams 1977) that have the potential to be named, claimed and mobilized to confront the hegemonic values of neoliberal capitalism.

Chapter 3 explores the ways in which the making of love, through love labour, is a very particular form of intimate caring work that can be distinguished analytically from other secondary and tertiary forms of care labouring, owing to its inalienability and non-substitutability (Lynch 2007; Cantillon and Lynch 2017). Drawing on empirical research by the author on love and care, this chapter demonstrates how love labour's non-substitutability, as a social and personal good, means that the logics of love labouring are at variance with market logic, as love is non-commodifiable. It cannot be assigned to others without undermining the premise of mutuality that is at the heart of intimacy (Strazdins and Broom 2004). Given its uniqueness as a form of labouring, love labouring can be claimed as a political and sociological place of resistance. Staying silent about the uniqueness and non-substitutability of love labouring creates a myth that there are market substitutes, thereby allowing the carelessness of capitalism to persist.

Care, love and solidarity work require time and proximity, presence and attentiveness, inside or outside capitalism. Chapter 4 examines the conflicts between the time and space logics of capitalism and those of care, focusing on how a society that prioritizes capitalist values of competitiveness and speeded-up productivity can leave people time poor and spatially distanced from those for whom they care most, often leaving both the carer and those who depend on them under-cared-for. I draw on my own collaborative studies of caring to highlight many of the tensions that arise over time as a resource in a bureaucratized society governed by the ethics of productivity and competition. The limits and possibilities of technologizing care are also examined, showing how the technologizing of care, including the use of affective technologies, is strongly profit-led, and by no means care-enhancing in affective relational terms. Overall, the chapter illustrates how the competitive and appropriative culture of neoliberal capitalism compresses time, making affective relations appear incidental and marginalized, work that is done in leftover time, with leftover energy, after productive (market) work has been completed.

Part II investigates the interfaces between the political values of liberalism, individualism and neoliberalism; it explores how these values have been incorporated and reinvented under neoliberal capitalism in ways that are often contrary to caring and social justice. The goal is to underscore the ideological challenges that neoliberal capitalism poses to care and social justice especially when it is dressed up in the respectable languages of liberalism, individualism, competition, choice and merit.

Chapter 5 examines the methodological individualism that is endemic to liberalism, showing how the lack of a structural and group-related analysis within liberal thinking (Young 1990) leads in turn to a lack of attention to institutionalized, enduring injustices (Tilly 1999), including those in the care field. The chapter examines the rise of self-responsibilization as social reformism in the era of neoliberalism, and how this generates a culture of political carelessness towards the suffering of the unfamiliar public 'other'. Finally, this chapter investigates how duplicitous thinking within liberalism facilitates capitalism at the psychic level, by celebrating private charity and compassion, while sanctioning policy interventions to address structural injustices that generate a need for charitable giving in the first instance (Muehlebach 2012).

Individualism in its entrepreneurial self-interested manifestations is an integral element of neoliberal capitalism (Mau 2015: 20). Chapter 6 analyses the complex relationship between different conceptions of individualism, how these have evolved over time, and how they interface with the development of neoliberal capitalism and conceptions of care. The chapter shows how religious and secular interpretations of individualism have overlapped through time, moving from individual salvation to self-realization and self responsibilization. The ways in which neoliberal capitalism promotes the concept of the individual entrepreneurial self, the individual as a bundle of human capitals, devoted to the project of developing itself as *homo economicus*, are also explored. Finally, this chapter investigates how the moral individualism of neoliberalism is care-free and independent, albeit contested by a residual culture of love and care that can challenge it from within.

Chapter 7 analyses the role that *competitiveness, metricization and meritocratic evaluation* play in generating harms, first by defining many people as failures relative to others, and then by holding them responsible for not competing successfully in competitions they cannot win. The role that metrics play in exacerbating and enabling competitiveness, and in hierarchically ordering people in care-harming ways, is given special attention. The chapter also probes how the immeasurability of care means that it is discounted in the very care-related services where it is the foundational ethic of good practice. The failure to take cognizance of affective relations across multiple settings means that when named and claimed they can become sites of moral generation and resistance to the hegemonic ideals of care as a commodity.

Because it is impossible to pursue affective justice without examining its nemesis, violence, the third part of the book examines the relationship between care, capitalism and violence. As the experience of climate change and the coronavirus crisis demonstrates, life on planet Earth is relational and highly interdependent. Because of this, care is not just an issue for human relations, but concerns relationships with non-human animals and the natural environment. Chapter 8 is devoted to exploring the ways in which the ontological distinction between nature and society in Western intellectual thought has provided a moral justification for the domination, and frequent destruction, of other species, non-human animals and the environment (Patel and Moore 2018). The chapter outlines reasons why social justice theorists should recognize the moral status of non-human animals as sentient beings that can and do experience intense and prolonged suffering at human hands. Chapter 9 opens with a discussion on why debates about violence and care occupy separate academic spaces in sociology, briefly examining the implications of this for understanding the interface between care and violence. While recognizing that war, abuse and violence long preceded capitalism, the chapter explores how agents of neoliberal capitalism and the state are active in the precipitation of violence, both separately and conjointly, especially in institutional contexts. The racialized and gendered character of the violence that underpins profiteering in trafficking, and in both the care and sex industries is explored. The chapter concludes by noting how unregulated profiteering can deprive people of a livelihood, health care, clean water and/or clean air, but is not registered in the calculation of the costs of capitalism. It is regarded as an unaccountable externality rather than a process of violation (Tyner 2016). This chapter tries to draw attention to how an ethic of care could help mitigate violence, not only in the personal relations but in the wider political order (Held 2010), not least because violence, including terrorist violence, is often instigated by those who are experiencing the geopolitical harms of globalized capitalism, directly or indirectly.

Ways in which neoliberal capitalism is imposing an alien market logic on affective relations are re-examined in the conclusions in part IV, and reasons for moving beyond a capitalocentric way of seeing the world are reiterated. As loving, caring and showing solidarity are endemic to being human, capitalist logics cannot be allowed to redefine the meaning and making of humanity itself. The 'war of position' (Gramsci 1971) between neoliberal capitalism and the values and practices of love, care and solidarity, *and* related political, economic and cultural justice, needs to be planned, organized and funded if it is to persist over time. Creating a new narrative will require both formal and cultural education, and ongoing mobilizations across social movements by progressive activists and scholars, and especially by women, carers and those who need care, which is all of humanity at some point in their lives. And it will be important to remember when doing this work that there is no end time in the pursuit of social justice and the creation of a caring world.

The book ends with a short postscript on the care lessons from the Covid-19 pandemic. This postscript examines some of the dangers of 'privileged' ignorance (Medina 2013) in defining social justice and care matters that the pandemic exposed, as well as demonstrating how primary care was constrained during the pandemic. The lessons learned from the early deaths and isolation of older people in residential care, and the increased corporatization of care, are also examined, as is how the pandemic demonstrated that both a care/needs-based and a rights-based justice perspective are necessary because one is incomplete without the other (Casalini 2020).

1

Care and Capitalism: Matters of Social Justice and Resistance

As the creation, repair and maintenance of human life cannot be undertaken without care (Tronto 1993), the affective relations that produce (or fail to produce) nurture are structural matters that are central to social justice and politics. This chapter examines ways in which the failure to substantively engage with the intellectual, political and economic significance of affective relations of love, care and solidarity has contributed to their misrecognition as sites of injustice (Folbre 1994; Federici 2012; Oksala 2016).

Affective relations are those nurturing-oriented care relations, and nurturing dimensions of other social and species relations, that humans engage in to co-create, support and enrich each other and the non-human world. There are three sociologically distinguishable contexts in which affective relations operate in the social world: the primary sphere of intimate love relations; the secondary sphere of professional, neighbourly and community care relations; and the tertiary sphere of solidarity-led political relations with largely unknown others (Lynch 2007). Care of other species and the environment is a further site of affective relations, albeit not a social-specific one. While each set of care relations is discrete, they are built on mutual trust. When they are broken or defaulted on, they are potentially harmful and abusive. Like all human relations, affective relations are embedded in relations of power, status and wealth that generate conflicts and contradictions within (Lynch, Baker and Lyons 2009; Care Collective 2020).

The chapter opens with a discussion of how affective relations of love, care and solidarity have been peripheralized across different disciplines in the social sciences. It examines the implications of this neglect for sociological and socio-political understandings of nurturing as a site of praxis and politics. Following this, an analysis of the different dimensions and forms of affective relations is presented, and the reasons why affective inequalities matter for social justice are explored. The third section is devoted to analysing how neoliberal capitalism promotes carelessness and affective injustices by undermining people's capabilities and resources for nurturing work. Finally, the chapter explores how the unincorporated and previously silenced political character of affective relations makes it a residual space (Williams 1977), a site of resistance for radical political thinking at an ideological level.

The neediness of the human condition leads to interdependencies that generate feelings of belonging, appreciation, intimacy and joy, but also feelings of ambivalence and anxiety, tension and fear. It is only when we acknowledge the challenging reality of our shared dependence, and the irreducible differences between us, that we can fully appreciate what a new politics of care might involve (Care Collective 2020: 21–31).

Neglect of Affective Relations

From Hobbes and Locke to Rousseau and Kant, and up to and including Rawls, Western liberal political theorists upheld a separatist view of the person, largely ignoring the reality of human dependency and interdependency (Nussbaum 1995a). As contractual models of social relations tend to inform dominant moral theories, and as these are built on liberal models of social relations between strangers (Held 2006: 80), the role of moral judgement and concern for others is marginalized in political understandings (Benhabib 1992). The separatist concept of the person and the focus on contractual models of social relations have combined to blind political theorists also to the material significance of care relations as central matters of social justice (Tronto 2013: 7–11).

Within classical economics, the core assumption has been that the prototypical human being is a self-sufficient rational economic man (*sic*) (Ferber and Nelson 1993; Folbre, 1994, 2001). Within sociology, neither Marxist, structural functionalist nor Weberian social scientists identified any major role for the affective system of social relations independent of the economy, polity or status order. The affective domain was defined almost exclusively in terms of the heterosexual family, as exemplified in the work of Talcott Parsons. Caring was assumed to be 'natural work' for women, not an autonomous system of social relations that operated both inside and outside families. In Marxist, and even neo-Marxist feminist, traditions, domestic work and care labours were defined as unproductive, creating use value but not exchange value (Engels 1942; Mitchell 1971).

The indifference to matters of vulnerability and inter/dependency in the human condition led to the framing of social injustices primarily in terms of the coercive political relations of the state and the economic relations of market economies, and thereby in terms of inequalities of income and wealth, status and power. This is exemplified in the three key conditions Nancy Fraser lays down as essential for realizing the social justice principle of participatory parity, namely equality in economic relations, political relations and cultural relations (Fraser 2005). The ways in which affective relations operate as a discrete and relatively autonomous site of social relations that impact on participatory parity is not conceptualized within this framework, as it is not defined as a key site of politics. As the production and reproduction of labour power are integral to the survival of capitalism (Dalla Costa and James 1972; Federici 2012), and as they cannot be completely commodified and 'brought into the sphere of market transactions' (Oksala 2016: 299), any theory of justice must take account of how care relations impact on partici-patory parity in everyday life.

Ontological impediments to recognizing affective relations

As sociable beings do not exist prior to their relatings (Mead 1934; Haraway 2003: 6), caring and relating share ontological roots (Puig de la Bellacasa 2017: 69). As relatings inevitability create interdependencies (Puig de la Bellacasa 2017: 72), and at times dependencies, care is a necessity, not an optional extra for human survival (Tronto 1993; Collins 2015). Without care, in all its forms, people would not survive, given the high dependency of humans at birth and at times of vulnerability (Kittay 1999; Fineman 2004).[1] To develop a sense of affirmation and recognition as an individual person of value and worth, love is also necessary. It is through love that the individual can grow and gain confidence in her/himself as an incarnated individual capable of feeling emotions (Honneth 1995, 2003). While caring, and especially loving, can be individual-istic or dyadic in character, caring is not necessarily individualistic. Caring about the needs of unknown others is foundational to public welfare and to the principle of solidarity; it is a moral and benevolent motivation to alleviate or prevent the suffering of others (Rorty 1989; Halldenius 1998; Arnsperger and Varoufakis 2003).

Despite these care realities, there are doxa-like[2] ontological assumptions within the social sciences that frame the subjects of sociological and political analysis individually rather than relationally. This has profound implications for the understanding of the politics, economics and culture of social life and social change (Archer 2000). The scope, meaning and normative dimensions of social actions are framed differently depending on whether an individual or relational ontological frame is employed (Mooney 2014: 36–8).

The first ontological impediment is the resistance to recognizing the vulnerability of the human condition. There appears to be a refusal to acknowledge that all humans are subject to events, and to the power and influence of other persons, over which they lack control, regardless of their 'virtue or rational will' (Nussbaum 1995a: 366). While dependency may be contingent and episodic, vulnerability is a constant feature of the human condition (Fineman 2008), making even the most autonomous and independent person liable to harm, not least because of the vulnerability of the human body (Vaittinen 2015; Engster 2019).

The scope, intensity and persistence of the non-recognition of vulnerability and inter/dependency has been documented by feminist scholars across many disciplines, (Gilligan 1982; Benhabib 1992; Tronto 1993; Sevenhuijsen 1998; Kittay 1999; hooks 2000; Fineman 2004, 2008; Held 2006; Ferguson 2014). Their work shows how care and love are both endemic to human relationality and have liberatory potential, not least because they generate a motive and desire for justice (Collins 1990: 197) and give people the strength to oppose domination (hooks 2000: 104). Love and care energize and motivate people to act other-wise rather than self-wise, both personally and politically (Boltanski and Porter 2012). However, this scholarship is corralled as 'feminist', outside the mainstream. It is often ignored by male scholars (Hawkesworth 2006), including those writing about the significance of affective relations in politics (Hardt and Negri 2005).

A second impediment arises from the disrespect for how central emotions are to social and political life, and particularly the emotional work involved in producing human beings through nurturing. The concept of rationality that dominates much of public life, namely economic utilitarianism, defines people as 'rational maximizers of satisfactions' and presumes that emotions are distinct from rationality (Posner 1997). Yet reason and value are not polarized concepts analytically (Vandenberghe 2017), something economists (Kahneman 2003; Loewenstein 2010), sociologists (Barbalet, 2002) and political theorists recognize (Nussbaum 2001), while contemporary neuroscience demonstrates how the neural mechanisms for reason and emotion are not entirely separate in the human brain: feelings aid reasoning rather than being its antithesis (Damasio 1994). Furthermore, empirically established facts can be both empirically true and normatively and emotionally engaged (Sayer 2011: 36–41). Failing to recognize the link between reason and emotion has contributed to an incomplete and even alienated view of social life (Sayer 2017: 474), including an appreciation of how emotions matter in politics (Ahmed 2004).

A third impediment arises from the presumption of self-sufficiency as an ideal human state. Western political theorists have idealized independence as a sign of maturity and growth, placing a premium on a human condition that is never fully realizable (Kittay 1999; England 2005). The presumption of independence mutates from an analytical presumption into an ethic of good social practice; what is presumed to be typical becomes desirable. In so far as it downgrades relationality, this type of political thinking has glorified a concept of the person that is potentially unethical: it is assumed that to be detached, and accountable primarily to the separated self, represents the ideal form of self-realization.

The fourth impediment to recognizing the significance of affective relations arises from the way principles of value neutrality have exercised axiological standing in social scientific analysis generally, and in sociology in particular (Sayer 2017; Vandenberghe 2018). While maintaining the separation between fact and value is vital to avoid representing a priori assumptions and values as empirically valid 'facts', the dichotomy also presents unique problems for research because the analytical distinction between fact and value is a false binary in sociological terms, not least because facts are 'entangled' with values (Gorski 2017), and values, when transformed into subjective beliefs, are also factual realities (Fuchs 2017).

The failure to recognize the role of values as constituting social life, and not just regulating it (Vandenberghe 2018), has led to a situation where it is often assumed that social actors are maximizing utilitarians, leading to the analytical neglect of the other-centred normative social actions (Archer 2000; Sayer 2011). Indifference to others is taken as normal, leading to a wider political understanding of indifference as both 'standard and appropriate' (Held 2006: 83).

In sum, the failure to appreciate the role of nurturing work as a politically salient dimension in the production of social life, the resistance to recognizing the full vulnerability of the human condition, the lionizing of self-sufficiency as virtue, and the failure to appreciate the complex ways in which values, especially those arising from other-centredness, are not just regulatory but constitutive of social life comprise four ontological impediments to recognizing the importance of love, care and solidarity for the production of people in their relationality. The summation of these ontological influences has led to a failure to appreciate the significance of the relational self, thereby missing 'a whole dimension of moral life' (Kittay 1999: 51) that is central to research on social justice.

Affective Equality

As the experience 'of being *needy*[3] is shared equally by all humans' (Tronto 2013: 29), theories of justice must take cognizance of the endemic inter/dependency and vulnerability of the human condition. Relationality has both *distributive* and *contributive* implications for justice: the neediness and vulnerability of life make love, care and solidarity crucial for survival at the very least, and for a good life at best. Being deprived of these experiences individually and collectively is therefore a *distributive* injustice. Just as love is an important resource in human life (Gheaus 2017), so too are care and political solidarity. Those who receive all three of these forms of nourishing can flourish more than those who do not.

Because doing loving, caring and showing solidarity all require time, effort and energy, they involve work. When this work is not recognized and rewarded, those who do most caring experience a *contributive* injustice similar to those identified by Gomberg (2008) and Sayer (2009). Caring people,[4] in all their different manifestations, are not recognized for their contribution to the good of society. As women are the default carers globally, intellectual and political silences about the primacy of nurturing work in producing and maintaining life make them vulnerable to exploitation (Oxfam 2020).

Affective relations are not social derivatives subordinate to economic, political or cultural relations in social life. Affective relations produce people in their humanness, as sociable beings in-and-of themselves (Oksala 2016: 297) These relations operate as a relatively autonomous field of social practice within and through which inequalities and exploitations can and do occur, just as they occur in the economic, political or cultural sphere (Baker, Lynch,

Cantillon and Walsh 2004; Lynch, Baker and Lyons 2009). They are productive, materialist human relations that constitute people mentally, emotionally, physically and socially, both positively and negatively. When relations are liberatory and non-alienating (that is, not simply instrumental and driven by exchange value) they are positively productive of our humanness (Dussel and Martinez 2003). The absence of liberatory, non-alienating relations produces neglect, harm and loss and is keenly felt at institutional, professional and personal levels (Mol 2008; Feeley 2009; Lynch, Grummell and Devine 2012; McDonald, Lolich, Timonen and Warters 2019).

The material impact of affective relations of love, care and solidarity is one of the major reasons they are of such significance for the politics and sociology of social justice and social change. Without the nurturing resources invested in them, not only as children but also as adults, people would be unable to participate on equal terms with others in social life (Gilbert 2010). Because love in particular 'has significant, and non-instrumental, non-substitutable and widely recognised value' (Gheaus 2017: 740), those who are unloved and *uncared for*, including in public institutions such as schools or residential care homes, lack a sense of care and love security that is required in order to learn (Commission to Inquire into Child Abuse 2009; Feeley 2014). In contrast, public investment in solidarity expressed through good welfare, health and education produces social goods such as trust and better physical and mental health (Wilkinson and Pickett 2009, 2018).

Bonds of intimacy, friendship and/or kinship and belonging are frequently what bring meaning, warmth and joy to life, while sustaining intimate relationships, friendships and trusted community relations all contribute to human well-being (Layard 2005; Rodríguez-Pose and von Berlepsch 2014). Being deprived of the capacity to develop nurturing affective relations, or of the experience of engaging in them when one has the capacity, is therefore a serious human deprivation and an affective injustice.

Because knowing how to love, care and show solidarity, and having the resources to act on this knowing, does not happen by accident, creating an affectively egalitarian society means creating social systems and institutions where people are resourced and enabled to receive as much love, care and solidarity as is humanly possible. While it is not feasible to force people to care for others, as there is a voluntary dimension to personal care relationships, nevertheless it is possible to create the political, economic, cultural and legal conditions that either enable or disable care capacities within individuals, institutions and organizations. Affective equality is therefore both an *interpersonal* and a *structural* matter; it is about maximizing the capacity of peoples *and* societal institutions to create, maintain and resource the affective relations that produce love, care and solidarity.

At the intimate level, it is about protecting and enabling primary care relations to ensure they are as nurturing as possible, including enabling and resourcing the love labouring work that non-substitutable affective relations involve (Lynch 2007; Cantillon and Lynch 2017). Affective equality also involves ensuring that people have the capacity to create nurturing caring relations outside of family, friends and intimate others. Nurturing needs to be resourced and enabled in secondary sites of caring, including childcare centres, hospitals, care homes for older/vulnerable adults, and other social institutions where the work involved has a care dimension, including education, health care and welfare particularly. Finally, affective equality is about promoting and sustaining care for strangers in the wider political domains, in one's local community, and at regional, national and international levels.

Figure 1 below gives a visual representation of the three major lifeworlds where love, care and solidarity operate. First, there is the world of primary, intimate relations where there is strong attachment, deep engagement and intensity. These love relations involve high interdependency and are characterized by strong attachments, intimacy and responsibility over time. While they vary in form cross-culturally, they arise from inherited or contractual dependencies or interdependencies and are people's primary care relations. The prototypical relationship in this circle is that between parents and children. Even if little love labour is invested in this intimate world, or if there is abuse or neglect, these relationships retain a high level of personal and social significance.

Secondary care relations are lower-order interdependency relations. While they involve care responsibilities and attachments, they do not carry the same depth of moral obligation in terms of meeting dependency needs, especially long-term dependency needs. There is a degree of choice and contingency about secondary care relations that does not apply to primary relations. Secondary relations characterize outer circles of relatives, friends, neighbours and work colleagues where there are lower-order affective engagements in terms of time, responsibility and commitment.

Tertiary care relations are solidarity relations that generally involve unknown others and do not involve intimacy. They are the political expression of care relations (Boltanski and Porter 2012). Sometimes solidarity relations are chosen, such as when individuals or groups work collectively for the well-being of others whose welfare is only partially or not immediately related to their own, or solidarity can be imposed through laws or moral prescriptions that are collectively binding. Solidarity is both a set of values and a set of public practices. It connotes the work involved in creating and maintaining local communities and neighbourhoods, on the one hand, and the advocacy work in formal politics and civil society for social justice at national and global levels, on the other. It finds its expression in people's willingness to support vulnerable others within their own country or to support people in other countries who are denied basic rights and livelihoods necessary to live a life of dignity and without unnecessary suffering. The levels of solidarity in each society are reflected in everything from the vibrancy of its community activities to the taxes people are willing to pay in order to fund and support vulnerable members of their own and other societies. It is where the moral, the affective and the political systems overlap in public life. (For a fuller discussion see Lynch and Kalaitzake 2018.)

Within each of these circles of care, people live in varying states of dependency and interdependency. And each care reality is intersectionally connected to the other, moving along a fluid continuum from deep and consistent love, care and solidarity to carelessness, neglect, abuse and violation (figure 1).

Within primary care relations, labours of abuse and neglect can replace love labouring, not only denying someone the benefits of love labour but damaging the person through violation (Feeley 2009). Equally, in the secondary care relations fields, other-centred care labouring may or may not take place. Highly competitive work environments do not generate cultures of care and concern (Ball 2003; Gill 2009; Grummell, Devine and Lynch 2009). Neighbourhoods mired by poverty, war or violence are not likely to produce the kind of trust that underpins neighbourly care; exclusionary forms of social capital persist (Leonard 2004). Higher levels of economic inequality within countries generate greater distrust and less willingness to show solidarity with vulnerable others, either within one's own country or outside of it (Paskov and Dewilde 2012). There is, therefore, nothing inevitable in the love, care and solidarity world; the relational sphere provides contexts where these qualities can be either fostered or destroyed, not least because economic, political and cultural injustices interpellate with affective relations and frame their character (Wilkinson and Pickett 2018).

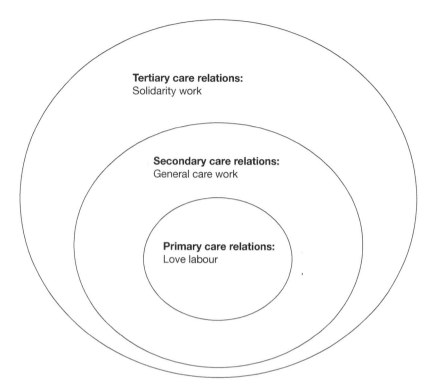

Figure 1 Affective relations: love, care and solidarity
Source: Adapted from Lynch (2007)

Neoliberal Capitalism, Inequality and Care

Although there is a danger in making capitalism the centre of all meaning-making when framing the politics of social justice (Gibson-Graham, Cameron and Healy 2016), the sociological reality is that neoliberal capitalism exercises a pervasive influence on social thought. It observes and locates people via mobile phones, credit cards and satellites; it exercises control over tastes and preferences through subliminal advertising, mediates communication and measures and records movement, all for the purposes of profit-making (Zuboff 2019). Even if its influence is indirect, the world is governed by its precepts. What makes capitalism so powerful is that it is deeply embedded historically. Its ecology and values shaped the modern nation state through force and coercion, as well as through enticement and consent (Graeber 2011; Patel and Moore 2018).[5] In its neoliberal form, capitalism is culturally pervasive and ideologically ingrained in major media, educational, cultural and recreational institutions (McGuigan 2010). While it is contested intellectually, it exercises an ideological hegemony that is very difficult to undermine (Leyva 2019).

Neoliberal capitalism is also institutionally hegemonic in the politics and economy of global life. It has been embedded and legitimated through the diffusion and enforcement of its principles in debtor countries in South America (Kentikelenis and Babb 2019), and more recently, with the support of the European Central Bank and the European Commission, within Europe (Kalaitzake 2017; Storey 2019). While the scope, scale and form of inequality arising from capitalism vary over time and with the politics of particular jurisdictions (Hall and Soskice 2001; Streeck 2016), since the 1980s advanced capitalist economies have, to a greater or lesser degree, been reorganized to reflect a distinctly neoliberal and deeply inegalitarian-led model of socio-economic (re-)production. Social class polarizations have grown, with income inequality increasing rapidly in North America, China, India and Russia since 1980, and growing moderately in Europe also during that period (Alvaredo, Chancel, Pikettty, Saez and Zucman 2018). The rise of wealth and income concentration at the top of so many national economies takes 'oligarchic' forms with high concentrations of wealth in family networks. The rich have become so rich that they perceive the fate of themselves and their families 'to be independent of the fate of the societies where they extract their wealth' (Streeck 2016: 28–9).

Upper-class detachment is paralleled by the rise of middle-class and working-class insecurities in a precarious working environment in Western democracies (Standing 2011). Fear of losing class privileges and related securities is heightened with the rise of precarious work among the previously secure middle classes (Mau 2015). The detachment of the super-rich and the exacerbation of middle-class insecurities have created a strong bulwark against promoting solidarity and care within welfare states in Europe (Frericks 2010).

The anti-care culture of neoliberal politics

As atomistic market relationships, aligned with and valorized within capitalism, tend to cultivate social relations built on risk/reward calculations, they encourage individuals to be highly competitive, be it in relation to job security, material wealth, social status or moral worth (Wilkinson and Pickett 2009; Bröckling 2015). This feeds disinterestedness and detachment from unaligned and unusable others. Capitalism produces a social 'nature' in humans that is characterized by coldness and indifference in politics and public life (Adorno 1978; Ferrarese 2017b). At the same time, rising inequality generates widespread feelings of suspicion, anger and resentment among the body politic and is an important factor in propelling the rise of new-right politics (Golder 2003).[6] These combined processes fuel political detachment and undermine the trust that underpins social solidarity and care for vulnerable others (Lynch and Kalaitzake 2018).

These dispositions are exacerbated in neoliberal politics as it is built on the essentialist assumption that human beings are primarily possessive and instrumentally rational individuals, who, while capable of being altruistic, work primarily in ways that are in accordance with their own self-interests (Friedman 2002). To channel this self-interest into politically valuable forms, individuals and institutions must be free from constraints; deregulation, privatization and competition are the guiding organizational norms of the neoliberalized economy and of social and economic life (Harvey 2005: 64–70). Neoliberalism is not only an analytical model, therefore: it is also a normative framework; it prescribes who you should be and how you should be. And it is a political-economic model that demands the state facilitate, implement and enforce free market economics and logics regionally and globally, and across all types of institutions and organizations (Leyva 2019). Neoliberalism does not abandon the state but enlists it to serve its own logic and purposes in a way that is increasingly welfare-indifferent (Korpi 2003; Frericks 2011; Gingrich and Häusermann 2015; Mau 2015).[7]

Domination and carelessness: pre-capitalist antecedents

There is nothing new about the human desire to exercise dominion and power over others and over the environment; such dispositions and practices have a long history across cultures and time wherever untrammelled power reigns. In gender terms, the enslavement of women, be it as a form of family currency in marriage arrangements or as a peace offering in times of war, showed scant regard for their care; and it preceded the formation of classed systems of oppression by a few thousand years (Lerner 1986: 212–19). In racial terms, hierarchical binaries between human, thinking beings and non-human, extended things (Patel and Moore 2018: 44–63) led

to 'natives' being defined as 'a sort of quintessential evil' that had
to be eradicated (Fanon 1967: 32). Defined as less than human by
their skin colour (Tsri 2016), many African people became 'things'
to be exploited for profit by powerful men and women for their own
ends, while those who were defined as 'Oriental', or Eastern, were
presumed to be culturally inferior to Western peoples (Said 1978).

Though disregard for the needs and sufferings of others is not the
preserve of capitalism, it is strongly associated with it as a political-
economic system, not least because the making of profit at the
expense of others and of nature requires a cheapening and abusing
of life in all its forms, especially given the finiteness of humans' and
nature's resources (Patel and Moore 2018). When all that counts
is what is countable in monetary terms, human relations become
care-less.

The everyday activities of properly functioning capitalism do not
produce forms of concern that lead to a sense of responsibility to
others. People are constructed as interchangeable within capitalist
logic and, as such, individually dispensable; fashioned as units of
human capital, they are instrumentalized, habitually formed and
re-formed in the service of the market and thereby distanced from
others (Ferrarese 2017a). There is a coldness towards the needy
other that is endemic to the logic of capitalism (MacDonald 2011).

While undermining care ethics is not unique to capitalism, it
does take distinct forms under *neoliberal* capitalism: as the latter is
globalized, and increasingly unregulated, it can be more predatory
in character, exploiting and exacerbating crises in pursuit of profit
in ways that are deeply harmful (Jessop 2019). Even in theory,
profit-making is no longer regulated by the self-discipline and
responsible stewardship that Weber (1930) regarded as the hallmarks
of capitalism in the nineteenth and early twentieth century. Rather,
the rational pursuit of self-interest is regarded as having a high moral
purpose (Rand and Branden 1964).

Ideological matters

Neoliberal capitalism has many *disorders* and contradictions undermining it internally (Streeck 2016; Jessop 2019); however, it also has
many powerful ideological tools at its disposal to perpetuate disorder
in its own interests. One of its defining features is its ability to conflate
economic, moral and political understandings (Harvey 2005) so that
what was once regarded as ethically reprehensible is now regarded as
normal. Neoliberal capitalism has encoded the pursuit of profit at all

costs as an *exciting* individual choice, a moral purpose governed by *meritocratic principles*, and a system that guarantees personal *security* for those who are worthy (Boltanski and Chiapello 2005).

As Weber (1930) and, more recently, Boltanksi and Chiapello (2005) argued, people need powerful moral reasons for rallying to capitalism. What gives neoliberal capitalism much political credibility is that it has managed to colonize public discourses on morality in a way that makes winner-takes-all profit-making virtuous. In lieu of solidarity, globalized capitalism offers unique forms of *excitement* and liberation (especially from the local) and opportunities to realize personal ambitions. The enticement and excitement of capitalism culturally are that it offers choices, especially in consumption terms. Even if such choices are between equally valueless goods, choice symbolizes that one has access to the power and autonomy that the market offers. The poor and not-so-poor are incorporated into society via credit and indebtedness, while ideologies of consumer power, consumer protection and consumer goods create the illusion of power and sovereignty (Soederberg 2014).

Neoliberal capitalism also lays claim to servicing social justice and the common good by rewarding the *meritorious*, the 'intelligent and hardworking'. To be a winner is to be entrepreneurial in a self-interested way. Winning is framed not only as virtue, a social good, but also as a game that simultaneously offers adventure and excitement without human cost. An actuarial spirit of calculation is normalized for all classes in a way that was unthinkable a generation or two ago (Peters 2005). For those who 'fail' in the merit stakes it offers charity. While charity long predates capitalism, contemporary philanthrocapitalists have framed it in a new corporate form as a politically appropriate method of redistribution; they regulate charitable 'giving' on their own terms in a highly strategic and business-like manner, a giving that reinforces rather than challenges the injustices of capitalism (Giridharadas 2019). Yet their charity provides them with a valorized public persona and a sense of pride in their own generosity, no matter how unwarranted that may be (Browne 2013).

Security is a prize also available to those who behave *responsibly*, and who are active in managing themselves and availing themselves of opportunities within neoliberal capitalism. 'Moral' people are those who secure their futures by regular reinvention, mentoring and retraining. They also manage their privileges responsibly by securing their transfer intergenerationally via property, including cultural capital, the management of education and money, and social networking. Solidarity with the more vulnerable is replaced by the ethic of self-responsibilization, especially among the middle classes, as they fear the loss of class standing in increasingly precarious work and welfare regimes (Mau 2015). Solidarity has become more and more conditional on self-responsibilization (Paskov and Dewilde 2012; Frericks 2014).

Unlike the early years of organized, European-led, colonial capitalism, when powerful oligarchs and monarchs sought moral approval prospectively and often retrospectively from their marauding and murdering in the acquisition of wealth (Patel and Moore 2018), the accumulation of wealth is now a universally approved precept for the labourer as well as for the venture capitalist. Not to follow this precept is to be deemed foolish and irresponsible. It is the universalization of self-interest as virtue, and the related distancing and invisibilization of harm, that make neoliberal capitalism particularly care-less.

Conclusion: Contradictions, Residuals and Resistances

The deregulation of capitalism, especially financial capitalism, since the 1980s, aligned with the exponential rise of digitalized communication technologies, has given corporate globalized capital untrammelled power in a world order where effective regulatory governance remains the preserve of nation states (Streeck 2016).[8]

As global competition intensified under the winner-takes-all-provisions of monopoly capitalism, by the end of the twentieth century the human detritus created by growing hierarchical divisions started seeping out of the cesspit of capitalist democratic neglect. It did not always arrive in the expected and manageable, individualized (nation-state-controllable) forms of drug and alcohol addiction, homelessness and petty crime, or even in a coherent party politics of socialism. It arrived unexpected and uninvited in the form of desperate and frightened asylum seekers and refugees; it found collective expressions in ethnic and religious-induced nationalism, xenophobia and welfare protectionism reflected in the rise of new-right movements across Europe and the US (Mudde 2007; Golder 2016). The internal contradictions of capitalism (Polanyi 1934) began to erode its political and moral façade in a neoliberal era producing cynicism, violence, anger and revolt, as well as a new populist politics of nationalism and anti-immigration. The cultural residues (Williams 1977) of nationalism and racism that were latent within already existing neoliberal capitalist states were awakened.

But the contradictions of capitalism do not generate dissent solely in negative terms through violence, war and terrorism, managed and orchestrated for the greater part by powerful men. They are not the only makers of dissent historically or contemporarily. Capitalism is not homogeneous even when defined in its own terms (Hall and Soskice 2001; Bresser-Pereira 2012). In every society there are alternative forms of economic and social organization that stand outside the capitalist nexus, be these voluntary and community associations, worker and producer cooperatives, or cooperative banks (Sánchez Bajo and Roelants 2011; Roelants, Eum, Eşim, Novkovic and Katajamäki 2019). These are living proof of institutionalized dissent from neoliberal capitalist values. There are also many sites of resistance to capitalism outside the market economy, as exemplified in civil society movements as diverse as the Occupy campaigns, Black Lives Matter, Me Too, the International Women's Strike 2017, land struggles in South America and Africa, and community gardens.[9]

Recognizing the multiple sites of human productivity, politics and cultural engagement compels us to recognize the household as a major site of production of non-market services. It produces goods and services that are arguably equivalent, in volume of outputs and numbers of people involved, to the formal economy (Folbre 1994); the unpaid care work undertaken in the world by women aged fifteen and over was estimated in 2020 to be worth three times the value of the entire global technological industry (Oxfam 2020: 8). Capitalism, and especially the capitalist economy, may be hegemonic but they are not monolithic and incontestable. Neither is the capitalist economy (specifically the relations between labour and capital) the only political and social space for the generation of action or resistance to the social injustices of capitalism (della Porta 2017). Classed and related inequalities are produced and reproduced not only in the market economy, but in the multitudinous economic, cultural and social sites that are aligned with it, and sometimes against it. There is more than one economy in a capitalist economy (Ferber and Nelson 1993; Folbre 1994, 2001, 2020; Gibson-Graham 1996; Federici 2012). And meaning-making is not confined to economic relations alone. People have a care consciousness (Crean 2018) as well as a gender, class, racial or sexual consciousness that informs their decisions. Things matter to people outside of formal politics and the economy (Midgley 1991; Sayer 2011).

There is a need to examine the possibilities of socialism (Streeck 2016: 234) and 'envision [both] local and proximate socialisms' (Gibson-Graham 1996: 264) and new feminisms, new types of revolutionary action that are built on foundations that must involve challenging exploitative relations within the economy in practice but are not confined to these.

There are many sites inside and around the capitalist nexus where transformative interventions can occur. One of those sites is affective care relations, those relations that produce, reproduce and repair the world relationally (Tronto 1993). These operate not only at the micro level of the local environment or family, but also at the meso and macro level of public institutions, multilateral agencies, community and voluntary organizations and the state. While the care relations that have coproduced humanity over thousands of years vary in cultural form, they have cultural purchase. Even if they are not named and claimed in public or celebrated, they exist in the realms of the care underworld in the form of care consciousness (Dodson 2010; Crean 2018) even among children (Luttrell 2020); people know what care relations matter to them. In many respects care is a kind of 'cultural residual', an area of human life, experience and achievement that the dominant culture neglects, represses and cannot even recognize for its political salience (Williams 1977: 123–4). Care relations are active in the subaltern world; they are the relations wherein people coproduce each other as human beings. But they operate in a subterranean sphere, without political 'citizenship', as they lack a political name and a political voice. Like other cultural residuals, however, they can and do influence current cultural processes (Williams 1977: 122). It is for this reason that they should be claimed, named and made visible intellectually and politically. The dilemmas and contradictions of doing loving, caring and showing solidarity[10] are spoken of daily in kitchens and bedrooms, in crèches and schools, in staffrooms, in union meetings, in canteens, tea rooms, coffee houses and pubs, in hairdressers, in cars, buses and trains. It is time to open this affective cultural residue of hope to provide a countervailing narrative to subvert the neoliberal message.

Affective relations of love, care and solidarity: unincorporated residuals

Because no dominant social order can erode and erase all human practice, energy, and intentions (Williams 1977), neither can neoliberal capitalism. While capitalism has commodified much of the care world, it has not been able to incorporate it completely, not least because certain forms of care relations are non-commodifiable; they are based on intentions and feelings that are voluntarily given and/or are non-substitutable (Lynch 2007; Mol 2008; Flores 2013; Cantillon and Lynch 2017).

Care relations are unincorporated residuals in Raymond Williams' terms; they remain outside and, for the most part, in opposition to legitimated cultural and party politics. Because these relations have not been fully incorporated, they lack status as political subjects, being regarded as apolitical, private and personal family matters (Okin 1989; Kittay 1999; Held 2006). It is because they have been disregarded, unaligned and unincorporated that affective care relations matter as potential sites of resistance. They are waiting to be articulated politically, to be mobilized and organized, as the co-creation and nurturing of relational life are dependent on them. Affective justice is an everyday concern for many, many millions of people owing to the care crises of the twenty-first century (Fraser 2016; Dowling 2021).

While the power of capitalism to reinvent itself and incorporate resistance is ubiquitous (Boltanski and Chiapello 2005), and seemingly overwhelming (Streeck 2016), meaning-making does not take place solely within markets. People live extensive lives outside the capitalist economy where non-market meaning and values are also materially created, especially through caring. There is scope for developing alternative thinking, new paradigms of justice and social action built around affective relations (Gibson-Graham 1996). If we put capital–labour relations at the centre of all meaning-making (Gibson-Graham, Cameron and Healy 2016: 194), we undermine our capacity to think outside that framework.

Part I
Care Matters Inside and Outside Capitalism

2
Care as Abject: Capitalism, Masculinity, Bureaucracy, Class and Race

Capitalism does not survive solely on exploitative class relations. The production and reproduction of classes require care labour, both the care of people and of those parts of nature that are available for exploitation and commodity production (Dalla Costa and James 1972; Federici 2012; Patel and Moore 2018). Humans, non-human animals and the Earth itself require attentiveness to survive and flourish, and capitalism requires caring to happen, even it does not pay for it directly and exploits it indirectly.

While care is central to capitalism's survival materially, the devaluation of care is also endemic to capitalism. There is a value disassociation within it through which the labour of caring and reproducing humanity itself is 'dissociated from value and abstract labor' (Scholz 2009: 127). The severance of production from reproduction and caring in modernity has created a deep dichotomy of values. 'The commodity-producing civilizational model' that is glorified under contemporary capitalism is underpinned by a system of care and domestic relations built around the marginalization of those who do the care work, mostly women, and the neglect of the natural and the social world (Scholz 2009: 130).[1] Unpaid reproductive work, and unpaid love and care work, are not value-producing in capitalist terms. They have vital use values but not an exchange value.[2] Affective care relations exist as a different order of values, values that are jettisoned within the ethics of capitalism.

The globalization of capitalism in the neoliberal financialized era has exacerbated this trend. The instrumental exploitative logic of *homo economicus* (Brown 2005) contradicts the logic of being *homo curans*; it undermines cooperative, nurturing, non-exploitative ways of relating to other humans and the natural world (Tronto 2017). In economic terms, care is defined as a private value for which capital is not responsible. And capitalism especially devalues relational embodied care, by treating it as both a cultural and an economic externality (Müller 2019). To pay for care directly would reduce profit (hence the persistent resistance to paying for public childcare in most countries, and, increasingly, resistance to paying for eldercare). In cultural terms, caring is associated with dependency, the vulnerable other who threatens productivity (profit) by either needing care or being tied to caring. Those in need of embodied care are treated as abject, as is the hands-on work of bodily caring, especially in societies that see both death and bodily fragility as problems to be eradicated (Banerjee and Rewegan, 2017).

At a wider cultural level, capitalism produces moral dispositions of indifference to the interests of others, what Adorno (2005) termed '*bourgeois coldness*' in the pursuit of one's own interests. This coldness is not the preserve of any one class or group, though the power to exercise *coldness* is most available to those with the capacities to exclude, and with most to gain from exercising indifference towards the vulnerable other. In the twenty-first century, the upper classes, especially the oligarchic elite, reflect these capitalist values as they live without allegiance to any nation state or people. In many respects, 'their fate and that of their families have become independent from the fates of the societies from which they extract their wealth' (Streeck 2016: 28). They can 'buy' political majorities through advertising and campaign contributions at election times, while gaining social legitimacy through philanthropy. They provide charity for their chosen 'causes', frequently funding public institutions, such as higher education and hospitals, impoverished by the elite's failure to pay taxation commensurate with their personal and corporate wealth (Winters 2011; Browne 2013). And although a small number of women are among the oligarchic elite and the upper-middle-class professionals who service them, and thereby benefit from their class dividend, they are rarely the leaders or those who exercise controlling power over capital.

Patriarchy and Capitalism Interface

Capitalism is not simply a form of hierarchical organization; it is a hierarchy in which people from particular backgrounds fill particular positions. Gender and racial hierarchies feed into the class hierarchies, playing a major role in determining who fills the empty class places. The capitalist economy works in and through a gendered and raced division of labour, including care labour and domestic labour, building on and exploiting pre-existing divisions of race, gender and status (Duffy 2005, 2011; Glenn 2010; Gutiérrez-Rodríguez 2014; Romero and Perez 2016; Folbre 2020). In so doing, it is not only a classed accumulation process but also a gendered and raced accumulation process.

Racialized care

While there is an internal, classed care economy within most wealthy countries, much of care labour supplied to the rich North/West of the world involves mining the care 'gold' (Hochschild 2002) of other countries, especially that of poorer countries. Care has become an export, not unlike other raw materials,[3] often extracted from former colonies, especially from women (Hochschild 2003; Mahadaven 2020), a twenty-first-century 'mining' of poorer parts of the world to supply the needs of the rich. In the United States, women from Mexico, Central America and the Caribbean account for much of the growth in domestic workers, cleaners, personal care workers and childcare workers since 2000 (Duffy 2020), while nurses from the Philippines,[4] and to a lesser degree India (Brush and Vasupuram 2006; Garner, Conroy and Bader 2015; WHO 2018), fill many nursing positions in the UK. Although men comprise the majority of migrants globally,[5] women comprise the majority of migrants to Northern, Southern and Western Europe and half of those to the US (IOM 2020), a very large proportion of whom are working in care services, including in the highly unregulated home care and domestic sectors (Misra 2003; Da Roit, González Ferrer and Moreno-Fuentes 2013). These globalized care workers do benefit from their employment, as do their families in the sending countries through emigrant remittances. However, their involuntary migrations often leave care deficits behind in their country of origin (Anderson 2000; Hochschild 2002).[6] When women with young children migrate without their families, it is other women who are left behind who take on informal family caring, while the women who migrate suffer the loss of intimacy of their own families (Anderson 2000).

Migrant care workers and domestic workers generally work without labour protections. They share common challenges including irregular hours of work and precarious working conditions, low wages, problems with immigration status and experiences of discrimination (Hondagneu-Sotelo 2001; Glenn 2010; Romero 2018). Although the

ILO convention on domestic work (Domestic Workers Convention, 2011, No. 189),[7] offers protections for domestic workers, it has only been ratified by thirty-one countries, and is not ratified by several European countries (including the UK, France, Austria, Spain, Denmark, Norway and the Netherlands), by Saudi Arabia, by the United Arab Emirates or by the Federal government of the USA. For those who migrate to do care and domestic work, there are also emotional and personal challenges in adapting to living in intimate family settings, especially where they do not share the family's cultural values or practices (Lutz 2016). Paid care work is not just classed and gendered, therefore; it is also racialized, especially given the role that migrant labour plays in care provision.

Patriarchy: historical considerations

We live within a gendered global order in which the overall subordination of women to men is one of the principal axes of power. Gender relations are a major component of social structure, and gender politics play a central role in determining our collective fate (Connell 1995: 67–86; Folbre 2020).

While patriarchy is facilitative of capitalism (as are other hierarchies, including racism), it did not originate within capitalism. The enslavement of women, combining both racism and sexism, preceded the formation of classes and class oppression, while patriarchy as a social system of norms, values, customs and roles preceded capitalism by a few thousand years (Lerner 1986: 213). The historical subordination of women as a social group originated in the shift from a matrilineal/matrilocal (mother-right) social structure to one that was patrilineal/patrilocal (father-right). And while women were again domesticated and subordinated much later in history as a result of agricultural enclosures and the divisions that ensued between unpaid and paid labour under industrialization, their original subordination was not generated in capitalism. For many hundreds of years, women were used as a form of family currency in marriage arrangements; they were frequently proffered as a peace offering, or to create alliances, between warring tribes. While men were often killed after conquests, women were taken as slaves for reproduction and sexual work. Their so-called 'sexual services' were part of their labour although their children were the property of their masters (Lerner 1986: 212–29).

The use and abuse of women that operated in prehistoric times, and that found expression during colonization and at times of war, have continued into the late twentieth and early twenty-first centuries, often on a deeply racialized basis. The organized sexual enslavement and rape of between 100,000 and 200,000 Korean teenage girls (so-called comfort women) by the Imperial Japanese Army during World War II, where they were forced to have sex with several men (raped) each day, exemplifies this (Hicks 1997). More recent studies of Afghanistan, the Democratic Republic of Congo, Sri Lanka, Palestine, Algeria, and Bosnia and Herzegovina, all demonstrate the continued widespread abuse and rape of women at times of military conflict (Ní Aoláin, Cahn, Haynes and Valji 2018).

The role of ideas in legitimating subordination

The North Atlantic gender order has its roots in the European colonial period beginning in the later 1400s. Empire building was a highly gendered enterprise (Connell 1995). The domination, control, use and abuse of women were endemic to colonization, justified on the dubious philosophical and moral rationale that women were part of nature rather than society, especially if they were women of the colonized peoples (Patel and Moore 2018: 111–37).

While a commercial dividend was paramount in driving colonization and exploitation, including the exploitation of care work, the role that ideas played in both framing and legitimating the cheapening of things, including caring, was also crucial. Moral concepts and ideas were deployed that not only named the world but created it ontologically, implicitly prescribing as well as describing who and who was not fully human (Patel and Moore 2018: 47).

One of the sources of inspiration was the work of Descartes (1991). He drew a philosophical distinction between mind and body, between thinking things and extended things, *res cogitans* and *res extensa*. Not all humans were defined as thinking, including women and indigenous peoples, and non-humans, so-called *extended things*, or *nature*. *Nature* was subsequently defined as something to be possessed and used by humans; it was to be controlled and dominated by *society* (Patel and Moore 2018: 45–55). The two laws of capitalist ecology, one distinguishing between man (*sic*) and nature, and the other classifying nature as *a thing* to be dominated and controlled by man, provided moral justification for the exploitation of swathes of humanity and the destruction of much natural life.[8]

To justify making care cheap it had first to be defined as worthless, part of nature rather than society. This was achieved through the equation of care labour with femininity and women, people who were not fully human: as women were exploitable things, then by default their caring *'nature'* was exploitable. Like water, trees and clean air, care was defined as freely available from the *nature* of women, regarded as being produced without effort or work. Within the binary Cartesian mind/body logic of value, as carers were part of *nature*, exploitable things, so caring was not an individuality-defining or citizenship-defining activity (Sevenhuijsen 1998; Hobson 2000).

Hegemonic masculinity

While the concept of hegemonic or idealized masculinity changed over time from rule by physical violence, and the threat of violence, to rule by male-promulgated laws operated within the machinery of the state; and while it changed location, from the colonies to the factories, from the high seas to the financial markets, the boardroom and the stock exchange (Connell 1995: 185–203); the governing principle of control has remained in place as a defining feature of hegemonic masculinity.

The idea that it is natural and legitimate for men to dominate women informs structures, policies and practices across social, economic, affective and political life (Connell 1995: 73–8). Though hegemonic masculinity is not singular in form, changing with history and culture, from imperial times to neoliberal times, taking localized and globalized forms, and being contested as well as accommodated (Connell 2016), it remains extremely powerful including among the younger generation (Harvey, Ringrose and Gill 2013).

The patriarchal codes that are bound up with hegemonic masculinity do not just create boundaries between women and men; they also create hierarchies between men, external and internal hegemonies that define some forms of masculinity as subordinate (Demetriou 2001). In neoliberal capitalist times, the powerful transnational business elite epitomize a strong form of *entrepreneurial masculinity* not just in the Western metropole but in China, India and wider Asia (Connell 2016). Hoang's (2014) research in Ho Chi Minh city shows how wealthy men demonstrate their status and power over women and other men by socializing in expensive bars and sex venues, while research in multinational-controlled garment factories in Malaysia (Elias 2008) exemplifies the deeply gendered forms of work in these export zones, in which women are persistently subordinate.

Men Leading Capitalism

The Forbes list of the world's richest people in 2019 showed that almost 90 per cent of the world's billionaire elite were men.[9] Although there are now more women billionaires than twenty years ago, they are still a small minority. Most of those who own and control the transnational corporations globally are not only men but also White (Patterson 2013). Though there are local billionaires in several countries, the transnational capitalist class who both own and control much of capital globally form a hegemonic fraction (Poulantzas 1975) and are in an extremely powerful position to become a global ruling class given their dominance of so many fields of production and services, including financial services (Robinson 2012; Murray 2015).

As wealthy men (and the few women), and their professional allies in the financial, investment, accounting and legal professions (Sklair 2000), move globally, organizing takeovers and forming alliances, new business and allegiances, they are above and beyond the control of most nation states (de Graaff 2020). They are unlikely to renege on their power and wealth without a struggle; indeed, they have developed a sense of entitlement to that power and strongly contest its erosion in both gender and racial terms ((Kimmel 2013; Anderson 2016).

The material dividend of patriarchy

To understand how capitalism works, we need to go beyond capitalism and explore how it is constitutionally linked to the racial, gender and care ordering of society. The internal dynamics of gender itself are far from binary (Mitchell 1971). While patriarchy is a hierarchical system within which men dominate and control women, it is also *a relationship between men*. Men are hierarchically constituted within capitalism by class and co-constituted hierarchically by sexuality and race especially (Connell 1995). While hybrid types of masculinities exist, the White, upper-class, heterosexual male is symbolically at the pinnacle of the masculinities' hierarchy. Men who are poor, working-class, Black or Brown, and/or gay or transsexual are variously located at the nether end of the male hierarchical order.

While some men find new ways to elevate themselves above other men, they often do so in a manner that does not threaten the symbolic boundaries that maintain the patriarchal dividend of their own kind. It is quite common for well-educated White middle-class men to differentiate themselves from 'traditional' men by highlighting their gender-aware ideologies, tastes and behaviours, while simultaneously retaining and protecting their male power in the gender hierarchy (Bridges and Pascoe 2014; Eisen and Yamashita 2019). As Hondagneu-Sotelo and Messner (1994) observed, White middle-class men want to stop paying a price for being at the pinnacle of the gender hierarchy (including the disrespect and criticism that comes from being defined as part of the privileged, undeserving elite) while at the same time wanting to remain part of that elite. As with all groups who benefit from privileges, they do not want to lose the material benefits of their superior (gender) status.

Although the vast majority of men do not belong to a normatively prescribed hegemonic group of (White) upper-class males, they benefit from the patriarchal dividend of being part of the male social group per se (Connell 1995: 79). They do not have to be proactive to benefit from the patriarchal dividend, nor do they have to defend it. Just as White people benefit silently from the racial dividend of whiteness, so all men can benefit from the patriarchal dividend of being a man, if they remain passive and silently *complicit* with its injunctions (Hartmann 1979; Connell 1995). Men's complicity with the unequal gender order is highly visible in the care field and within families.

The gender order of caring in families

While the heterosexual household is a contested family formation, it remains the modal form of family organization. Within all types of families, there is an internal economy within and through which household goods and services are produced: food is prepared and cooked, floors are cleaned, toilets are washed, family events are organized and so forth (Folbre 1994). The relations of production, consumption and the transmission of goods within families operate by different rules of exchange from market production; they are differentiated by age and marital status, and especially by gender, where heterosexual couples are involved (Delphy and Leonard 1992). While there have been changes since the early 1980s, and men now do more childcare and more housework than several decades ago, on average, US data show that wives do 1.7 times the housework of husbands, while married mothers average 1.9 times as much housework as married fathers (Bianchi, Sayer, Milkie and Robinson 2012). Although there are changes in the amount of time men spend in certain areas of childcare when both partners are employed full time, notwithstanding this, a US study spanning the years 2003–7, involving over 13,000 women and men, found mothers' time in childcare always exceeded fathers' time, although the gender gap is narrower in dual-earner families (Raley, Bianchi and Wang 2012: 1440).[10] The pattern is similar across Europe and nearby countries; while women do much more care work and housework in Greece and Turkey than in Sweden and Norway, the gender disparities remain even within these.[11] Even in the Nordic countries (Sweden, Norway, Finland, Denmark and Iceland), where there are enhanced childcare supports and extensive paid parental leave for both parents, men remain reluctant to take the full leave available, and where the leave can be shared between mothers and fathers, mothers are far more likely to take it (Cederström 2019). Undertaking hands-on primary caring is not central to men's identity as men (Hanlon 2012). The gendered male order impacts on men, even in the more gender-egalitarian Nordic states, with men fearing that their managers and co-workers might judge them adversely if they took longer and more optional care leave; they fear they would suffer career penalties (Cederström 2019: 40).

The unequal gender division of both domestic and care labour benefits men individually (Connell 1995: 67–86), as women's unwaged care and domestic labour frees men up to take public power in an hierarchically ordered economy and society. Men can use their power relative to their class and racial position in ways that involve exercising control over women (Badgett and Folbre 1999; Folbre 2012). The unequal division of care and domestic labour also impoverishes women, especially working-class and poor women, not only in the present but in future time, particularly in old age, due to their lack of economic independence and pension entitlements (Oxfam 2020).

Without recognizing the unique and highly unequal gendered dynamics of household economies, work organizations and the state itself, and the materialist gains that ensue for men of all classes from these, there is misrecognition of the interests of men, *qua men*, in upholding a capitalist system from which they are net beneficiaries relative to women of their class.

While patriarchy has long historical roots predating capitalism, capitalism has reinforced, legitimated and consolidated a value order in which there is a deep disassociation of value between female-dominated caring labour and market labour. Neoliberal-led globalization has exacerbated that value divide by making the chains of connectedness invisible. It has widened the physical and mental distances between provisioning and consumption, as most are ignorant of the exploitations and abuses that often underpin the food they eat, the clothes they wear or the phones and laptops they use to communicate (Federici 2019: 109–10). The foundational work that is required to care for the Earth, prevent suffering and produce humanity itself in non-exploitative relations is unnamed and unspoken (Mies and Bennholdt-Thomsen 2000; Federici 2019).

Bureaucracy, Hierarchy and the State

While hierarchical divisions are endemic to the organization of capitalism, hierarchical organization is not its prerogative. Bureaucracies are means for organizing power relations, that are constitutionally hierarchical, and for those who exercise control within them, they are 'a power instrument of the first order' (Gerth and Wright Mills 1958: 228). Weber goes so far as to say that 'where the bureaucratization of administration has been completely carried through, a form of power relation is established that is practically unshatterable'. He also claims that bureaucratization is 'often carried out in direct alliance with capitalist interests' (Gerth and Wright Mills 1958: 230).

We know from anthropological research that for 99 per cent of their history, humans lived in small foraging groups where there was no organizational capacity and ill-defined leadership roles; they were largely unstratified, fluid in form and non-violent (Schoenhals 2019). There were and are societies that manage their conflicts and differences without violence. One of the features of more peaceful, non-violent societies is that they are generally more gender egalitarian, with women playing key roles in decision-making (Malešević 2010a: 298). It was the emergence of sedentary social organizations, especially the establishment of state power (Carneiro 1970) and related bureaucracies, that has generated both deep gender stratifications and organized warfare (Malešević 2010a: 295–6).

But modern life is lived within the frame of increasingly large bureaucratic organizations, be these public or private services, business corporations, educational institutions and/or non-governmental and community organizations. While there are many polities, entities that have authority over a specific social group or territory or set of institutions that are not states, including organized religions, hegemons and global institutions (Walby 2009), the state remains a powerful polity in determining the outcomes of people's lives. And in the twenty-first century, it is men who control the means of decision-making and meaning-making within most states (and within all major globalized religions, and most global political and economic institutions).

The subordination of women has been enabled and consolidated by the development of bureaucratized organizational power (Acker 1990, 2006), including the organizational power of the state. While women can and do use the machinery of the state to fight for their rights, it is through the state that women's subordination is often consolidated in law and regulations, rather than being simply a matter of habit and cultural convention (Walby 2009). The very idea of the 'social contract', a cornerstone of democratic thinking, was based on the deeply gendered concept that the civil government replaced the king/father as the protector of the nation (Pateman 1988). This assumes that the protector (the state) is a father figure, an abstract, disinterested player who will always act in the interests of his dependents, who are first defined as women and children. The logic of the state as 'protector' enjoins a gendered discourse of care and concern to rationalize power, and oftentimes the abuse of power. The metaphor of the protective father is a political ruse granting legitimacy to the exercise of power and control, though it may be arbitrary and abusive.

There are several ways in which male control of state institutions impact on women as primary carers, both institutionally and ideologically. As bureaucratic entities designed and planned by men, state organizational practices are constitutionally masculine in character. They are governed through gendered concepts of production and reproduction, and gender-configured in terms of recruitment and promotion, the division of labour and systems of control. The state does not always have to operate explicitly in men's interests to be patriarchal because it is shaped by masculine interests and practices. Multiple dimensions of socially constructed masculinity have historically shaped the multiple modes of power circulating through the domain called the state (Brown 1995: 177). The masculinist character of the state is reflected in the generalized lack of interest in, and commitment to, childcare; in the declining investment post-austerity in many welfare states in basic infrastructural public (care) services; in the adversarial approach of parliamentary debates; and in the timing of political meetings and assemblies, most of which assume that people are not tied to time by care commitments.

Because domain assumptions influence our paradigmatic

assumptions (Gouldner 1970) at an ideological level, intersecting identities of social class, race, age, gender and marital and family status influence paradigmatic perspectives: how people live, who they live with, what they read, listen to, see and know help make up their world view. What they are hardwired to see, feel and notice about the world and its politics is highly contingent and driven by strong emotions (Ahmed 2004), not necessarily by reason (Lakoff 2008). As men do not inhabit the world in the same way that women do in care terms (Hochschild and Machung 1989), and as they are much less likely to be hands-on carers (Oxfam 2020), their domain assumptions about care work, paid and unpaid, are fundamentally different from those of women (Hanlon 2012; Cederström 2019). As 'care commanders' (Lynch, Baker and Lyons. 2009: 132–57), men's political paradigms are less likely to be informed by everyday experiences of attending to the ongoing corporeal and emotional needs of dependent others. As men do not tend to carry the family care-map around in their heads every day, this impacts on their decision-making. Their underlying paradigmatic assumptions are framed by their own relatively, and sometimes entirely, care-free experiences. Nowhere was this more evident than during the Covid-19 pandemic when male-dominated governments closed crèches and primary schools in many countries with no plan for childcare, forgetting that someone had to care for children if people (especially health care staff) were to work. The net effect of this was a drop in employment rates for women in seventeen of the twenty-four Organisation for Economic Co-operation and Development (OECD) countries that reported a drop in employment due to the pandemic; care-work commitments contributed greatly to women withdrawing from the labour market during the pandemic of 2020–21.[12]

Women in Bureaucratic Organizations

Organizations are neither gender neutral (Acker 1990; Witz and Savage 1991; Britton 2000) nor race neutral (Acker 2006; Ahmed 2012). The seemingly 'disembodied, universal worker' is in reality a male and a White worker, especially at senior levels; women and men whose skin is Brown or Black are judged by their degree of adherence to the prevailing organizational norm for any given position that has been White-male-dominated and male-defined historically (Joseph 2018). Those who enter positions within organizations do not do so, therefore, on their own terms; they may negotiate, but positions have a status and identity that predate and post-date the potential postholders, and senior posts are coloured-coded White and masculine in White-dominated societies.

While power may not now be entirely in male hands in the twenty-first century in all countries, or in all organizations, men exercise a controlling interest in all the major organizational centres of power. Men have claimed organizational power for themselves at senior levels, be it in business, culture, sport, the arts or the media (Kanter 1977; Collinson and Hearn 1996). Even when some women are present at senior levels, men, being in the majority, exercise the power of veto in most political, cultural and economic institutions.

Even a cursory glance at the leaders of the G20 or the EU 27 highlights the hegemony of White male political power. Outside of politics, men are twice as likely to be managers as women within the European Union: only 6.3 per cent of CEO positions in major publicly listed companies were held by women in 2019 (European Commission 2019: 5). Women's lower status is reflected in their earnings: around 25 per cent of the top one per cent of wage earners in the EU are women, though in some countries it is lower, with just 17 per cent of the top one percent of earners being women in the UK (European Commission 2019: 20). Men's dominance of senior posts and their higher earnings are likely to continue, especially with the rise of globalized corporations where geographical mobility and 24/7 availability are expected (Vahter and Masso 2019). A long-hours' work culture is not conducive to good caring, simply because it takes time from care.

Kate Millett's assertion some fifty years ago regarding the persistence of men's patriarchal power remains largely true organizationally today:

> the military, industry, technology, universities, science, political offices, finances – in short, every avenue of power within the society, including the coercive force of the police, is [almost][13] entirely in male hands. ... What lingers of supernatural deity, the Deity, 'His' ministry, together with ethics and values, the philosophy and art of our culture – its very civilization – as T.S. Eliot once observed, is of male manufacture. (Millett 1971: 25)

Being a Man

What underpins White male control is a very particular concept of what it is to be a man, what it is to be masculine. Because we become what we live, the work that we do, and what and who we value while doing it, have a major impact on our character and who we become (Sayer 2009: 5). By practising the norms of competitive masculinity, it is inevitable that most men will absorb related capitalist values over time (Hartmann 1979: 21). By filling the places created by other powerful men, each new generation of men is engaged in enacting the practices and codes of hegemonic masculinity that make these posts what they are (Connell 2000). What happens in parallel with living out hegemonic, dominant-led masculinity is the denigration of the qualities associated with its opposite, namely social need and dependency. Despite the emergence of hybrid masculinities, and the selective incorporation of elements of identity associated with various marginalized and subordinated masculinities as well as femininities into hegemonic masculinities, the new hybrids do not signal the end of male dominance (Demetriou 2001; Messerschmidt 2010). Combining toughness with tenderness in a male public persona often masks the perpetuation of male systems of power and inequality (Messner 2007). Borrowing some 'soft' feminine symbols and practices may even conceal male power by giving it a symbolically acceptable face. Much research on hybrid masculine practices shows that they often work in ways that 'fortify symbolic and social boundaries, perpetuating social hierarchies in new (and "softer") ways' (Bridges and Pascoe 2014: 255). The principle of dominance that is central to masculinity remains intact; it is defined against femininity and its perceived vulnerability and dependency. As it is men who carry capitalism's torch, and define its parameters in elite positions, capitalism and hegemonic masculinity are deeply embedded with each other.

Independent of bureaucracies, capitalism produces moral dispositions of indifference to the interests of others, what Adorno (2005) termed 'bourgeois coldness' in the pursuit of one's own interests. While upper-class women negotiate the services of cleaning, caring and catering for the family, upper-class men generally do not meet poor women in person, but only know them as the providers of abstract, invisibilized services as cleaners, caterers or childcare workers. These men are not confronted by the in-person feel of poverty. Even in average-income households, men do not manage the household harms of capitalism as much as women, especially where they are felt most keenly and cannot be ignored, namely in poor families (O'Neill 1992; Dodson 2010). The moral imperative to do hands-on caring does not apply to men as it does to women (Bubeck

1995; Glenn 2000; O'Brien 2007). Men are allowed to be 'cold', to be careless (in hands-on care terms), more than women.

While there are developments in Europe promoting a caring masculinity model to replace the hegemonic ideal of male dominance, especially in the academic field (Ruby and Scholz 2018), how and when that will translate into familial, organizational and state politics remains to be seen. Whatever the outcome, unless caring and hegemonic concepts of masculinity are better aligned, it is hard to see how a caring world order can be part of a new political imaginary.

To date, the overlap between the constituencies of capitalist and patriarchal interests, not just in maintaining the hegemony of men in heterosexual families, but in the developing of hegemonic constructs of competitive, controlling masculinity in employment and within the machinery of the state, means that capitalism and patriarchy are inextricably linked. And the same can be said of the relationship of capitalism and racism; the success of the capitalist project globally is not only deeply classed and gendered; it is also deeply racialized and tied to a long history of colonialism (Patel and Moore 2018).

Care as Abject

As noted in chapter 6, the Cartesian philosophical distinction between *mind* and *body*, between *thinking things* and *extended things*, had important implications for women and indigenous people. Within that paradigm, not all humans were defined as fully human thinking beings, and this included slaves, women and indigenous peoples; they became part of the non-human, so-called extended things, part of *nature* rather than *society*. Thus, Cartesian logic was built on and legitimated the exploitation and domination of *nature*, and of those things equated with nature, among them women (Patel and Moore 2018: 45–55).

Given the conceptualization of women as an object of use, it was inevitable that their caring work would also be open to exploitation. What was feminine was inferior, and what the feminine character produced was of less value simply because it was produced by a woman (De Beauvoir 1993). Even when women entered into the work of *animal rationale* or *homo faber*, they still found that their work was not granted equal standing (Smith 1987). Women poets were not seen as writing about matters of universal interest (Boland 1996).[14] There is no profession or job that women dominate that is comparable in status and power to that of men, even when that job of work is in the public domain (Witz and Savage 1991).

Denigration of care and domestic labour

While the intellectual denigration of care work as natural to women, part of their essential *nature*, facilitated the exploitation of colonized women/carers, care was denigrated whether women did it or not as the dependency that called for care was seen as an aberration in the adult human condition, 'a sign of incompleteness in an adult', in neoliberal thinking (Moynihan 1973: 17). Being an adult and a citizen was closely aligned with the ideals of independence and autonomy in the post-industrial era; there were no 'good' dependencies for adults (Fraser and Gordon 1997: 135).

As being dependent is shameful in a society where productivity and 'active citizenship' reign as superior values, by extension, caring for non-citizens (adult dependents and children) is shaming by association, with significant political and economic consequences (Müller 2019). The abjection of dependency, carers and their caring work is not just a psychic matter however; it has had material and violent consequences, especially as reflected in the violence that women experience during pregnancy when they are likely to be more dependent (Tyler 2009: 87–94).

The abjection of care has been closely linked to the abjection of domestic work, where women also predominate. Although care work and domestic work are analytically distinguishable, in the embodied world of lived material reality they overlap (Duffy 2011). Because they do so, the lowly status of domestic work compounds the lowly status of caring. When care involves body work, it is often dirty work; it involves cleaning and managing the leaking fluids from the orifices of the body that are often uncontrolled and even uncontrollable.[15] The leaky body smells, soils, and demands a huge amount of time and energy to keep it managed without harm, to keep it under control; the management of this human waste adds to the designation of hands-on caring as low-level life work (Hughes, McKie, Hopkins and Watson 2005: 266–8). The abject status of body work and domestic work is reflected in the fact that it is work very few people choose to do. Paid carers for frail older people in Europe are disproportionately migrant workers who often have no choice about doing this work (Da Roit, González Ferrer and Moreno-Fuentes 2013), as are domestic workers in many wealthy countries (IOM 2020).

While feelings of disgust and abjection at leaky, disintegrating bodies are not a modern phenomenon, the achievement-led, competitive individualism that characterizes contemporary culture is premised on the managed, contained, intact, cleansed and controlled body; bodily disintegration and leaking threaten this (Twigg 2000: 396). There is a 'dematerializing tendency' in how the vulnerable body is interpreted in contemporary Western culture; excretions, especially where they are involuntary and uncontrolled, and death and decay are distanced and sanitized in a way that hides the body. Status, especially professional status, is inversely related to the amount of body work involved, especially work with vulnerable, frail bodies (Twigg 2000: 391). Those who do hands-on body care work are made abject by their association with vulnerable bodies in a society that valorizes individualistic independence and productivity.

As Simone de Beauvoir observed in 1948, domestic work is governed by endless repetition (De Beauvoir 1993). In so far as domestic work is part of care work (Gutiérrez-Rodríguez 2014), it is repetitive work, a remark we heard frequently in our care conversations for *Affective Equality* (2009).[16] It goes on incessantly in cycles of hours, days and years. And when one cycle ends another begins, be it in the meals that have to be produced, the cleaning that is required, or the cycles of age and illness that follow each other as life ebbs and flows.

Yet many tasks in life involve endless repetition: teaching the same school syllabus or fixing the same parts in cars year on year, meeting patients in surgery with the same illnesses time and time again or answering the same queries about computing on a software support line. What makes domestic work abject is not the repetition, but the conditions under which it is undertaken. Cleaning is not demeaning per se, but it becomes so when it is unrecognized, underpaid or unpaid. This is something women spoke of a great deal in our care conversations studies for *Affective Equality*,[17] as did the minority of men who were primary carers.[18]

There is no doubt that the demanding, at times dirty, and thankless character of unpaid care labour and related domestic work helps explain its abjection. However, it is also made abject by the deep cultural assumption that this necessary work is not citizenship-defining labour; it is not the kind of work that those who are fully human (part of society rather than nature) have to do. This problem is greatly exacerbated in capitalist society given the deeply classed and gender-stratified division of care labour.

Abjection and capitalism

Capitalist societies are driven by the demands of the accumulation process, where production is oriented to exchange, not use or provisioning (Nelson 1993; Mies 2014). Production matters in so far as it can be monetized; the *use* value of products is a non-market consideration. Capitalism, while it benefits from the *use value* of unpaid family-care labour in particular, does not see itself as having any obligation to pay for it as it is not defined as real work (Dalla Costa 1972; Folbre 1994; Hochschild 1997; Federici 2012; Fraser 2016).

Love and care live and produce life in the underground of political and economic life, creating use values that are invisible in the exchange market. They are concealed beneath comings and goings, doings that only become visible in their absence, when they fail to happen, or happen badly over time. The absence of care or love is not defined as a political or a structural problem. Instead, it is individualized and reconstructed as a responsibilized failing of 'dysfunctional' families, 'poor parenting', a signifier of the immorality of the class, race and/or gender and marital status of the carer (Dodson 2010).

Care's centrality to life is further invisibilized when resolutions to care deficits are framed in terms of supplying care on market terms, as a purely technical service, through monitoring, recording and surveillance in a supply-chain management system. The emotionally demanding character of hands-on care work is not recognized for the time it takes and the demands it makes on those who are expected to do it (Gutiérrez-Rodríguez 2010). The assumption is that people can be organized and compelled by market rules to care well, and if that care is not available, e-health care or robotic care will suffice. The limitations of commercialized (Dowling 2021) and digitalized health care are frequently overlooked (Moisil 2019). Care is constructed as a technical product, a package to be delivered in minutes and hours, as if counting time on task makes care happen. But care is not reducible to a product that can be bought and sold as it involves ethical and relational dilemmas and 'the maintenance of life *for* itself' (Dowling 2021: 45).

Yet there is a growing corporatization in which for-profit businesses are increasingly entering the world of care, seeking 'to impose business rationalities and the corporate logic of profit-making and (labor) cost-cutting upon the whole sector' (Farris and Marchetti 2017: 110). In this corporatized model, there is no time allowed for the relational work that is so central to caring; it ignores the voluntary human engagement and mutuality that is at the heart of caring, even when it is paid (Müller 2019). Care is made abject by being reduced to a package of marketable, measurable products, in which time for relational work is not named or granted.

As care is not a product like others, it cannot be mass produced cheaply. It is inherently labour intensive, requiring face-to-face, and sometimes hands-on, contact. It is generally not substitutable by capital and does not offer easy productivity gains, given its labour intensiveness (England, Budig and Folbre 2002). Given that the time logics of care, and the disposition of engagement and attentiveness that it requires, are at variance with capitalist logic, care crises are inevitable when care is placed on the market (Dowling 2021: 137–8).

Conclusion

The capitalist economy works in and through a gendered division of labour, including care labour; it is a classed, raced and gendered accumulation process that distinctly advantages men *within* each class, especially within the household economy. Given this, many men are vested in the patriarchal-capitalist nexus, and as the rise of male-right groups shows, they have developed a sense of entitlement to power and are likely to contest its erosion (Kimmel 2013).

But hierarchies of power are not the preserve of capitalism. Bureaucratic organizations play a central role in the organization of everyday life, and while bureaucracy and capitalism are constitutionally linked, bureaucracies exist outside capitalism and are neither gender neutral (Acker 1990) nor race neutral (Ahmed 2012). The development of bureaucratic institutions, including the bureaucratic institutions of the nation state, has played an important role in institutionalizing pre-existing hierarchies of class, gender and race (Malešević 2010a) to the detriment of women and their care work. Because most large bureaucratic institutions are designed and run by powerful men, men who are free from daily hands-on care work, care work is often invisible at the centres of power. The strong instrumentalism that is endemic to output-driven bureaucratic organizations further invisibilizes the care infrastructure that lies underneath them and enables them to survive.

There are also cultural and ideological factors underpinning the devaluation and abjection of care in a gendered way. The masculine/feminine binary, where hegemonic masculinity is equated with dominance and being in control while idealized femininity is identified with compliance and service, feeds into the devaluation of women and care, as women are morally impelled to care in a hands-on way that men are not (Connell 1995, 2000). Hegemonic masculinity requires men to be dominant, especially men in positions of power (Connell and Wood 2005), even if they have to conceal this in order to have legitimacy in a contested gender order. Doing some breadwinning allows men to do hands-on caring without undermining their masculinity in a way that full-time hands-on caring does not.

The gendered dependent/independent binary also contributes to the denigration of care work as there is no legitimate state of dependency for adults in contemporary society (Fraser and Gordon 1997). Being cared for implies dependency, non-adulthood and non-citizenship; while it is acceptable at times for women, such as in pregnancy, it is not acceptable for adults generally unless they are very ill. Those who do hands-on care work with people who are highly dependent become abject by association; they are devalued by doing work that is often dirty, tiring and demanding, but lacking in status and power.

The *value disassociation* at play within capitalism also helps explain the abjection of caring. The *commodity-producing civilizational model* that is glorified under neoliberalism devalues work that has a *use value* rather than an *exchange* value. As caring is focused on producing a use value, it is defined in opposition to abstract surplus-value-producing labour, and thereby defined as unproductive and valueless (Scholz 2011), especially when it is unpaid.

If care is to challenge capitalism as a source of ethics and a site of resistance, not only must the capitalist value of profit at all costs be contested, but so too must the deeply gendered and racialized hierarchical social order that underpins it. The equation of masculinity with dominance and power is a key concern; a hegemonic masculinity that also equates the ideal man with excessive wealth urgently needs to be contested.

3

Making Love: Love Labour as Distinctive and Non-Commodifiable

This chapter explores some of the ways in which the making of love through love labour is a distinctive form of intimate relational work that is distinguishable analytically from other secondary and tertiary forms of care labouring, such as paid professional care, community care and solidarity. While secondary care labour can be assigned to others and provided on a paid basis, this is not true of love labour. Both love labour's non-substitutability and the inalienability of love as a social and personal good mean that the logics of love labouring cannot be reduced to market capitalist logic. The non-substitutability of love labour has profound implications for humanity. It places a brake on capitalism's exploitative potential in the realm of intimacy and contradicts the popular narrative that everything is commodifiable. The love labour that produces humanity in its relationality can inspire and resource resistance to the commodification of life itself. Love is not only conceivable as a social good; as it meets a fundamental need, 'it can also be conceptualised as a resource, as a form of advantage or as a capability' (Gheaus 2017: 740). As such it can enable and resource resistance to its ethical nemesis, capitalism.

To recognize the potential power of love is not to underestimate the abuses that take place in its name. Love is a dangerous concept; its explicit normative intent can conceal the abuses of power and neglect that remain hidden beneath a cloak of concern and affectionate care (Wilkinson 2014). Much harm and violence have been committed in the name of love, not least of which is the harm done to women in the name of heterosexual love in particular. Such love is sentimentalized and romanticized as an emotional and social utopia, an existential panacea for women. What romantic love offers women realistically, as opposed to rhetorically, is often a life of self-sacrifice that can be self-harming; it entices and traps them in heterosexual relationships where their autonomy is often undermined, their independence curtailed and their opportunities limited (Bubeck 1995). Disability activists also fear the mention of care and love due to their association with patronizing attitudes, especially the way the rhetoric of love, care and concern is used to justify institutionalizing disabled people without regard for their rights to exercise control over their own lives (Oliver 1990; Morris 1993: Shakespeare 2000). Given the misuse of the term 'love', it is not surprising that there is a great ambivalence about the concept in society and in the academy (hooks 2000).

There are many contradictions, conflicts and paradoxes involved in caring, loving and expressing solidarity that are endemic to such practices in and of themselves. Feelings of concern, sympathy and compassion, and the desire to fight injustices, fluctuate like other emotions; the desire for power, personal gratification, pleasure and recognition live within the compassionate person and the social justice activist, as well as within the care- and justice-indifferent. It is because of the volatility of emotions and commitments underpinning love, care and solidarity that there is a need for infrastructural supports to sustain these practices, resolve their contradictions, and ensure that people are able and want to care for the distant stranger as well as the local friend or relative (Care Collective 2020: 27–9).

This chapter focuses first on the role of social science research in peripheralizing love intellectually. It examines the standpoints on care in the academy, and especially the peripheralization of the subject of love in the social sciences. Even though primary love relationships are non-substitutable, there are attempts to commercialize them, and the second section of this chapter examines the implications of these developments.[1] The final, and substantive, discussion in this chapter is focused on explaining how love differs from other forms of caring and solidarity work, and why it cannot be commodified without changing it into something other than love.

Introduction

Feminist scholars have deconstructed love and exposed its contradictions, including its association with a rigid maternalism and gender essentialism, while also valorizing love, recognizing that it is endemic to human relationality, and that it has liberatory potential in terms of promoting social justice (Collins 1990; hooks 2000;

Ferguson 2014; Ferguson and Jónasdóttir 2014; Robinson 2015; Puig de la Bellacasa 2017; Casalini 2020). They have reclaimed love as a political practice that energizes people, generating a desire for justice (Collins 1990: 197), and nurturing the oppressed in the fight against domination (hooks 2000: 104). However, as this scholarship is corralled as 'feminist', outside the mainstream, it is often ignored by male scholars, including those writing about the significance of affective relations and love in politics (Hawkesworth 2006). It exists in a zone of exclusion, where women produce research on affective relations that is treated as a 'special interest' topic, something for women, but not a theme or subject that could define or redefine other disciplines. Yet love and care are universal social practices; they are sets of affective relations that are as central to the social scientific investigations as political, cultural and economic relations (Lynch, Kalaitzake and Crean 2021).

Love as Other in the Academy

There was very little attention given to the subject of love among the so-called founding 'fathers' of sociology: Marx, Durkheim and Weber. Sorokin (2002) was one of the few early sociologists who was seriously interested in the concepts of love and altruism. He became very isolated and much maligned in the academic community once he shifted his interests away from empirical studies of stratification and mobility and towards the study of love and 'creative altruism' (Rusu 2018: 9). He was pushed aside by Harvard (and by the American Sociological Association), and Talcott Parsons was elevated to replace him.[2]

While love did receive attention from twentieth-century leaders in sociology, including Bauman (2003), Giddens (2008) and Beck and Beck-Gernsheim (2002), their work is predominantly focused on love in intimate and sexual relationships between adults, and its management and commercialization in highly mobile and globalized societies. Love is engaged as a concept that helps explain changes and tensions in modernity, rather than being investigated discretely as a set of affective relations. The practical, hands-on character of love as work is not examined in depth, nor are the feelings of those who are dependent and in need of love.

Hochschild's work (Hochschild and Machung 1989; Hochschild 2002, 2003, 2012) and that of Illouz (2007, 2012) are exceptions to the mainstream tradition. These scholars have put care and love on the sociological map, although the important distinction between care and love work is not the central theme of their research. Despite the path-breaking work of Hochschild in particular, to write about feminine subjects such as care and love locates the speaker/ writer on the periphery of male-dominated disciplines like sociology (Aulenbacher, Lutz, and Riegraf 2018; Rusu 2018). While it is now safe and welcome to write about gender, as it is an officially approved subject and fully incorporated into the research mainstream,[3] love still retains a sentimental standing (hooks 2000). The development of a new interdisciplinary journal, *The International Journal of Care and Caring*, as recently as 2017 demonstrates how care and related subjects such as love have not been mainstreamed in other fields in the social sciences.

The heuristic practices at the disposal of social scientists are their 'conceptual practices of power', which are generally learned from the founders or leaders of the discipline (Smith 1990). However, as the dominant paradigms within a discipline do not necessarily encourage reflexivity, enabling scholars to see or know the hidden doxas (unspoken and unnamed assumptions) of their scientific trade (Bourdieu 1990), most scholars are not trained to recognize how their domain assumptions influence their theoretical assumptions. Because of this, the world academics are cognitively hardwired to see is limited; they can and do live in 'privileged ignorance' of many matters of social justice (Medina 2013). Perspectives are constrained not only by their discipline and the paradigmatic assumptions of their research traditions, but also by their domain assumptions, namely their biographical and cultural experiences, including their gender, age, social class, colour, abilities and ethnicity.[4]

Bourgeois values, androcentrism, Eurocentrism, racism, hetero-sexism and disablism are widely shared in research communities, and while problematized, they do not unseat the reigning paradigms. The deep cultural, political and economic injustices documented by African, Indian, Aborigine and South American scholars (Said 1978; Ngũgĩ wa Thiong'o 1986, 1993; Spivak 1988; Tuhiwai Smith 1999; Mignolo 2007, 2009) are boxed off as postcolonial scholarship, a strand outside the mainstream (Connell 2007). Epistemic struggles persist (Escobar 2007; Quijano 2007; Lugones 2010; Icaza and Vazquez 2013; Rojas 2016), though they often do not gain academic traction until academia is shamed by social justice activists, people who can read the limits of the academic standpoint, from below. Very often, powerful scholars/disciplines only recognize the limitations of dominant academic standpoints when they are forced to do so from outside. (Harding and Norberg 2005; Harding 2008).

Knowledge relations are also power relations, and, as men (especially) but also women of a particular class, colour and nationality (White, Western, middle- and upper-class) dominate the professoriate and other leading positions in academia and research (Bagilhole and White 2011),[5] they largely determine the definition of what is valid knowledge and who has a right to produce it, teach it *and* be securely funded to do it. And, as with those who hold senior positions elsewhere, senior academic men's power, and especially their eminence (and this can also apply to senior women), discharge them from domesticity. They are frequently detached from hands-on care work; it is taken as given, something that comes 'naturally' to women.[6]

The care ceiling in the academy operates not only in terms of who does the care work at home and at work (Raddon 2002; Pocock 2005; Fox, Fonseca and Bao 2011; Toffoletti and Starr 2016; Bomert and Leinfellner 2017; Cardozo 2017; Dubois-Shaik and Fusulier 2017; Lynch, Ivancheva, Keating, O'Flynn and O'Connor 2020), but also in terms of subject-based divisions of labour. Low-status work like caring is mirrored in the lowly status of care-based subjects, such as social work, social care, nursing, childcare and teaching, all of which are female-dominated. Because love work cannot be professionalized, unlike other forms of caring, it has an even more subordinated standing. The patriarchal and colonial traditions of universities and research institutes make them ill equipped to see love at work, both literally and intellectually.

Making Love Commercial

Like other services, the caring and loving involved in the production and reproduction of life are being defined as potential commodities with market returns; they are invested in in terms of their share price and dividend potential, in ways that are not dissimilar to those applied to other products, be these mobile phones, cars or financial services. Paid care is a globalized industry, with an estimated 11.5 per cent of total global employment now being in the care sector (ILO 2018). The home care industry alone was valued at US$281.8 billion in 2019 and is expected to expand at a compound annual growth rate of 7.9 per cent from 2020 to 2027 (Grand View Research 2020). This global paid-care economy is deeply racialized and gendered, in both personal and geopolitical terms (Ehrenreich and Hochschild 2003; Yeates 2009; Lutz 2011; Oxfam 2020).

There is an emotional capitalist market paralleling this, where 'emotions have become entities to be evaluated, inspected, discussed, bargained, quantified and commodified' (Illouz 2007: 109). This is especially evident in the field of dating, much of which now begins online: the dating sites enable connections/dating to occur where the self is disembodied and textual performance in visual and psychological terms is key to success (Illouz 2007). Outside of sexual relationships, there are extensive markets in the worlds of intimacy emanating from the fields of psychology and psychotherapy (Nehring and Kerrigan 2019). Psychology-related disciplines have succeeded in defining the terms on which the healthy psychological self is assessed, marketed and constructed, and in selling their expertise to develop these skills accordingly.

What is interesting about these new attempts to commodify intimacy, care and love is that they are wide-ranging in scope and reach. The ways of loving and caring that women mostly, and men, have crafted to provision for their relational lives outside the market are deemed to be replaceable in the same way that new furniture or shoes can be replaced; 'touch' on screens is assumed to be a good replacement for physical touching and caressing; replacing breast milk with breast milk substitutes for new-borns and infants is sold as both personally convenient and a healthy option.[7] Making babies has also become an important market for profit-making. Advances in fertility have enabled a new economy in pregnancy surrogacy to develop; poor women's wombs have become a part in the global supply chain for babies, particularly in India, although some regulations have been introduced in recent years to control this market. It is estimated that the surrogacy industry in India alone made in excess of US$2 billion profits in the early years of this millennium (Rudrappa 2015). As bodies are tradable so are body parts, including blood and organs (Healy 2006).

Native knowledges of ways of living, birthing, sustaining and caring for humans and other species, and for the environment, are regarded as 'primitive', soft (feminine) and unscientific. Just as the native ecological knowledges of indigenous people about their land and ways of living sustainably are dismissed as anachronistic, so localized care knowledges at family and community level are regarded as trivial and primitive; they are cast as knowledges that need to be replaced with paid-for, scientifically informed knowledge. While there is much to learn from science about ecology and care of the world, what is produced by researchers in relation to care is not value free, as much research is funded directly or promoted indirectly (via governments) by commercial interests (Olivieri 2003; Lieberwitz 2005); nor is it always disinterested in Merton's (1973)[8] sense of that term.

Notwithstanding the limitations of the interests embedded in knowledge in contemporary science, experts are presented in wider society as being 'disinterested' and objective. In the love and care field, expert knowledge from food science, medicine, psychology, child development and welfare are called upon to guide parents, especially mothers. They are told what their children should eat, where and when they should sleep, and how, if and when they should be comforted. A deeply White middle-class way of caring and loving is idealized implicitly in much of the professional knowledge presented to parents (Gillies, Edwards and Horsley 2016). Expert knowledge is presented to mothers by (mostly middle-class) professionals as the benchmark by which they will be judged. The information is governed by a concept of intensive mothering that is 'expert-guided, emotionally absorbing, labour intensive, and financially expensive' (Hays 1996: 8). Although this kind of mothering is unaffordable and unattainable for many low-income households, and induces a sense of guilt and inadequacy, poor women feel compelled to pursue it even if they have little chance of success (Cappellini, Harman, Marilli and Parsons 2019). Trying to follow professional advice on 'creative budgeting' (Daly 2015), they live with considerable strain and anxiety (Leigh, Gauthier and Pacholok 2012). In all of this, experts stand by, hovering overhead, judging and evaluating women in terms of how they perform love for their children (Henderson, Harmon and Houser 2010; Budds, Hogg and Banister 2017). This surveillance has high costs for all mothers, but especially for low-income women and families; they feel blamed, guilty and inadequate when they cannot pass the ideal mothering test (Romagnoli and Wall 2012; Henderson, Harmon and Newman 2016), including the ideal consumption test (Hutton 2015).

Prior knowledges that have had a history of care 'successes', judged by people's mental health and well-being over generations, are seen as dated, valued only where they can be translated into marketable forms of relationality, be it in parenting programmes, the therapeutic couch or the economy of cheap care. Yet native knowledges of how to love and care well do exist; they have helped protect people from loneliness, fear and isolation and secure their mental and emotional health, which, in turn, secures their physical health, as these knowledges have done for past generations. Households, parents, grandparents, great-grandparents, neighbourhoods and communities have built up ways of caring and loving across time, and even across migrations, that vary by cultural tradition, but have care-security outcomes. This sustaining and sustainable knowledge of good care and love practice is not named or claimed; the focus of research is most often on the pathological, so-called 'dysfunctional' families. Positive native care knowledges are allowed to die slowly of neglect through lack of research and education. They are replaced by paid professional 'parenting' experts from the psychological sciences in particular, supplemented by family therapists, social workers and others with degrees and diplomas granting them the authority to advise on how to love and care.

And while love most certainly requires competences, and professional care workers are necessary, the nurturing care that young children or those who are old and lonely need requires more than this. It requires a disposition, energy, attentiveness and desire to care that cannot be simply supplied by 'training', professional interventions or therapy alone. Though education can enhance the quality of care provided, loving-led care cannot be supplied to order like a set of new clothes (Weicht 2019). Care and love are 'elements' of life, sets of relationships that are endemic to life itself. They are 'fictitious commodities' (Polanyi 2001: 75) in the sense that their commodification changes them into products, where life-creating essential elements are lost.

While the air hostess can 'put on a smile and use' her (his) emotionally trained professional self to help make people feel comfortable and welcome on an airline (Hochschild 1983), the managed smile cannot be sustained in long-term relationships of care without its calculability becoming evident. Genuine, emotionally engaged 'caring about' someone cannot be bought or forced, as it has a large voluntary dimension to it even in paid settings. It is a complex matter, especially when provided on a professional basis for children or young people in need of non-family care in residential settings (Emond 2016; Mulkeen 2019).

In many senses, love is most visible in its absence, in the harms that are created and the loss that lingers over time. Just as those who are without food can speak of the experience of hunger, so those who have been deprived of love are well placed to speak about love in its absence. They are highly sensitive to what it is and what it is not; they can distinguish between those who are 'phoney' and those who are 'genuine', between people who are putting on a face of care, just doing their job, and those who are interested in them as unique individuals (Mulkeen 2019).[9]

Adults who have been reared without much love or care for most of their lives, either outside or in their birth families, identify love as consistency of nurturing, commitment and interest over time (Feeley 2014). Being deprived of such love meant they could not flourish, not only relationally, but also in practical ways such as becoming fully literate (Feeley 2014).[10] This finding was confirmed in a major review of abuse and neglect of children in state care in Ireland: the absence of nurturing, in and of itself, was defined as abuse by those who had been deprived of such nurturing (Commission to Inquire into Child Abuse 2009).[11]

While there is much to learn from research and scholarship on how to care and love well, many of the assumptions about the best ways to love in families are based on deeply class-biased and racially specific ways of caring and mothering (Hays 1996; Skeggs 1997; Dodson 2010; Luttrell 2013, 2020). Those who cannot care in the idealized way, owing to lack of structurally determined lack of resources, time and/or good health, are judged, leading to deep feelings of blame and inadequacy. Their everyday experiential knowledge of loving and caring is dismissed and replaced by professionalized knowledge. The latter comes with a price tag for those who are better off (paying for counselling, parenting advice, psychotherapy) and with surveillance and potential moral reprimands if they are poor.

Love in the Context of Care

As noted in chapter 1 (figure 1), there are three major sites or contexts where different forms of care can operate: the intimate circle of face-to-face family and friendship relations; the circle of community and professional relations through which life is lived in employment, in residential neighbourhoods and in associational settings; and the circle of geopolitical relations, regional, national and international, within which life is spatially located in terms of towns, cities and nation states. The world of primary, intimate relations is the place where love relations are most likely to be generated,[12] involving strong attachment, deep engagement, commitment and intensity. While primary care relations vary in form cross-culturally, they arise from inherited, chosen, accidental[13] and/or contractual dependencies or interdependencies; they are people's primary love relations, best represented by the relationship between parents and children. Even if little love labour is invested in this intimate world, or if there is abuse or neglect, these relationships retain a high level of personal and social significance.

Secondary care relations are lower-order interdependency relations. They characterize outer circles of relatives, friends, neighbours and work colleagues where there are lower-order affective engagements in terms of time, responsibility and commitment. But neither love nor care is a purely personal or intimate matter, and caring is not simply a dyadic, individualistic relation. Care is about living to maintain, continue and repair the world so that we can live in it as well as possible (Tronto 1993, 2013). Solidarity is the political expression of such public care. It exists as a practice, be it in terms of health care, environmental care, community care, educational care or public welfare, expressed through a politics of redistributive solidarity recognition and parity of representation. Solidarity relations generally involve unknown others and do not involve intimacy; they can be regarded as the political or social form of love relations (Boltanski and Porter 2012; Lynch and Kalaitzake 2018).[14]

While most of the scholarship about care defines it as a singular phenomenon – and it is so in the sense that it is a disposition, a set of values and attitudes that inform practice – love is a unique form of care. Health care, care in education and welfare care are all important forms of care, but they are not specifically loving relationships. They do not have nurturing the other, and the relationship with the other as a specific goal, except and in so far as it improves some other professional or personal purpose. The labour involved in nurturing and coproducing one or more persons relationally is a project in itself, be it individual or collective. It is distinguishable from generalized forms of caring in that it is focused on the person and/or group and the relationship per se, not on the services that the relationship provides.

Love Labouring as Distinctive

Drawing on the author's research for *Affective Equality* (Lynch, Baker and Lyons 2009), table 1 summarizes some of the defining features of love labour compared with other care relations. What it highlights is that all care work is demanding but love labouring is especially so. It requires an investment of attentiveness, commitment, affection, time, energy, physical work and resources that is more intense and demanding than other forms of care labour.

Love labour involves *emotionally engaged attentiveness* that has as its principal goal the survival, development and/or well-being of the other, in the context of a mutually engaged relationship with a history and assumed future.[15] There is an intense sense of *belongingness* and *trust* in primary care relations when they are positive, and one of isolation, distrust and pain when they are neglectful, exploitative or abusive, feelings that do not hold to the same degree for other care relations.

Though love labour is fundamentally affectively driven work that enhances humans as relational beings, this is not to suggest it does not also involve domestic work or body work. Neither are love labour actions entirely altruistic, as the bonds that develop in such relationships have the potential to be mutually beneficial, even if the benefits to any given primary caregiver are disproportionately small, contingent or temporally distant. Love labour is generally characterized by relations of strong *mutuality*; there is a sense of mutual dependence no matter how poor the relationship may be.

Table 1 Affective relations of love, care and solidarity

Features of care work	Love labour	Secondary care labour[a]	Solidarity work[b]
Using the skills of knowing how to care (cognitive work)	Having knowledge of what love is and what it is not	Knowing how to care	Knowing how to do solidarity work (as opposed to charity/ philanthropy)
Attentiveness and emotional engagement (emotional work)	Intense and prolonged (may be positive or negative)	Moderate and variable	Politically engaging
Commitment and responsibility	Long-standing and sustained but may be reneged upon	Temporary and contingent	Variable – can be long-standing or temporary
Spending time	Prolonged time	Variable time	Variable time
Moral imperative	Strong and compelling, especially for women	Limited and bounded	Determined by law, culture, custom and personal values

Features of care work	Love labour	Secondary care labour[a]	Solidarity work[b]
Trust	High (expectation)	Moderate and variable	Variable but can be reasonably high
Belongingness	High (expectation)	Moderate and variable	Variable but can be reasonably high
Attentiveness including advance planning (mental work)	High (expectation)	Variable	High at the political level if it is to be effective
Scope	Extensive	Bounded	May be bounded or extensive
Intensity	High	Low and bounded	Variable
Mutuality	High interdependency whether voluntary or not	More circumscribed	Not necessarily present
Practical tasks including organizing, body work and physical tasks	High (expectation)	Moderate and variable	Variable but can be reasonably high

[a] Secondary care work varies considerably depending on whether it is set in the context of professional care relationships or voluntary relationships.
[b] Solidarity work also varies in character depending on whether it is determined by state action, custom or culture and whether it is voluntary and/or democratically or socially mandated.

Source: Adapted from Lynch (2007: 558)

The mutuality that is at the centre of love labour relations is also a relationship of power and control exercised through the medium of care. However, the structurally defined care or love recipient is not necessarily a silent or powerless partner, a tabula rasa for someone else's love labour. They can show appreciation for love or fail to show it; they can call on the moral imperatives to care available in the culture to enforce their care expectations and in that way exercise care commands on carers (Lynch, Baker and Lyons 2009: 114–31).

Love labour involves higher levels of *responsiveness* than would apply to other forms of care (Engster 2005). It denotes not just the activity of thinking about people or having them on one's mind, although this may be part of it. It also refers to the very real activities of 'looking out for' and 'looking after' the other(s). In the conversations for *Affective Equality*, a number of those who were cared for by family members spoke about how being secure in being cared for mattered. Monica, in her later seventies, was widowed and living alone. She spoke of how she felt protected and looked after at night by knowing her daughter always had her phone with her in bed, as had Monica herself: 'I would keep the mobile on and have it beside me when I am in bed. ... And I'd say, "If I ring in the middle of the night, you do know it is me"; so, I always have those safeguards' (Lynch, Baker and Lyons 2009: 125).

Love also involves the management of the tensions and conflict that are an integral part of love labour relations. In the *Affective Equality* research, Tom was a single man, a small farmer, caring for his elderly father alone. He articulated the contradictory emotions that primary caring involves and the sense of mutual love it entails:

> Sometimes I tear my hair out but then he will come up with a gem or I might be at the end of my tether after a very hard day with him. 'Tom,' 'What Dad?' 'I love you.' That defuses the whole thing then. As he says himself those are the three loveliest words in the English language 'I love you', and he does. (Lynch, Baker and Lyons 2009: 62)

For the person who has the primary responsibility for the care of vulnerable others, love involves drawing up the care-map for the other(s). It involves carrying the care-map in one's mind and overseeing its implementation in terms of scope and quality throughout the care journey. In the case of children or adults with high dependency needs, it is quite literally a twenty-four-hour care-map (McKie, Gregory and Bowlby 2002); it can feel like a 'military operation' in terms of the demands on time and energy that it makes (Lynch, Baker and Lyons 2009: 59).

One of the biggest issues raised by carers (and older people living and being cared for at home) in the *Affective Equality* conversations was institutionalization. Parents of children with intellectual disabilities went to great efforts to plan ahead for their children in later life to try to ensure institutionalization did not happen. Debra, whose young son had Down's syndrome, said it was her greatest concern and she and her partner had a long-term investment plan in place for their son to secure against it: 'I think the biggest, my biggest, the biggest thing that I want or don't want for (son) is I don't want him to be institutionalised' (Lynch, Baker and Lyons 2009: 69). Nora, who was in her seventies, and the carer for her adult son with intellectual disabilities, spoke about her fears, not only for her son but for herself, as she had worked in a care home earlier in life:

> I lived through it. I told my family, … should I be on my hands and knees, I don't want to be a burden to anybody, just get me a spot out the back there, I will do my own thing as long as I can. As long as I live, I do not want to be put in a home … Because I saw too much. (Lynch, Baker and Lyons 2009: 68)

Love labour variously involves body work, physical, and mental work such as washing and cleaning a person's body, cooking favourite meals for a child or partner (not just feeding them so they are not hungry), listening to cares and worries, massaging the body or giving financial help if needed. At the mental level, it involves holding the persons and their interests in mind, keeping them 'present' in mental planning, and anticipating and prioritizing their needs and interests. It involves listening, affirming, supporting and challenging, as well as identifying with people at times of distress. There is an assumption of mutual affirmation and acceptance; while appreciation is expected, love is not given on some kind of cost–benefit system of incessant individualized calculability. However, this kind of loving is most likely to exist when there are nested dependencies and interdependencies, where exchanges of love and care over time are community-based rather than individually accounted (Kittay 1999: 66–8).

Love labour involves making some kind of *commitment* to maintaining and sustaining the relationship over time, although the length of that commitment can vary: the moral and legal imperative to care for dependent children is clearly much stronger than it is to care for a sibling, a friend or even a parent, especially in Western societies. Love labouring can be experienced as both pleasure and work, depending on the time and day (Lynch, Baker and Lyons 2009). When we asked people in our care conversations for *Affective Equality* if love was work, many said it was at times, and at other times it was not. The response of Elizabeth, who was co-parenting two children with her partner, was typical:

> I feel that there are times that it has to be work and sometimes you come home, or at the weekends and you just want to watch TV, you really just don't want to [do things] … Yes, sometimes it is work … and

you just have to do it. Most times it's not, most times you're delighted to be with them, and that whole involvement is wonderful. But then sometimes you are sick, you're fed up, but you have to do it because they are your babies. (Lynch, Baker and Lyons 2009: 63)

Neither the moral imperative to care, nor the expectations of trust that are part of love labouring relations, are present to the same degree in other care relations. There are also higher levels of time invested in love labouring relationships, and more of the self, than applies in other care contexts. Love labouring involves levels of commitment, responsibility and attentiveness that do not apply in other relationships. The care that is available to others in love labouring is personally defined and non-transferable, as it is given in the contexts of pre-established relationships with a unique history and assumed future involving continuity and attachment (Barnes 2006: 8–9). However, the boundaries between loving and other caring relations are fluid. Love labouring relations can and do change to secondary care relations when friendships or intimate relationships mutate over time. Sometimes the primary love labourer becomes the care recipient, such as when a parent becomes dependent due to illness or infirmity. Equally, secondary care friendships at work or elsewhere may evolve into love labouring relationships.

The professional love dimension of secondary care relations

While primary care relations are love relations in the sense that they are intentionally and primarily focused on nurturing and co-creating intimacy, relations that are not defined by love, notably professional care services, can and do contribute to nurturing, even when their principal purpose is not loving per se. This is especially true of professions such as childcare (Page 2011, 2018), but also of nursing, and social care with people who are ill or vulnerable. A pedagogy of love is also vital for good teaching (Darder 2002), because, as Freire (1970) observed, liberatory education involves mutual respect, learning and dialogue, and dialogue cannot exist 'in the absence of a profound love for the world and for people. The naming of the world, which is an act of creation and re-creation, is not possible if it is not infused with love' (Freire 1970: 70).

Equally in health settings, many care assistants, nurses, general service staff and doctors provide exceptional care for those who are sick in a way that is not directly connected to the illness per se or the contract of employment (Mol 2008). There may be extra responsibility taken, and attention given to those who are suffering due to a family illness or loss, or those who are lonely and need intimacy. Though the care assistant may not be required to provide intimacy and time, by listening to people's concerns they can and do choose to do so. This primary care work is not part of their contract but given voluntarily due to a perceived need. While listening to, being with and sharing time with older people is often not recognized as necessary care work by employers, it is often what people value most of all (McDonald, Lolich, Timonen and Warters 2019). Because it is voluntarily given, it is in some respects a gift, something that cannot be commodified, though it can be and is exploited by employers (Müller 2019).

Equally, in work relations or in neighbourhood relations, people can and do engage in extended care for colleagues, especially at times of bereavement, loss or illness, by giving time and showing attentiveness, and through practical actions such as visiting, listening, cooking meals or raising money if necessary. This primary care may be temporary and short-lived but it cannot be commodified, as it is voluntary, neither contracted nor contractable. Yet it is such incidences and occasional expressions of love-like care that make a difference to people; they give people a sense of belonging and support, a sense of feeling welcome and at home in their neighbourhoods and appreciated and recognized at work.

Why Love Matters and Is Not Commodifiable

Love matters because it is (1) inalienable as a need and (2) non-substitutable as a practice. The need for love is not something people can reassign to others, as it is a foundational necessity to their own life. Love is also inalienable in that it cannot be removed by force or some other power; nor can it be stolen, as it is a relational experience, something that is bound to, given by and shared with others as part of pre-existing relationships. It has a history that cannot be taken away. To attempt to steal love would be to try steal a set of relationships, something that is intangible and only exists as it is living through co-creation in habitual practice. While the conditions and resources that are required to produce love can be undermined and under-resourced, and people can literally steal your lover (as happens in sexual relationships, or even in friendships, or when someone steals a valued pet), the living, existing relationship cannot be stolen. People will continue to love and need love from given person(s) or beings, even in their absence.

What distinguishes love most from other forms of caring also is its non-substitutability. To attempt to substitute, or commodify, the intimate part of the love relationship would change it into something else. The attentiveness, emotional engagement, attachment and belonging involved in loving people cannot be assigned to another by a commercial or a voluntary arrangement without undermining the premise of mutuality that is at the heart of intimacy (Strazdins and Broom 2004; Lynch 2007). Love relations are not fungible; they are not replaceable by another identical relationship. When a sister or father wants to meet you, you cannot arrange for a friend to be with them as a substitute for yourself; you cannot contract someone to go for a coffee/tea with friends or meet a partner for a chat without fundamentally changing the meeting into a quasi-commercial transaction. Because a core part of love relationships is the maintenance of the bond of intimacy and mutual affirmation, being in the presence of, and listening to and being with, the other in time and space are vital elements of the love relationship.

To say that love is distinct from other forms of caring is not to say that, in the practice of loving, desiring and caring, the boundaries between forms of love and care can be neatly drawn. As Traustadóttir (2000) observes, while we can make a distinction between emotions and activities, they are not so easily separated in practice. Professional secondary care relationships can and do transform into friendships. There are numerous records of long-term carers of older people changing from professional carer to friend in specific contexts.

Conclusion

'In order to grow, flourish, and survive and endure illness, disability and frailty, each individual requires a caring relationship to significant others who hold that individual's well-being as a primary responsibility and a primary good' (Kittay 1999: 108).

Much of the scholarship on care treats it as a singular phenomenon. The danger in treating care as a unitary entity is that this potentially invisibilizes the aspects of care labour that cannot be commodified, especially the love labour dimension. While love is a part of care, not all care is loving.

Loving care matters because it is what produces people in their relational humanity (Oksala 2016: 297), enhancing the capacity of their lives and enabling their moral transformation (hooks 2000). Being loved is enabling and enriching; it is creative in terms of the capacities that it produces within people: both individually and collectively, people are disabled as relational beings in families, professional, political or other areas of life without the experience of being nurtured and loved. Having a good life generally involves experiencing some loving relationships with other people (Honneth 1995; Gheaus 2017). Because the affective relations involved in reproducing love (care and solidarity) are a core part of what produces people as human beings, to be deprived of love (primary care), and also of the secondary and tertiary care that facilitate and enable love, is a major social injustice.

Loving, and the affective relations in which it is embedded, are highly materialized practices. They are not especially romantic. Love relations involve work, as they are engaged in the production and exchange of affective energies, of attentiveness that is deeply nurturing; they are not driven either by profit or by pure self-interest but exist as something intrinsically valuable and good (Ferguson 2014: 250–1). The labour that produces love is undertaken through affection, commitment, attentiveness and the material investment of time, energy and resources. It may be pleasurable, but is also demanding in terms of effort, time and energy. It involves, at different times and in various forms, friendship, desire and nurturing, where there may be little or no reciprocation, or seeming merit or deservingness for receiving love. Love, like other forms of care, operates under principles of other-centredness, even when it fails in this purpose. But unlike other forms of care, love work is inalienable and non-substitutable. The emotional and related attentiveness and commitment involved in loving particular persons cannot be assigned to another, by a commercial or even a voluntary arrangement, without changing it into something other than itself. Love relationships cannot be commodified or outsourced without eliminating the relationship that co-creates them and maintains them.[16]

4

Time to Care

Because neoliberal capitalism is governed by a culture of incessant competition, productivity and speed (Rosa 2013), time is a scarce resource for which care time must compete. This chapter examines the ways in which the organization of time under neoliberalism impacts on the practice of care. While recognizing that capitalism alone is not responsible for competition over time, the chapter demonstrates how the competitive and appropriative culture of capitalism compresses time, making love, care and solidarity work appear incidental and marginalized, work that is done in leftover time, with leftover energy, after productive (market-related) work has been completed.

To give an empirical context to the chapter, and for illustrative purposes, following a brief overview of the concept of time itself, the opening section is devoted to a discussion of some of the author's own studies of family carers and care receivers, as this work highlights many of the time conflicts that arise in a society governed by the ethics of productivity and competition.[1]

On Time

Time is a resource that is lived and known to humans in socially defined ways. There is no one time but a multitude of overlapping, interpenetrating times (Adam 1995: 12), be it work time, sleep time, leisure time, growing up time, travelling time, family time or historical time. While industrialization led to the dominance of clock time, experience of clock time is not simply quantitative; time is framed by tasks and mediated through relations of power

(Adam 2004). Caring is embedded within 'timescapes' and spatially bounded 'caringscapes' that are politically defined, by age, gender (Adam 1995; McKie, Gregory and Bowlby 2002) and race (Duffy 2005, 2011).

From a human perspective, time is experienced cyclically (night and day, winter, and summer), linearly (with a past and a potential future) and as a fixed point (a birthday or death). Time not only moves, it moves constantly and in an embodied way; it is mapped out in corporeal changes as bodies grow, and as they age; and it is lived and known objectively and subjectively as relationships, locations and bodies change (Adam 2004).

Time matters because of the finiteness of human and other species' existence; it is a limited resource that ends inevitably in death. As all tasks take time and moving between spaces to do different tasks also takes time, both mobility time and mental and emotional readjustment time, time is a resource that has to be managed. Moreover, because human beings are indivisible in terms of their bodily person, they cannot bilocate; they are constrained by the spatial confines of their bodily existence within specific time frames. They literally cannot be physically present in two places at the one time, something that is hugely significant in care terms. How time is organized has serious implications for how we relate to others, who we relate to, when and on what terms.

Hands-On Care as Process and Practice: A View from Primary Care Studies

Care, time and values

We live in a world where thinking and action are future-oriented and productively led (Puig de la Bellacasa 2017; 203–11). Biological time, emotional time and ecological time are subjected to a production logic that is future-led. Life in the present is often lived for the future: children learn to study so they can 'get on', so they can get a good job; workers think of jobs in terms of how to get a higher wage/salary or promotion, or how to maximize holiday time in the future; businesses are managed in terms of maintaining and/or extending markets, being more productive than competitors; both land and sea are seen as resources for the increasingly intensified production of food.

Productive 'timescapes' are only possible, however, because speeded-up and intensified production often disregards the biological and ecological times it takes to produce food and other goods in a way that is ecologically and care balanced (Mellor 1997), and non-exploitative in terms of other species. Yet production logic only works through time when the infrastructures of care co-exist at its foundations, enabling it to happen. Despite being the foundation stone for living well, however, care-led maintenance and repair work often remains imperceptible until it breaks down, as happened in the Covid-19 virus crisis in 2020; it was only when crèches and primary schools closed, and when hospitals, care homes and care workers were overwhelmed by virus-related illness, that the dynamics of care infrastructures became visible publicly in many countries.

Decisions about time are decisions about values and what and who is prioritized in the use of time. The act of caring involves *making time* for others, often at the expense of productivity, and with that at a cost to power, status and money. One cannot know or show concern for others by simply thinking about them in the abstract; care requires action specific to the needs in question and action takes time specific to the needs of the relationship. It has micro, meso and macro manifestations: it involves listening, waiting, being present, tending to someone's frail body, preparing and planning food, naming care needs to others, organizing services, mobilizing in solidarity politically, and/or engaging in protests over the lack of a care infrastructure, and related injustices globally. It comes at a cost to productivity, at least in the short term. The ways in which time resources are crucial for caring were very evident in the caring studies undertaken with colleagues (Lynch, Baker and Lyons 2009; Lynch, Grummell and Devine 2012; Lynch, Ivancheva, Keating, O'Flynn and O'Connor 2020).

The time it takes

Hands-on care work is time-consuming, boundless and incessant with those who are highly dependent. It has to be done *on time* and at *specific times*: it commands immediate attention and bodily presence. While the contexts where urgent care needs arise vary, the ways in which high dependency requires presence and immediate action are universal.

Valerie, who was caring for both her ill parents, explained how challenging and tiring non-stop care was:

It is ... like a military operation, you're talking oxygen, you're talking
nappies, you're talking clean underwear, their juice or a drink, their
medication, I mean, the plan has to be there ... Well, it's basically
twenty-four hours a day, seven days a week. I mean you are on call all
the time, ... you cannot leave them, it's a case of you have to be here,
which is very trying. (Lynch, Baker and Lyons 2009: 59–60)

How time is socially interpreted produces and recognizes certain
social realities while closing down and shutting out others (Bastian,
Baraitser, Flexer, Hom and Salisbury 2020: 290). The lack of publicly
funded, accessible and affordable childcare in many countries,
including the UK and Ireland, became a major political issue during
the Covid-19 crisis. Parents had nowhere to go for care help as
private crèche operators closed their premises for safety reasons.
Governments had limited plans in place to manage the care needs of
parents with young children who were trying to work at home. The
net outcome was a dramatic lowering of life satisfaction, especially
for women.[2]

The care studies undertaken by the author and colleagues in
2016–17 show that managing childcare and employment where there
are very limited public care services is a 'nightmare' for working
parents, especially mothers, as this young mother working in an
administrative post explains:

It's an absolute nightmare and, truthfully, because I have no family
at all ... here ... . If they're sick at all, the crèche ring you and you're
snookered. It's really, truthfully, it's so hard, very, very hard. ... I was
naïve ... . I didn't think it was going to be [like this] ... I had no idea
the pressures on parents, until I became a parent. (Lynch, Ivancheva,
O'Flynn, Keating and O'Connor 2020: 165)

The position of another mother, who was a university lecturer
parenting alone, was very similar: 'I mean I'm stretched all the
time, you're rushing between here and there so, you know, I think
that anybody – I don't know if that's just exclusive to me – I think
any parent of small children is stretched finely' (Lynch, Ivancheva,
Keating, O'Flynn and O'Connor 2020: 165).

But the care of most young children has an ending in terms of time.
Those who are caring for adult children who are highly dependent
due to intellectual disabilities have a very different timescape (Adam
2004: 143) in care terms. Melanie, a mother of two adult children
with intellectual disabilities, noted how

When you are minding children, like they grow up and then they will be
gone but I know that this is not going to happen with them. You know?
That means that it goes on, there is no end to it. ... I don't know to be
honest if they will ever get to the independent stage that I would like
them to get to. (Lynch, Baker and Lyons 2009: 110)

Those who exercise political power define what time matters, what
time becomes visible and invisible, and whose work is made visible in
time. There is a 'chronopolitics' (a time–power interface) operating
locally and globally that exercises control over the interpretation of
time (Mills 2020).[3] Not only can the politically powerful define time,
the economically wealthy can buy the time of others to provide services
like cleaning, laundry, food preparation, childcare or eldercare. Time
is a form of wealth that can be bought and sold. While control over
time as a resource varies by age, employment and care status, it varies
especially by gender and social class (Chatzitheochari and Arber
2012). The moral imperative on women to care denies them 'free'
time, time over which they exercise personal control (Bryson 2007),
while those who are wealthy can buy the time of others to undertake
caring, especially time-inconvenient and demanding forms such as
night-time caring. Time for uninterrupted sleep and predictable
leisure are rich resources, though often not available to parents
(especially mothers) of young children or family carers of adults
with high dependency needs, or to those employed on shift work or
working unsocial hours.

One of the most persistent themes in the *Affective Equality* studies
was how time-consuming hands-on caring is. Mothers spoke of how
'there weren't enough hours in the week', or how they were 'rushing
them [the children], constantly rushing'. Others spoke of 'running
them [the children] here and running them there' (Lynch, Baker and
Lyons 2009: 147–51).

The contrasts between those who have money to buy out of the
tedious, dirty aspects of care and those who cannot afford to were
illustrated clearly in two different conversations in the *Affective
Equality* research. Jill and Jane were a professional couple with two
young children. They explained how they bought 'quality time' with
their children by paying for domestic work:

We wanted quality time at dinner time every day of the week, so that we
had at least from 5 o'clock in the evening until 8 o'clock at night ... We
... get help for two mornings and dinners get made, and the place gets
cleaned up. [This] allows us to totally enjoy being with them and being

at home. (Jill, partner of Jane, primary carer of two primary-school children). (Lynch, Baker and Lyons 2009: 153)

In contrast, Sasha was parenting one pre-school and two primary-school children alone, and struggled with time and money. She was constantly 'going', and unable to find employment that fitted in with her care commitments.[4] Worrying about money every day took time and energy:

> When I do stop at half seven and I want to watch Eastenders or something ... then it is nearly time to go to bed. Then I am thinking 'what am I going to do tomorrow, I have no money, where am I going to be able to get this from?' You know. If there is something coming up, ... it is just mental torture on your brain, just wearing your head down ... [all the time]. (Lynch, Baker and Lyons 2009: 152–3)

Those engaged in caring for highly dependent others are often locked out of the time–money-earning nexus. Their care time does not count as real time in the market system, as it has no immediate exchange value, remaining invisible in monetary terms (Adam 2004: 127). For those who are poor, there is no way to buy time from others, except through bartering, which, in itself, comes with time costs, as bartering is a reciprocal arrangement that has to be negotiated in time.

Whoever does hands-on care work is tied to care by time, as there is no substitute for time if the care relationship is to have a humane dimension, be it paid or unpaid. Equally, where body care is involved, the carer must be physically present. Time needs to be available within a defined place and for designated periods. Where relationships are intimate, and are of primary importance in love terms, they not only require time, they also command proximity, as they are person-specific. Very often one needs to be in the presence of others to meet their needs; for example, one cannot pay someone to replace oneself as a close friend to another person. The attentiveness to bodily presence, and the affections that are possible in the physical presence of another, cannot be given virtually or at spatial distances, not least because they do not allow the sensory experiences of touching, holding, seeing, smelling or hearing in person, something that became painfully obvious in virtual meetings during the Covid-19 crisis.

Also, when care takes the form of love labouring it has a longer and more unpredictable trajectory, given it is not tied to a time-specific contract and is built on mutuality and commitment (Lynch 2007; Cantillon and Lynch 2017). Any process or mode of organization that undermines time and/or presence for giving love and care generates affective injustices for those in need of care. Capitalism is a system that does this in different ways, though before examining how it impacts on care, it is important to recognize how institutional practices can undermine caring.

Bureaucracy, Time and Care

Caring work has a fluid, relational and cyclical temporal logic (Bryson 2007) that contradicts the logic of bureaucracies. It is not completed in clearly measurable time, as it is a process, a disposition, a way of living out relationships (Mol 2008). Since the need for love, care and solidarity arises from vulnerabilities and dependencies that do not operate on clock time, care cannot be contained or packaged in advance in a predetermined manner. It is a response to needs that keep on changing. The differences between clock time and lived, cyclical time are pivotal, therefore, to understanding caring. The open-ended practice and process of care time (Ruddick 1989) and measured, linear bureaucratic clock time are not easily aligned.

Yet all the major institutions of the state, capitalist and non-capitalist entities, including voluntary, community and charitable organizations, are organized as bureaucracies. Schools, workplaces and rest places are all governed by bureaucratic principles of 'rationally ordered societal action' (Gerth and Wright Mills (1958: 228). As such, life within them is mediated, managed and produced by clock time.

While bureaucratic structures enable services to be provided in an organized, systematic manner, care is simultaneously constrained by bureaucratic rules that are required to operate on universalistic principles (Weber 1978: 975); these rules do not take account of the particularities of persons and contexts at given times. In bureaucratic time, caring is expected to have a clear beginning and ending that can be calculated and measured (Andersen and Torbenfeldt Bengtsson 2019). This visibly conflicts with 'compassionate time' that requires slower engagement and is 'more developmental and cyclical' (Yuill and Mueller-Hirth 2019).

Even though bureaucratic organizations are not coterminous with capitalism, not least because they are central to the organization of public welfare, education, health and care services, they are enablers of capitalism. Not only do the hierarchies endemic to bureaucracies facilitate the stratifications on which capitalism thrives, they provide the infrastructures and logistics for capitalism's expansion and globalization. As Malešević's (2010a) studies of war demonstrate, bureaucratic power and organization play a central role in perpetuating contemporary warfare, much of which has been historically beneficial to colonization and capitalism (Patel and Moore 2018). Neoliberal capitalism also relies heavily on the bureaucratic power and capacity of financial, legal, transportation and telecommunications networks to realize its ends, demonstrating the multiple ways in which contemporary capitalism and bureaucratization are deeply integrated with each other (Malešević 2014: 77). The intimate, interdependent relationship between capitalism and bureaucracy is exemplified in the organization of time.

Capitalism and Time

Capitalist time is clock time, linear, progressive, measurable and commodifiable (Rosa 2013). This was something Marx recognized as a defining feature of capitalist production. The idea that time had to be compressed and maximized in its utility underpinned his labour theory of value:

> The less time the society requires to produce wheat, cattle etc., the more time it wins for other production, material or mental. ... Economy of time, to this all economy ultimately reduces itself. ... economy of time, along with the planned distribution of labour time among the various branches of production, remains the first economic law on the basis of communal production. (Marx 1973: 103)

Valuing time as an economic resource, as Marx, and economists like Becker (1965) did, is not a new phenomenon, however, nor is it confined to capitalism. It has its origins in pre-Christian Babylonian times, when systems of interest and credit were time-defined and time-limited (LeGoff 1980). Christianity challenged the practice of escalating interest on loans over time, and made usury[5] a sin, while a Catholic meeting in the Council of Vienne made the belief in the right to usury a heresy in 1311.[6] From an early Christian perspective, trading in time was theft because it was trading in something you did not own (Adam 2002: 18): the usurer was regarded as evil as he or she was trading in time, a good that was held in common and did not belong to any given individual. The recategorization of usury from being a sin to being tolerated, and even accepted as inevitable, was a major achievement for capitalism. As long as the notion of earnings based on time (selling money on a timed basis) was rejected outright, capitalism and the money economy could not develop.

But the money economy did develop,[7] as did time-based interest, and in a market economy there was an 'expectation that human beings behave in such a way as to achieve maximum money gains' (Polanyi 2001: 71). For this to happen, the economy had to become a separate sphere; it had to be defined as a unique space and a law unto itself, something that had not been the norm historically: 'Neither under tribal nor under feudal nor under mercantile conditions was there ... a separate economic system in society' (Polanyi 2001: 74).[8] What is significant about defining the economy as a separate sphere is that it conceals the way in which the economy never has operated and never will operate autonomously, not least because it is dependent on the daily social reproduction and care of workers, current and future, to service it (Dalla Costa and James 1972). It is intimately tied to families and their care institutions, and deeply dependent on their unpaid care work and domestic work for its own survival (Folbre 2001; Federici 2012). But by not acknowledging its interdependence with cultural, political, familial and care institutions, economists can dismiss care relations as being irrelevant to political–economic debates, defining care talk as 'soft talk', something that only concerns women, and can be addressed in leftover time, at the end of the day, the week or the year.

Capitalism and Speed

As the relentless pursuit of profit is a structural imperative for the entire capitalist system, the economic and political relations that govern it are greedy. This is not to suggest that the individuals who own and control businesses are necessarily mean or greedy; rather, they are simply following the logic of the free market economy (Block 2018: 129).

Capitalist businesses are under pressure to maintain or increase shareholder value, especially under financial capitalism. They want to achieve high levels of productivity, growth and expansion to survive and outcompete other businesses. Just as the speeding up of production was endemic to industrial capitalism, finding expression in Taylorism and Fordism,[9] so it remains a priority value. It is fed and led by competitiveness and enabled by information and communications technology (ICT).

Competitiveness drives productivity and creates abundances (even though these abundances are not evenly distributed). The goal is to win, to get control of markets; in this context, time becomes a scare resource that has to be maximized in its usefulness. To survive, companies seek to create products that retain, and where possible increase, their market share in as short a time as possible. Getting to the market first and making a product synonymous with your brand is a way of controlling that market. The ways in which the Hoover company made vacuum cleaning synonymous with its brand throughout the twentieth century, especially in the UK and Ireland (where it became a verb, *hoovering*, that is still widely used), is emblematic of this. In a similar way, *google* has become a twenty-first-century verb (if you do not know something you are told to *google it*), with Google controlling 87 per cent of the internet search engine market in early 2020, compared with Bing's 5.5 per cent. In both the Fordist manufacturing-led and post-Fordist services-driven eras, the escalation of speed was and is a defining feature of capitalist production (Harvey 1990, 2010; Rosa 2013).

To weaken and eliminate competitors, companies try to be 'dynamic' in terms of appropriating the land, resources, skills and capacities to create new goods and new markets. This means accelerating the pace at which appropriation happens, especially technologically but also socio-culturally, while politically ensuring that workers and citizens (and non-citizens) are activated to respond to the time frames of market requirements (Rosa 2013; Rosa, Dorré and Lessenich 2017).

Capitalism is not just a political-economic-legal system, organized through principles of market coordination and bureaucratic rationalization; it is a system that is not sustainable without constant movement. Capitalism has to stay in motion; like a bicycle, it gains its stability from movement, 'while it easily tips when slowing down or coming to a halt' (Rosa, Dorré and Lessenich 2017: 56). It also has to be growing, expanding and innovating to survive; its accelerated movement alters the organization of time throughout society:

> In the capitalist economic system, ... the continually rising speed of production necessarily goes hand in hand with the escalation of speeds in distribution and consumption, which are in turn driven by technological innovations and thus share responsibility for the fact that the

material structures of modern society are reproduced and altered in ever shorter periods of time. (Rosa 2013: 74)

When production speeds up, so do all of capitalism's component parts, including the business of marketing, sales, distribution and consumption. Even though those who consume capitalism's products are party to acceleration; they are incentivized to buy more in time-defined ways.[10] Greater and faster consumption means more profit in less time

Neoliberal Capitalism and Care Time

The intensification and speeding up of work, due to greater competition, increased flexibilization and precarity, that is part of neoliberal capitalism (Standing 2011) adds to the pressure to do more in less and less time (Rosa 2013). There is a 'heightening of the pace of life' (Rosa 2013: 219) that both undermines the quality of life (Garhammer 2002) and challenges the cyclical and unpredictable calls of care time (Bryson 2007; Andersen and Torbenfeldt Bengtsson 2019). While this has always been so under capitalism, the availability of new ICT has speeded up life, with a growing expectation not only of completing tasks as quickly as possible but of thinking quickly (Clark 2020). Speeding up thinking and transactions allows more money to be made more quickly. Working in 'instantaneous time' creates urgency and makes working at speed a priority (Rosa 2013: 219–20). Anything that reduces speed is a liability in money time. Taking time out to care for a child who is sick, or a person with dementia, challenges the profitability of capitalism, as it all takes time. As urgent care time cannot be predicted in advance, it can't be planned in clock time, and it is not done well in packaged, linear clock time (Mol 2008; Fazio, Pace, Flinner and Kallmyer 2017).

With the deregulation of financial services from the 1980s, financial markets and financial institutions gained a pre-eminent position in determining the workings of the global economy (Davis and Kim 2015). Financial rationales not only reshaped private enterprises and businesses, they led to new modes of management and performance appraisal throughout the public sector, thereby impacting on general social well-being and household welfare in ways often unknown to families, pensioners and households (Christopherson, Martin and Pollard 2013: 351–2).[11] Financialization promoted values and practices that emphasized individual responsibility, risk-taking and calculative financial management (Davis and Kim 2015: 212). Relatedly, it prioritized calculative, conditional solidarity over more altruistic and affective forms of solidarity (Lynch and Kalaitzake 2018), thereby providing an updated moral rationale for the promotion of self-interest (Mau 2015).

The compression and intensification of work, enabled by the widespread use of ICT, have facilitated permanent reachability and constant accessibility. This breaks up the boundaries between paid work times and unpaid care times, accelerating the pace of work and conflicts over time more generally (Rubery, Ward, Grimshaw and Beynon 2005). How and where time conflicts arise differs considerably across occupational contexts and by gender (McGinnity and Calvert 2009; Schöneck 2018). Conflicts over work–life balance[12] have an adverse impact on people's health generally, especially their mental health (Leineweber, Baltzer, Magnusson Hanson and Westerlund 2012). Data from the European Social Survey (undertaken in 2010/11 and covering twenty-three European countries) provides confirmation that people in countries with 'accelerated economic development', wider use of the internet and, interestingly, more new cars 'show a significantly greater inclination toward an unsatisfactory work–life balance' (Schöneck 2018: 12). Given that the 'life' part of 'work–life balance' refers to both care time and personal time for other activities,[13] this indicates that those who are employed are increasingly under pressure to subordinate personal time to deregulated paid-work time, following its rhythm and interruptions (Schöneck 2018).

The deregulation of work hours and increasing precaritization of employment through outsourcing and dismantling of full-time jobs under neoliberal capitalism (Standing 2011: 31–40) not only alters the relations between paid work and caring time in the private sector; it also does so in the public sector[14] (Standing 2011: 51). Precarious and temporary work provides employers with flexibility, but it undermines the management of primary caring, as the timing of care is based on needs, not on bureaucratic or market logic; it cannot be turned on and off when a person goes to work. Living with temporary and precarious work hours means that workers live without control over time; they are always effectively 'on call', and thereby lack control of their love and care relational time.

Speeding Up Care

Speeding up productivity does not only apply to industrial and service provision in the market economy; it also applies to public and community services, including those that are care-informed and/ or care-defined. Paid care work itself is also expected to be done in less time (Kubicek, Korunka and Ulferts, 2012; McDonald, Lolich, Timonen and Warters 2019).

Through the widespread diffusion of business-led modes of organizational thinking (Crouch 2004; Boltanski and Chiapello 2005), and the active promotion of neoliberal ideals of 'new public management' (Newman and Clarke 2009), public services including hospitals, care homes, welfare agencies and universities operate under pressure to produce more with less within a specified time frame (Sowa, Staples and Zapfel 2018). A brief perusal of the websites, mission statements and strategic plans of community and non-profit organizations shows that non-governmental organizations are also led by strategic plans with strategic goals in specified time frames. These organizations have been adopting managerial models based on business principles (Maier, Meyer and Steinbereithner 2016).

Following the deregulation and liberalization of trade and markets in the 1980s (Harvey 2005), and especially after the financial crash beginning in 2007, investment in public services was scaled back, privatization and commodification of hitherto public goods were rampant, and those working in the public sector were expected to produce more with less, while being excoriated for 'inefficiencies' if not doing so. Public service employees were disciplined through hierarchical observation and surveillance (Newman and Clarke 2009) in the manner identified by Foucault (1977: 170–7). Time was central to disciplining both workers *and* service users. There was pressure to increase the 'number of episodes of action and/ or experience per unit of time', leading to a heightening of the pace of life (Rosa 2013: 64). Agility became an interesting and related mantra, encapsulating the idea that time must be used with efficiency, innovation and flexibilization. The concept of 'training' in agility has even been incorporated into higher education.[15]

Although public services are *services to the public*, governed expressly by a duty of care, especially in fields such as education and health care, neoliberal forms of new managerial governance were adopted internationally (Sowa, Staples and Zapfel 2018) in ways that are often careless (Lynch, Grummell and Devine 2012). Public sector workers were and are defined as assets (or liabilities), their productive capacities measured 'in units of cost, time and effort', something that is greatly facilitated by the digitalization and tracking of information on their work routines (Tresson 2018; Mau 2019).

The outcomes of these systems of measurement and surveillance are not neutral in care terms. Research with over 500 primary-schoolteachers in Sweden found that new managerial reforms instituted a culture of 'strategic violence' that was 'structural' rather than individual, expressed through unreasonable productivity demands, exclusions, aggressive behaviour and lack of support; this led to many teachers taking extended sick leave or leaving the profession completely (Hetzler 2018). Studies of nursing in the UK show that the introduction of Care Record Service systems in the National Health Service led to a standardization of practice and the intensification of work, creating time-consuming scanning tasks that were neither necessary nor feasible within the specified time frames (Petrakaki and Kornelakis 2016). The implementation of algorithmic-led clinical decision-support software in the Australian health service (to move from face-to-face nursing to tele-nursing) meant nurses were making decisions that were led by programmed technology developed in the US that was not really appropriate in the Australian context (Russell 2012).

The metricization of care in terms of 'packages' and time 'slots' has been instrumental in enabling its privatization, marketization and commodification across the world (Williams 2010; Hoppania 2013). While the commodification of care for children, older people and people with disabilities is very advanced in Anglophone countries, especially in the UK (Dowling 2021) and Ireland (Mulkeen 2016), it is also happening in what are the 'strongest' welfare states, the Nordic countries (Hoppania and Vaittinen 2015; Meagher, Lundström, Sallnäs and Wiklund 2016; Szebehely and Meagher 2018). When care is meted out in time slots, and corporatized (Farris and Marchetti 2017), it becomes a unit of supervision rather than a form of care (Badgett and Folbre 1999). The time required to provide the relational and emotional dimension of care (Fazio, Pace, Flinner and Kallmyer 2017) is put at risk, thereby disregarding the voluntary human engagement and mutuality that are at the heart of caring, even when it is paid (Müller 2019). Care is made abject by being reduced to a 'package' of marketable, measurable products, in which time for relational work is neither named nor granted.

Technology and Care Time

How time is managed changes with the acceleration/deceleration of time, especially in terms of how it is managed by modern technology (Redhead 2004). Because software takes up very little space, we do not notice it. Yet it conditions our existence, through programmed outputs and expectations, in timed but often invisible ways (Thrift 2005).[16]

The boundaries between care times and employment are increasingly permeable through new communication technologies that make work ever-present through emails or mobile tracking systems. New forms of intelligence software put employees under surveillance *within* work in ways that can curtail rest, self-care or social time. Amazon's time wristbands for tracking employees' rate of productivity, GPS tracking of delivery and courier services[17] and timed care 'packages' for family carers[18] all exemplify forms of work organization that submit people to rigid schedules of time that often crowd out time for listening, being, or caring for self or others in ways that are not explicitly task-oriented.[19]

The widespread use of GPS technology to monitor and manage home carers has primarily been driven by cost-cutting in the public sector and profit in the private (business-led) sector to the detriment of the relational, emotional and affective aspects of care work (McDonald, Lolich, Timonen and Warters 2019; Dowling 2021: 119–21). When monitored and paid by fixed time on task (time spent in someone's home), both the paid carers and those who are in receipt of care experience the frustration of having task-time rather than care-time counted. The person who is being visited may be lonely and want companionship (more than being washed) but there is no time allowed for this, while the person caring feels they are being inhumane by not staying to listen (Folbre 2012; Moore and Hayes 2017).

Assistive Technologies of Care

Digitalized and robotic care technologies do provide technical assistance, and thereby give people considerable independence where they have the capacity to use them. These technologies may be all that some people need. In other cases, assistive technologies can complement personal care; however, they cannot not replace it completely. Helping someone with washing or showering, with dressing, getting up, going to bed or going to the toilet is not just a matter of physical assistance, though it is that. It also involves respecting them, as well as encouraging, reassuring, supporting and explaining; how important these care dispositions are in any given day or event will vary with the person involved. There is no formula that works all the time.[20] The individualized empathy, intuition and understanding that are involved in such care cannot be programmed, and in this regard it cannot be automated. This is especially true for those who need physical care and also have depression or dementia (Dowling 2021: 126).

Moreover, intimate companionship cannot be provided through mechanization: older people desire face-to-face communication, as this is what care means to them; being with and enjoying the company of other human beings is what produces and reproduces their sense of belonging to humanity (Lolich, Riccò, Deusdad and Timonen 2019; Müller 2019). Equally with children, it is not possible to mechanize cuddling, consoling, feeding and reassuring a small child (Federici 2019: 162). While interactive nursebots[21] are a useful form of care assistance in certain contexts, including lifting, moving, bathing and washing, and pet robots are used in Japan especially in assisting older people in long-term care, they have significant limitations on cost, technical and ethical grounds (Scerri, Sammut and Scerri 2021). They also come at an emotional cost, due to the loss of human contact and relationships that cannot develop over time with robots (Folbre 2006).

Mining Care Data for Profit: Affective Computing

New forms of *affective computing*, using biometric and depth sensors, are part of the new machine intelligence. They can scan the face, voice and gesture to survey how someone feels. This emotional mining can transmit messages about what precipitates different human feelings. It has the potential to undertake sentiment and emotional analysis without people's knowledge or consent, because it tracks emotional responses in a way people cannot control. While affective computing research was originally designed with good intentions, to assist in medical and therapeutic settings, it did not stay under public-interest control. It is now a significant dimension of surveillance capitalist practice (Zuboff 2019: 281–9).

It is their lack of innocence in politico-economic terms that makes virtual forms of communication problematic in care terms. Digital connectedness comes at a cost, much of which is unknown at the point of use. Personal data within care communications (such as FaceTime, WhatsApp or Instagram) is 'fabricated into *prediction products* that anticipate what you will do now, soon, and later'. This data is the stuff of surveillance capitalism, used to inform '*behavioral futures markets*' (Zuboff 2019: 8; emphasis in the original). What makes feeding off the everyday information of human experience so concerning is that information sharing is not confined to mining people's material interests; it involves 'bodily rendition', reimagining human bodies as 'behaving subjects' that are then 'tracked and calculated, for indexing and research' (Zuboff 2019: 241).[22]

Tracking personality and emotional life is extremely useful in profit terms, as it is a way of learning about (and ultimately influencing) powerful subliminal desires. As an influential market research report explains, 'knowing the real-time emotional state can help the businesses to sell their product and thereby increase revenue'.[23] What this means is that engaging in digitalized caring enables online communication to be used for personalized and behavioural identity mining, marketing and ultimately profiteering. This invasion of privacy has only recently been challenged in Europe,[24] and very belatedly in the US courts, albeit in the latter case because of concerns about monopoly rather than privacy (in an antitrust lawsuit, not a privacy one).[25]

There is a strange irony in the accessibility and online/virtual/robotic care for others that technology allows. It enables care of a virtual kind while recording and partly owning the feelings and sentiments people express and passing them on for commercialization. As Zuboff observes:

> It is no longer a matter of surveillance capital wringing surplus from what I search, buy, and browse. Surveillance capital wants more than my body's coordinates in time and space. Now it violates the inner sanctum, as machines and their algorithms decide the meaning of my breath and my eyes, my jaw muscles, the hitch in my voice, and the exclamation points that I offered in innocence and hope. (2019: 290)

The value of this information is that it can be used ultimately to direct and control individual behaviour.

A process of instrumentation is occurring (Zuboff 2019: 352):[26] behaviour is increasingly modified, predicted, monetized and, in the end, controlled. The instrumentalization of human behaviour ultimately means manipulating preferences and choices, not only about products but also about people, thereby creating a pool of who is or is not worthy or valuable, who is or is not worth caring for or caring about. This development is potentially totalitarian in terms of the power commercial interests can exercise over feelings, over preferences and, inevitably, through these, over one's sense of self and of one's relationships – people's sense of who does and who does not matter.[27]

Migration and the Geographies of Time for Care

Apart from those who work directly in agriculture and fishing, employment is increasingly available in cities and large urban centres, with an estimated 68 per cent of the world's population living in cities by 2050.[28] Capital invests in manufacturing and service developments where it has access to a suitable labour force, and where transport, networking and communication infrastructures maximize profitability and reduce costs. As labour has to follow capital, migration within and between states and between cities is accepted as inevitable. Ties to place and relationship commitments to loved ones, friends or neighbours are treated as incidentals, a type of collateral damage arising from economic migration.

The ways in which migration dismantles care and love infrastructures is rarely the subject of negotiation for employees, except for the sought-after in highly skilled employment who can negotiate 'packages' for themselves and their families. While elite migrant workers benefit hugely economically from migration (Gibson and McKenzie 2012), not all workers have beneficial experiences, especially those in horticultural work (Holmes 2013) and many of those in the care economy (Fernandez 2010; Vahabi and Wong 2017).

And although migrant (White) families have opportunities to form new care networks when they migrate to rich, largely 'immigrant-friendly' countries like Norway (Bygnes and Bivand Erdal 2017), this experience is not universal. Migrant care workers can benefit economically, often indirectly, from their migration (Dumutri 2014), but this experience is not the norm. Much migrant care work is 'live-in' and based on cash payment (Bettio, Simonazzi and Villa 2006), offering neither social security nor pensions. In-house care workers often have neither the time, the money nor the space to exercise autonomy to form new care relationships. They are regarded as 'cheap and disposable' workers (Fernandez 2010).

The other side of the care equation is the care status of those who are dependent but left behind. The 'care drain' from poorer to richer countries counts as a countervailing migration cost (Hochschild 2002). When parents migrate transnationally, this has adverse health implications for left-behind children in particular (Fellmeth, Rose-Clarke, Zhao, Busert, Zheng et al. 2018). The care loss is complicated by the fact that those who do not/cannot migrate in poorer countries are disproportionately old, very young or lacking the skills and capacities to advance their own economic standing.

Although hands-on caring requires presence, presence-based care time is also lost commuting, be it between home and work, between cities and/or between countries, for all types of workers. Evidence from several countries suggests work–family-care conflicts are increasing due to greater competition, intensification and job insecurity (Schöneck 2018). Commuting exacerbates such conflicts; while the age of children, gender and other neighbourhood experiences mediate the impact of commuting, conflicts still occur (Montazer and Young 2020). Moreover, transnational migratory employment often requires adults to leave young dependent children with other relatives, making it difficult to care and love in ways that are not fraught with tensions and incompatibilities. Given the moral imperative for women to be primary carers, this creates particular tensions and anxieties for women (Ehrenreich and Hochschild 2003; Lutz 2011).

Care time is also constrained by the lack of synchrony between the geopolitics of housing and employment, especially for service and manufacturing workers that have to be on site to work, most of whom are low paid and cannot afford to live near their work due to the high cost of living in cities (Montazer and Young 2020). One of the outcomes of the financialization of capitalism is the rise of high-paid finance-related workers, in law, accounting services, investment, ICT, insurance and so forth, who rely on low-paid service workers in retail, cleaning and catering to service them. These service workers, many of whom are migrants, often have to live far from the business districts where they work, or in overcrowded accommodation if near their employment, both of which impact adversely on their care time.

The casualization and precaritization of employment also undermine labour solidarity, especially trade union mobilization, as the latter is dependent on stable, secure employment where people get to know and trust one another and where they have the time and space to organize to protect their work rights (Standing 2011: 30). The lack of personal contact also limits opportunities to support each other in mundane, everyday work or personal matters.

Conclusion

One of the defining characteristics of neoliberalized societies is the compression of more and more tasks into less and less time (Rosa 2013); life is speeded up and care itself is expected to be speedy and time-bound. But given that care is cyclical, unbounded and led by needs rather than the logic of the clock, it is undermined by the principles of capitalist acceleration and accumulation while remaining a challenge to them. The lifeworld of care, at miso, meso and macro levels, is not fully incorporated into capitalism, and because of this it represents a residual space (Williams 1977) where resistances are possible.

Attempts by the market to fully colonize the lifeworld, including the care world, are resisted by 'those most immediately affected by the deleterious action of the market' (Polanyi 2001: 138). Even though such resistance meets strong counter-resistance, it happens nonetheless, within civil society in the *commoning*[29] movement (Gibson-Graham 1996; Gibson-Graham, Cameron and Healy 2013),[30] in the *slow* movement (Honoré 2004, 2013), and in the *slow food* movement in particular (Csikszentmihalyi 2002). While the success of these movements is limited politically, they do create a different narrative of deceleration, focused on achieving ecological balances, and living simply for both human well-being and environmental reasons (Rosa 2013: 86).

Degrowth movements,[31] left-led critiques and experimentations (Alexander 2017; Perkins 2019), are also a significant challenge as they offer alternatives to both the social democratic and the neoliberal economic growth paradigms (D'Alisa, Demaria and Kallis 2014). One of the first degrowth initiatives began in Ireland in 2006 with the Transition Town movement, which has now developed into a wider global movement of Transition Networks,[32] one of the major aims of which is to develop respect for the environment and better living conditions by creating ecological and sustainable houses and transport systems (Neyra 2019). Degrowth initiatives have also had a significant impact within the city of Barcelona with the development of urban gardens, cooperative enterprises and timebanks.[33] The importance of the degrowth movement is reflected in parallel political developments such as the success of the Indignados movement that developed in Spain after the financial crisis (Weiner and López 2017). The week-long conference in the University of Leipzig in September 2014, attended by over 3,000 people from very diverse backgrounds from across the world, and the initiatives and experiments that followed from that event are also indicative of a new kind of political thinking about social change (Alexander 2017) that is more care-led and deaccelerated.

Moreover, there are social movements that, while not focused on degrowth as such, especially in South America, challenge the environmental destruction that comes with accelerated capitalism.[34] Peasants, landless labourers and many other 'community' and non-governmental agencies are resisting enclosures of the commons (water and forests) and the extraction of minerals through mining that would lead to land dispossession, water pollution and further proletarianization. As Veltmeyer observes (2019: 1280), there are many ways in which 'the Latin American countryside remains a fundamental bulwark of resistance and a crucible of revolutionary foment in the class struggle against capitalism', including capitalism's focus on incessant 'growth', regardless of the ecological and human costs over time, and especially for future generations.

While the North American and increasingly Northern-hemisphere-related Black Lives Matter and #MeToo movements may not be explicitly anti-capitalist, they are so indirectly as they challenge both the racialized and gendered power of capitalism. As racial exploitation in particular is endemic to capitalism in its historical and contemporary colonial forms (Patel and Moore 2018; Dalrymple 2019), resistance to colour-based racism is undeniably a form of resistance to capitalism and its time-accelerating and compressing precepts. And, as colonizing the care labour of women is also endemic to capitalism (Federici 2012; Patel and Moore 2018: 111–37), care relations are also a potential site of resistance, albeit one that is not, as yet, mobilized transnationally, although there are care mobilizations within-countries, both in response to the austerity politics following the financial crash that began in 2007, and in response to the Covid-19 pandemic in 2020 (Care Collective 2020).[35]

There is scope for developing a new interconnectedness, a new care *commoning* mentality, a relational revisioning of the world built on recognizing the deep interconnectedness of life (Gibson-Graham, Cameron and Healy 2013), where principles of cooperation, and of responsibility to each other and to the earth, the forests, the seas, and other animals informs what is done to reproduce life. Care of children, the ill and other adults in need of care cannot be mechanized and speeded up incessantly without dehumanizing it. 'We cannot robotize care except at a terrible cost for the people involved' (Federici 2019: 110–11).

Part II
Challenges

5

Liberalism, Care and Neoliberalism

The relationship between care and neoliberalism (new liberalism) cannot be determined without examining how care is defined within classical liberalism. Because liberals tend to see care and love as private matters, they do not regard care as an issue of public judicial concern. Care is defined as a problem of ethics rather than a matter of justice. Though this position has been strongly critiqued by a variety of scholars, especially but not exclusively by feminists, for failing to take account of how care and love are social goods without which people (or indeed the world and all other species) can neither survive nor flourish (Benhabib 1992; Tronto 1993; Held 2006; Kittay 1999; Baker, Lynch, Cantillon and Walsh 2004), it remains a part of the mainstream liberal position.

While liberalism as a political philosophy has enabled minorities and women in Western and European countries to make some gains politically and legally over the past hundred years, many of these gains were about giving minorities and women chances to compete with (White) men in what remained White-male-controlled worlds of politics, employment and social and cultural life. As MacKinnon observed, 'Applied to women, liberalism has supported state intervention on behalf of women as abstract persons with abstract rights, without scrutinizing the content of these notions in gendered terms' (1983: 642). What men were, and had achieved, especially White upper-middle-class men, remained the benchmark for humanity, and the success of women and minorities was judged by their degree of adherence to male hegemonic norms (Connell 1995, 2000). Achieving equality of respect for care work and for carers was not part of the liberal ideal, as care was not seen as work; rather it was a private ethical matter. Neoliberal politics builds on this prior disregard for care in the liberal tradition.

The doing of caring is taken as a natural disposition that does not require education to develop capacities. It for this reason that affective relations of love, care and solidarity are not studied systematically in formal education (Lynch, Lyons and Cantillon 2007) and are only referenced in higher education where they are part of professional training. The non-recognition of care work is currently exemplified in the incessant promotion of ICT and STEM (science, technology, engineering and mathematics) subjects as fields of study and work for women, a long-standing preoccupation of many OECD countries[1] and a priority for the EU (European Commission 2021: 28). The care and public service subjects and fields (within which women have traditionally excelled), including education, health care and the arts, humanities and social sciences, are downgraded and increasingly underfunded (Downing 2017).

As a major goal of neoliberal politics is to create a small, cheap state, the reduction of funding to public services, including care services, has been systematic since the late 1980s (Harvey 2005). The cutting of funding to care services, including those for older people, is well documented; privatization of care services has gathered pace across Europe (Farris and Marchetti 2017), including within the Nordic states over the past twenty years (Szebehely and Meagher 2018; Merceille and O'Neill 2020).[2] Even solidarity work, such as that undertaken by non-governmental organizations to promote social justice, is also under pressure to self-fund, or become enterprising, rather than relying on state support (Harvey 2014).

This chapter begins by exploring how the methodological individualism that is endemic to liberalism has contributed to the misrepresentation of care within both academic and public discourses. It also investigates how the a-structural approach to the analysis of inequalities under liberalism conceals the intersectionality of care-related inequalities with other social, economic and political injustices. Liberalism's neglect of groups, and how group-based identities mediate social experiences, including care experiences, is also explored, as are the ways the prioritization of freedom over equality undermines social justice in the care domain.

Methodological Individualism

The belief that subjective individual motivations or intentions can best explain social phenomena, rather than class or group-based dynamics, has underpinned much of classical liberal social scientific and political thinking (from Weber to Popper, to rational choice scholars such as Elster). This methodological individualism valorized social understanding from the perspective of the individual separated person. While prescribed as a *method* rather than a *value* by Weber (1978), the method became a value, promoting both a resistance to structural analysis arising from group-based affiliations, and an ontological atomism, implicitly disregarding the sociological reality of interdependency and the ways in which individuals co-create each other relationally.

When political analysis focuses on instrumental contractual relations as the basis for politics, the role of moral judgement and concern for others is marginalized conceptually; relations are implicitly defined in transactional terms. This peripheralizes the analysis of the human work required to create and sustain people in their inter/dependency, work that is driven by moral concerns, including the prevention of suffering and the preclusion of harm (Vandenberghe 2018). Operating analytically within an instrumental and atomistic perspective intellectually conceals love, care and solidarity relations as matters of politics and social justice. It assumes that people are singular and isolated, primarily self-referential in their thinking and actions, disregarding the interdependent relational and moral order of social life.[3]

Because an iterative relationship exists between social scientific theorizing and political practice, the dominance of liberal thinking in political and social theory is not an incidental matter. As the non-relational model of the person operates at both analytical and normative levels, disregard for the ontological reality of human neediness, and the social, political and psychological reality of interdependency and intersectionality, becomes endemic to thinking about the political and social subject. The absence of a commitment to *solidarity* in English political rhetoric for most of the later twentieth and early twenty-first century was related to the fact that solidarity was not a key concept of liberalism, a dominant value in English political thinking. Neither solidarity nor any functional equivalent was integrated into political language, particularly not into Labour Party language, which would be its natural home. Middle-class liberalism 'triumphed in the struggle with the aristocracy' and became the dominant economic and political theory[4] in the UK (Stjernø 2004: 142–4).

The neglect of relationality and interdependency is not confined to liberal political theorists, however. It found expression across disciplines, within law, economics, politics, philosophy and sociology

(Lynch, Baker and Lyons 2009: 12–34; Lynch, Kalaitzake and Crean 2021). While early French sociologists appreciated that interdependency was endemic to the human condition (Durkheim 1964; Mauss 1954) as did Norbert Elias (1978) in Germany, with the latter claiming that 'underlying all intended interactions of human beings is their unintended interdependence' (Elias 1969: 143),[5] leading scholars within the Anglophone tradition, including Anthony Giddens, did not subscribe to this position. Giddens' disregard for relationality is reflected in his highly influential structuration theory (1984). The starting point for his action theory is the interaction of individuals 'rather than the plurality of people in webs of interdependencies' (Kilminster 1991: 98); interdependence was not a systematic part of his sociological framing.

While an extensive body of literature on affect, across several disciplines, has been developed recently that directly and indirectly addresses relationality, affective care relations are not the primary focus of this work.[6] Much of the analysis is also quite abstract, including that of political theorists such as Hardt and Negri, who identify affective labour as immaterial (2000, 2009). But affects are not ephemeral and abstract in psychological terms; they constitute *affective practices* and cannot be removed from relationships, and from the cultural and social contexts through which they are lived corporeally and mentally (Wetherell 2015).[7] This is especially true in care terms, as caring is defined in its doing, in its practice, not just in its thinking (Ruddick 1989: 13–16). Care is an embodied practice with ethical dimensions (Mol 2008; Lanoix 2013). The embodied character of and ethical dilemmas posed by relations of care and love work have been neglected in much of the debate about affect (Lanoix 2013; Oksala 2016).

While the lack of sociological scholarship on care has been recognized more recently (Aulenbacher, Lutz and Riegraf 2018), with the exception of Williams' (2018) paper, the special issue of *Current Sociology* devoted to care[8] does not examine the deep ontological and epistemological limitations of sociological scholarship on care and affective relations.

The Limits of Liberalism Reformism

To fully appreciate how liberal thinking has undermined the importance of affective relations of love, care and solidarity politically, it is helpful to locate it historically. In his account of the 'illiberal' origins of liberalism, James Simpson explores how liberalism's origins in the Reformation and evangelical religion are part of its DNA, though this is often ignored by secularists who choose to align its origins with the eighteenth-century Enlightenment (Simpson 2019: 8). Liberalism, like its much older religious sister, Calvinism, distrusts institutions and remains in 'a permanent state of revolution' against them, including institutions created by liberals themselves. But liberalism is not a world view like Marxism or Christianity: it has no clear anthropology or 'salvation history'. Rather, the history of liberalism shows it is a second-order belief system, a framework for managing first-order systems (Simpson 2019: 348–50).[9] Liberalism defined itself originally against the dominant form of Reformation Protestantism, with the aim of providing stability politically and culturally after 150 years of 'psychic and social violence'. Unlike evangelical religion, however, liberalism is a stabilizing norm, upholding democracy, the rule of law, division of powers, respect for liberty and privacy of conscience (ibid.: 346). It endorsed ideological pluralism, helping to institutionalize tolerance (if not respect) for different viewpoints as today's common sense, something that was yesterday's heresy, and remains heretical across much of the world.[10] The gains of liberalism in providing an ideological bulwark against the tyranny of unrestrained institutional power (be it that of the king/queen or of the state) are one of its most important political achievements.

However, the reforming merits of liberalism are also its limitations, especially in political terms. The ideological pluralism it upholds also allows for perspectives that are reactionary and politically harming for minorities and vulnerable groups to persist and grow (Brown 2005). Tolerance of differences can undermine the principle of respect for difference itself. And it can stabilize the status quo even where the latter is deeply unjust.

Moreover, the ideals liberalism upholds are those of fair processes, procedures and principles that guide the becoming of things; what is structurally present is taken as given. The ideal theorizing of liberal scholars does not confront 'the problem of historically rooted injustice' (Kelly 2017: 75). This leads to the development of principles of justice that are indifferent to the role of institutionalized social practices and cultural norms, including the norms whereby women are assumed to be 'naturally caring' in families and in society. Liberalism's a-structuralism houses the political inertia and resistance that face those who try to address a wronged group's disadvantage over time, especially those who try to address institutionalized injustices.

From the eighteenth century, liberalism was aligned and infused with the promise of the Enlightenment. As such, it relied heavily on the assumption that through the exercise of reason a world order led by truth, freedom and equality could be created. The limitation of this idealistic rationalism was evident in its failure to address the issue of institutionalized, organizational and geopolitical injustices. 'Modernizing' was defined by those in power in their own interests; it was used to justify highly inegalitarian political actions (Brown 2005: 103). Not only did liberal ideals of equality not come to pass; they were openly flouted through colonization and pillaging of the Global South by the proclaimers of 'truth and justice' of the Global North. The promotion of global and local wars, and the widespread disregard for human life, other species and the natural environment, where murder and destruction were legitimized 'as collateral damage' in the interests of geopolitical capitalist power, belied the emancipatory intent of the Enlightenment and its liberal political associates (Patel and Moore 2018).

The promise of liberal reformism and its narrative of incremental progress were also undermined by its inability to address the political-economic realities of capitalism within which it became deeply embedded. Liberal reforms were interest-protecting: they were accommodations designed to undermine some (mostly left-leaning) interests while protecting other powerful groups in the interests of political stability, a core concern of liberals. As such, liberal policies carry within them the seeds of political conservatism. The liberal welfare reforms first institutionalized within states in Europe did emanate from social movements built around shared identities and collective interests; however, they were also strategically and politically managed to preclude radical egalitarian social change (Baldwin 1990). The social insurance welfare reforms introduced in Germany by Bismarck in the 1880s were initiated primarily to stymie the rising power of the labour movement rather than protect the welfare of citizens (Stjernø 2004: 179)·

Liberal reformism did not involve some great comprehensive vision for society (Brown 2005: 110). The reforms were and are fundamentally 'affirmative remedies' to injustices; their goal is to correct the unjust outcomes of particular social arrangements without transforming the underlying institutions and structures that generate them (Fraser 1995: 82). As affirmative remedies are not 'transformative', by definition, they generate a requirement for 'surface reallocations again and again' (Fraser 1995: 89). The need to engage in ongoing reforms leads, in turn, to resentments among those who are not the beneficiaries of the reallocations, and especially among those who are losers in terms of allocations of power and money. When reallocations and reforms are repeated over time and over generations, this can even create a myth that the underprivileged are being overprivileged (Fraser 1995). Yet all that is happening is surface-level changes in the reallocation of power, status and money, changes that do not alter the underlying structural relations, and in the process generate the need for more reallocations, leading to further resentments among the more privileged. The ways in which White people have attempted to roll back democratic gains made by African Americans in the US, over several generations, reflect this: struggles for basic human rights have led to the reassertion of White supremacism and 'White rage' (Anderson 2016).

Liberalism's reluctance to engage, both intellectually and politically, with the reality of social structures in their institutionalized expression not only facilitates the macro processes of capitalism, colonialism and patriarchy, it also facilitates micro and meso injustices. As Weber observed, groups can and do establish and consolidate interests and 'lifestyles' which they protect as a group, *within* classes (Gerth and Wright Mills 1958: 180–95), through the practice of social closure (Parkin 1979; Tilly 1999). The failure to address structures means that the multiple ways in which powerful interest groups create monopolies around valued goods and opportunities, in gender, racial, ethnic and dis/ability terms, are less visible in the liberal frame. Hence the relatively modest success of so many initiatives to promote equal opportunities for women and/or minorities at work and in public life: the individualized liberal approach fails to address the ways in which racism, gender and ethnic biases, ableism and carelessness are integrated into the structures of institutions themselves.

Groups and Group Identities

One of the limitations of classical liberal political theory is that it does not fully recognize the ways in which being a member of a social group (or several groups at the same time)[11] impacts on all areas of social life. Groups have unique social forms; they are not 'aggregates' of individuals or types of 'associations', and the groups to which people belong have major implications for their 'incomes, power and status (Young 1990: 41–8).

Classifications that treat social group identities as add-ons (in the case of aggregates) or chosen groups (in the case of associations) disregard the scientific evidence showing how group affiliations operate sociologically and psychologically (Young 1990; Douglas 1993). Individuals do not choose to have a given ethnicity, colour, nationality, social class, impairment and/or gender[12] at birth; they are born as infants with group signifiers already *in situ*. These group identities carry with them norms and social mores that have little to do with choice. Individuals arrive in the world with socially embodied labels that assign them statuses, and maybe responsibilities, even if they do not choose them.

As most group identities are already inhabited when a person 'arrives' to join them, the individual can choose how to manage these, but has little ability to choose (at least in the short term) to live outside them. Some pre-given identities grant one considerable power and status (as a White, upper-class girl or boy, who is heterosexual and European) while others consign one to an oppressed position, such as being a child of a migrant worker without full citizenship status, whose skin colour is Black or Brown, and/or having an intellectual impairment.

Many group-based exclusions occur without those who are engaged in the individual exclusionary actions either intending or wishing to be discriminatory (Young 1990: 41). It occurs unconsciously and habitually, as exclusionary norms are often internalized unreflexively through habitual practice and cultural and institutional norms. Group-based exclusions are also institutionalized in law (the prohibition on marriage for same-sex couples is still in force in many countries), in cultural beliefs (the widely held assumption that caring comes 'naturally' to women, making women feel morally impelled to do the unpaid care work in families), and in political arrangements (whereby politics is organized so that people who are highly dependent, or who are carers of people with high dependency needs, cannot participate, as no allowance is made for their differences or their non-transferable care obligations). Both the habitual and institutionalized expressions of inferiority or superiority attributed to given groups are so normalized that they are invisible to the privileged and accepted by the subordinated.

Because liberal thinking is strongly individualistic (Young 1990), the ways in which membership of a given group also impacts on the care work people will do, and the quality of care they receive, become lost. Political thinking becomes blinded to the gendered, classed and racial divisions of care labour globally, and the way poor girls and women throughout the world are the most likely to provide care for no pay or low pay, and to suffer from care deficits themselves (Oxfam 2020). The care losses experienced by the many millions of people who are forced to flee from their own countries or regions due to persecution, war and/or violence are often not recognized, as is evident from the challenges they face when seeking family reunification on getting refugee status. The lack of a structural analysis, allied to the methodological individualism that underpins the aggregate and associational perspective on groups, presumes that the individual is ontologically prior to the social, in defiance of psychological and sociological reality.

Liberalism Accepting Structural Inequalities

While liberals subscribe to the idea that all human beings are of equal moral worth and are therefore equally worthy of concern and respect, they vary considerably in terms of how they define equality more generally, be it in terms of the distribution of resources such as material goods and money, the exercise of power or the granting of status or recognition. As colleagues and I observed in *Equality* (Baker, Lynch, Cantillon and Walsh 2004: 24–32), liberals could be classified as minimally, moderately or maximally egalitarian, especially in terms of the distribution of wealth and the exercise of power, but also in terms of how different statuses are respected and recognized.

One thing liberals agree on is that there will always be significant inequalities between people in terms of power, status and money, that there will always be winners and losers, people who fare well and people who do badly. The solution to the equality dilemma is the promotion of equality of opportunity, and Rawls has presented the most comprehensive framework for a liberal politics based on this principle. He argued that people should not be advantaged or hampered by their social background, and that their prospects in life should depend on their own effort and abilities; he called this principle 'fair equal opportunity' (1971: 73). Rawls also believed in the efficiency of the so-called 'free market economy' and that, within the constraints of this system, 'those with similar abilities and skills should have similar life chances' (Rawls 1971: 72–3). What Rawls and other liberal egalitarians accept implicitly is that equalizing opportunities is about equalizing the right to compete within a system of institutionalized inequality, not the right to choose among alternatives of equal value. So two individuals, or two different groups, can have formal equal opportunities even if one of them has no real prospect of achieving something valuable relative to others.

Liberalism is not about eliminating institutionalized or structural inequalities; rather, the focus is on providing a fair basis for managing them. It argues for strengthening the minimum to which everyone is entitled and employing the principle of equality of opportunity to regulate the competition for advantage. While Rawls presents an advanced and maximalist view of equality in liberal terms, arguing for a 'difference principle' that permits social and economic inequalities only where they work to the advantage of the most disadvantaged (Rawls 1971: 83, 1993: 6), others argue for a much more minimalist concession to the poorest and most disadvantaged. Utilitarianism-led liberals focus on protecting individual freedoms and interests as a way of promoting equality, regardless of how those interests are derived (Gutmann 1980).

Because liberalism prioritizes freedom over equality, even the most left-leaning liberal equal opportunities policies cannot deliver social justice in any substantive form in an economically and politically unequal society, as those groups that are privileged will use their already institutionalized power and influence to defend their own interests. Rawls' 'veil of ignorance' is a philosophical ideal, but it is not grounded in sociological or political reality. It reflects the social scientific naivety of those who try to resolve problems in the theory of social justice without a systematic engagement with theories of the psyche and society (Douglas 1993). The limitations of this approach are something Tawney (1964) realized many years ago. Writing of promoting equality of opportunity in a capitalist society, he stated: 'Equality meant not the absence of violent contrasts in income and condition, but equal opportunities to become unequal ... equality ... is encouraged to reign provided it does not attempt to rule' (Tawney 1964: 103). The inherent classed logic of social hierarchy under capitalism does not permit the election of the few to become the pattern for the many. The very constitution of a hierarchical society precludes the development of a meritocracy as privileged groups use their excess income, wealth, power and other forms of social and cultural capital to undermine meritocratic practices (Brown, Lauder and Ashton 2011; Brown 2013; Mijs 2016).[13]

Intersectionality of Inequalities: Why They Matter for Care

As people live cumulatively with multiple and overlapping statuses and identities (Crenshaw 1991; Yuval-Davis 2006), they are located institutionally across economic, political, cultural and affective systems at one and the same time. Consequently, affective injustices in both receiving and doing love, care and solidarity are exacerbated by the unequal re/distribution of resources and wealth, lack of respect and recognition, and lack of parity of representation in the exercise of power. To illustrate this point and provide a visual representation of how all social relations and group statuses intersect, table 2 maps four major forms of inequality (*resources*, *relationality*, *representation* and *recognition*), corresponding respectively to *economic*, *affective*, *political* and *cultural* relations. It illustrates how affective relations intersect with economic, political and cultural relations. Moreover, as explained in chapter 1, as affective relations are not confined to families or to dyadic intimate relations, the scale and scope of affective inequalities are considerable as they exercise power outside their own domain, and at micro, meso and macro levels.

Table 2 Forms of in/equality and the intersectionality of affective and other inequalities

Types of structures and social relations	Forms of in/equality and groups affected			
	Resources in/equality[a]	Relational in/equality[b]	Representational in/equality[c]	Recognition in/equality[d]
Economic	XX Working-class, poor	x	x	x
Affective (care)	x	XX (1) Those living in institutions involuntarily, seeking asylum, refugees (2) Carers and women	x	x

Types of structures and social relations	Forms of in/equality and groups affected			
	Resources in/equality[a]	Relational in/equality[b]	Representational in/equality[c]	Recognition in/equality[d]
Political	x	x	XX Children, intellectually disabled, stateless persons, prisoners	x
Cultural	x	x	x	XX Black, cultural minorities, Deaf, LGBTI, women

[a]   Re/distribution of material goods, income and wealth across groups to promote equality.

[b]   (1) Meeting love, care and solidarity needs; (2) sharing love, care and solidarity work equally, especially unpaid work.

[c]   Exercising power and control over decisions that impact on the group.

[d]   Parity of respect and appreciation of the group's culture, language, beliefs, ways of life, differences in colour, gender, sexuality etc. Non-recognition of the sentient character and moral standing of non-human animals is a major generative reason for their oppression but is not discussed here (see chapter 9).

XX = Site where a given social injustice is generated for a group. The groups listed are examples.

x = An indirect inequality arising simultaneously from the impact of other intersections of social relations on different groups. The groups listed are examples.

Source: Adapted from Baker, Lynch, Cantillon and Walsh (2004: ch. 4)

While affective relations are the generative or major sites of love, care and solidarity injustices, economic, cultural and power structures also impact on the affective domain. Affective inequality is especially exacerbated by economic inequalities, as highly unequal societies (lacking economic solidarity) produce 'socially evaluative threats',[14] leading to anxieties and insecurities that adversely impact on health, including mental health, while also undermining trust and solidarity (Wilkinson and Pickett 2009, 2018). The ways in which economic and care-related injustices intersect is very evident among those who are imprisoned. Prisoners are not only disproportionately from very poor, often ethnic minority households, lacking adequate education and other social goods (Wacquant 2009; Oleson 2016); they are also often people who have experienced much neglect and abuse, with high rates of mental health difficulties (WHO 2019 estimates 40 per cent of the world's prisoners have mental health problems), including high rates of depression (Bedaso, Ayalew, Mekonnen and Duko 2020).

While lack of love, care and solidarity is generated in affective relations, it has repercussions in economic, cultural and political relations: those who are uncared for, neglected or abused do not just experience an affective relational loss, they also experience indirect costs in economic and political life, often through lack of social confidence or inability to compete and succeed in employment and education (Commission to Inquire into Child Abuse 2009; Feeley 2009, 2014), or through the lack of practical economic and social supports from family and friends as a migrant worker, asylum seeker or refugee.

Just as there are power and economic dimensions to affective care relations, so there are affective dimensions to work relations and political relations. Care or lack of care for colleagues is a major issue underpinning the quality of life in work organizations (Bolton and Laaser 2019). Equally, in the wider body politic, trust and solidarity are vital for maintaining a sense of belonging and political engagement in democratic societies (Wilkinson and Pickett 2009, 2018).

Processes of acquiring social goods as sites of injustice

Social injustice is not just a distributive question because many injustices are not distributive in character (Young 1990: 21–33). The processes that create goods can themselves be unjust, something an end-state definition of equality fails to appreciate (Young 1990: 28). This is evident in employment where the conditions in which people earn a living differ considerably, not only in terms of income, but also in terms of the burdens and wider benefits of certain forms of work, and in terms of personal autonomy and respect at work (Gomberg 2008; Sayer 2009).

The distinction between *social goods* that are distributed justly and the *processes* by which one acquires social goods has serious implications for loving, caring and solidarity. Caring is a *social good*, but it is also a set of *processes and practices*. The processes or doing of affective relational work have profound equality implications, especially for women and girls, as they remain the default (mostly unpaid) carers throughout the world.

Doing low-paid and unpaid care work impacts adversely on poorer and ethnic minority women, especially (Oxfam 2020). Being economically dependent, unpaid family carers experience power-lessness, making them vulnerable to violence and abuse. Doing non-substitutable family caring also seriously limits opportunities for many women and carers to exercise their political voice. Primary carers' lack of time and resources to participate in and contribute to politics leads to silences about affective inequalities generally, and about the interface between affective inequalities and economic and political injustices (Crean 2018: 13).

The Public, the Private and the Politics of Care

Much of political theorizing about social justice is built on the liberal idea of impartiality: that a neat dichotomy can be drawn between universalistic and particularistic principles, reason and affectivity, and by extension, between the public and the private (Young 1990: 96–121). Universality and reason are defined as the appropriate principles for governing participation in public life, while particu-larism and affectivity are assigned to the private sphere. These distinctions are false dichotomies and are gendered by association with the dominant social actors in the so-called public and private realms. Universalism and reasonableness are equated with mascu-linity and the public sphere, while particularism and affectivity are equated with the private life of family care relations, and thereby assigned a female status. The net impact of this is that what is open for public debate and deliberation is that which is public and masculine; the world of affective relations is not part of public discourse.

Not only is an impartial, detached and universal reasoner a social and psychological myth, so too is the idea that the institution of the family, or any care-related institution, is exclusively private (Young 1990: 120–1; Tronto 1993; Okin 1994; Kittay 1999; Fineman 2004). Laws and regulations executed in public assemblies (parlia-ments and statutory agencies) govern the so-called private sphere of intimate relations (specifying who can and cannot marry, parents' obligations to children and so forth); what happens in primary care relations acts back on the public system. When women and men need to work to support themselves and their children materially, but lack childcare supports, this becomes a public issue that public institutions, including employers and parliaments, must address. The public and the private do not correspond to discrete institutional spheres. Moreover, care relations are not confined to the family or dyadic relationships: care is a core principle governing basic public services including health, education and social welfare. It governs relationships at work between employers and employees (through a duty of care) and between workers themselves, and the state's obligations to its citizens.

By creating a false dichotomy between the public and private spheres, liberalism enables a dualistic thinking to develop, one that allows *homo economicus* (governed by self-interest) and *homo relationalis* (governed by fellow-feeling) to live comfortably within the one person (Muehlebach 2012: 20–2). Compassion and care are defined as legitimate features of the intimate personal world while calculation and instrumentalism are the legitimated ethics of the public sphere. This means that private love ethically accommodates a 'cold public heart': solidarity is tied to self-interest, and is both calculable and restricted (Muehlebach 2012).

The growth of responsibilized individualism within increasingly neoliberalized welfare states systems (Frericks 2014), and the evidence that there is public support for this type of contingent welfare (Mau 2015; Streeck 2016), show how easily liberal thinking, mutating into neoliberalism, can accommodate capitalism by offering charity or conditional welfare for the deserving in lieu of structural justice and affective solidarity (Lynch and Kalaitzake 2018). .

Liberalism accommodates a dualistic ethics of care/carelessness: benevolence through charitable and philanthropic actions is encouraged, but, under neoliberalism, on increasingly demanding conditions, and only for those who are designated and approved as needy by the donors (Mau 2015). The structural relations of injustice within which the giver or donor are embedded with the charity recipient remain unclaimed. Yet the donor can feel morally upright by doing charitable and philanthropic works; they are redeemed by giving from their excess, while ignoring the underlying causes of the injustices to which they are administering charity. For the very rich, private virtue can be made public through philanthropy. This is especially visible in celebrity humanitarianism (Browne 2013; Kapoor 2013), where charity can also bring commercial dividends, not least by increasing brand recognition for the celebrities themselves.

Conclusion

Liberalism has merits, including its inherent scepticism of institutions and the arbitrary ways in which states and institutions can exercise power; its tolerance of difference; its focus on fair procedures; and its historical role in managing dissent and dissuading people from violent solution to conflicts of interests.

However, liberalism's strengths also produce its limitations. It has focused on reforming institutions rather than pressing for radical change in a global order characterized by increasing economic and care insecurity (Standing 2011; Fraser 2016; Oxfam 2020; Dowling 2021). By valorizing ideological pluralism, liberalism also frequently permits denigration and disrespect for vulnerable others, in the name of free speech.

As liberalism has operated with a separatist view of the person, focusing on individual rights more than needs, the ways human neediness drives interdependency, moral purposes and the need for mutual care are made invisible. As liberalism defines affective relations as private rather than public matters, this has led to disinterest in affective relations as relatively autonomous sites of injustice. Liberalism's individualistic premises have also led to a lack of attentiveness to the ways in which political, economic and cultural structures and group identities frame social life, and how these, in turn, impact on love, care and solidarity relations.

Because it has prioritized reformism, liberal politics has tolerated capitalism, attempting to modify it but in many ways becoming its agent and executor both ideologically and politically (Streeck 2016). Driven by the profit nexus, and relatedly by colonialism and consumer fetishism (Patel and Moore 2018), capitalism has controlled the terms and conditions of the relationship with liberalism. This is reflected in the psychic processes that are part of new liberal thinking, the ethical dualism whereby private charity and philanthropy comfortably co-exist within the one person with indifference to the general public welfare of others (Muehlebach 2012).

As liberalism and capitalism are now so interwoven, it is almost impossible to fight for something not on the liberal and capitalist agenda when such a fight is largely incompatible with seeking freedom from that agenda (Brown 2005: 107). The challenge is to locate frameworks for change outside the master's house of liberal-enjoined capitalism.

6

Individualism and Capitalism: From Personalized Salvation to Human Capitals

This chapter analyses the complex historical relationship between different conceptions of individualism and the neoliberal understanding of individualism as self-responsibilization. The goal is to illustrate the need to rethink individualism, so that what is positive is retained, in terms of protecting individual rights, while recognizing that individualism also has a darker side, especially when guided by the norms of *neo*liberalism. When individualism is equated with accumulating personalized human capitals, and with welfare policies based on self-responsibilization, it can and does undermine caring for vulnerable and needy others.

The chapter begins by locating the history of individualism in Western European political and religious thinking, demonstrating how religious and secular interpretations of individualism evolved over time, moving from individual salvation to self-realization and self-responsibilization. It outlines how neoliberalism modified the understanding of individualism in traditional liberal thinking, promoting the ideal of the entrepreneurial self, especially the idea of the individual as a bundle of human capitals. The chapter examines the implications of promoting human-capitalized individualism and the project of developing the self as *homo economicus*. It suggests that the moral individualism of neoliberalism is care-free and independent, but that it can be contested by a concept of the person as *homo curans*, as this is also part of cultural and political history (Tronto 2017).

Individualism in Historical Context

Neoliberal capitalism is governed by its own moral norms and within these is embedded a very particular concept of care and caring. The moral individual of neoliberalism is defined in self-responsibilized, entrepreneurial terms, an individual with initiative and a bundle of human capitals that she or he brings to the market (Bröckling 2015). To maximize the acquisition and use of capitals, the individual must be mobile, both geographically and socially. As mobility, especially transnational mobility, also requires detachment, the ideal individual is also care-free, without relational commitments that tie them to one place or country. Dependency and vulnerability are denigrated; as they are signs of weakness, they are to be avoided even though they are inevitable due to illness, age and infirmity.

Rather than recognizing the importance of the caring human, *homo curans* (Tronto 2017), self-responsibilization is lionized as a virtue for the rational economic worker/citizen idealized under neoliberalism (Frericks 2014). It is a mode of self-governance internalized and encouraged through declining investment in public services, migratory and precarious work, and ongoing competition for security. While a narrow responsibilized individualism is exacerbated under neoliberal capitalism, it has deep roots in the cultural, political and religious history of Western political and intellectual thought.

Individualism in Europe

Individualism and individualization[1] are pervasive features of Western intellectual culture, especially since the nineteenth century[2] (Lukes 1973; Beck 1992; Bauman 2001; Beck and Beck-Gernsheim 2002). However, individualism is not a clearly defined concept (Weber 1930: 222;[3] Lukes 1973) and it has been interpreted very differently over time by both its advocates and adversaries. Whether individualism was defined positively or negatively depended on the interlocutor and their politics. For those who upheld a collectivist view of society, individualism was a threat, though collectivists varied from conservative communitarians to committed communists.

In the eighteenth century, leading philosophers, including Voltaire and Rousseau, were defenders of individualism, particularly in terms of promoting individual freedom and challenging the power of the king and the Catholic Church. Conservative political theorists, including Edmund Burke, held a contrary view; they regarded individualism's attentiveness to the reasoning, interests, and rights of the individual as a threat to what they saw as 'the superior interests' of society. French socialists also viewed individualism with scepticism, but for the opposite reason to Burke's: while they validated individualism's emphasis on self-assertion, and the way it challenged dominant religious, economic and intellectual authorities, they defined individualism in opposition to communism, believing that the latter would best protect the interests and rights of the individual (Lukes 1973: 45–8). The ambivalent and, at times, negative interpretation of individualism in France contrasted with the more positive interpretation in Germany. There, individualism was understood in a more romantic sense by Humboldt and Schlegel. It was equated with *individuality*, the individualism of difference, emphasizing the person's uniqueness, originality and capacity for self-realization.[4]

Unlike in France and Germany, in England, individualism was interpreted most often as *non-conformity*, but also as self-help and freedom, including freedom from state interference. Individualism was closely aligned to Benthamism and utilitarianism, and a belief that the world would be best served by allowing every (wo)man to pursue their own happiness in their own way, and so doing would lead to collective happiness. The construction of individualism as self-realization was the one that took hold in the US, where it became closely aligned with liberal, democratically organized capitalism. While there were many overlapping influences on how American individualism was shaped throughout the late nineteenth and twentieth centuries, it was the ideals of free-enterprise individualism, competitiveness, personal freedom and free, unfettered industry that survived. This concept of individualism became synonymous with the concept of the 'self-made-man' (*sic*) of the American (capitalist) Dream (Lukes 1973: 59–63).[5] An idealized rugged individualism was widely promoted in the media, especially in Anglophone countries (Leyva 2019), that impacted on youth culture and values over time (McGuigan 2010; Konrath, O'Brien and Hsing 2011; Uhls and Greenfield 2011).

The concept of enterprise individualism was not the preserve of American or European thinking in the eighteenth and nineteenth century; it has a much longer history than this in Europe. It was deeply embedded in the ideal of empire building from ancient Greek and Roman times, up to and including the many colonizations undertaken by Western European countries from the 1500s onwards in the Americas, Africa, Asia and Oceania (Patel and Moore 2018).

Individualism within the European Christian Tradition

The loss of secular power by the Christian churches in Europe does not mean that secular principles of politics and welfare are detached from Christian principles (Kahl 2005: 122–3). Rather, values that are historically embedded, including those emanating from the religious and political traditions, continue to impact on contemporary cultural life and beliefs (Kahl 2005; Kapeller and Wolkenstein 2013), albeit in a new political form (Stjernø 2004; Brunkhorst 2009). Given the profound influence of Christianity in framing cultural life in Europe, the ways in which this tradition impacted on the framing of individualism, and how that, in turn, related to capitalism, are an important matter.

There are two quite different traditions within Christian thinking in terms of how the individual–collective relationship is defined. While love and *caritas*[6] are particularly strong in Catholic social teaching from the nineteenth century, especially following the publication of the papal encyclical *Rerum Novarum* in 1891, the concept of love and service (charity) was also central to Lutheranism, though the latter stressed the importance of individual charity rather than collective solidarity. Yet the Lutheran ideal of the two kingdoms[7] enabled political interventions to create 'God's kingdom' on Earth in a way that was not shared by Catholicism; the ideal of creating 'heaven on Earth' was also strong within Reformed Protestantism, especially Calvinism.

The European Protestant Christian ideal of 'creating God's kingdom on Earth' did find political expression within Europe after World War II through the development of Europe's post-war welfare states, especially in Northern Europe. While socialist and communist parties, and labour and other social movements, also played a crucial role in developing the welfare states at that time (Baldwin 1990), Christian democrats were leading activists in building the strongest welfare states in the post-war era (Stjernø 2004).

Despite its political activism, the importance of individual conscience remained pre-eminent within the Protestant tradition: the collective could not force the individual to do anything that contradicted personal conscience. A profound individualism of belief within Protestantism differentiated it from Catholicism, where papal encyclicals specified what was or was not religious truth or belief (Stjernø 2004: 74–8). Moreover, Protestantism was not singular in its form. There was a 'pessimistically inclined individualism' deeply rooted in the Calvinistic-Puritan tradition in particular (Weber 1930: 105–6), which, unlike Lutheranism, was characterized by spiritual isolationism warning 'against any trust in the aid of friendship of men'; brotherly love was only to be 'practised for the glory of God' (Weber 1930: 108). When God is 'your confidante', relationality is undermined; neighbourliness means giving what is due, nothing more. Weber goes so far as to say that within this thinking, 'Humanity in relation to one's neighbour has, so to speak, died out' (Weber 1930: 226, fn. 34).

The individualism of Puritanism is different, therefore, from that of Lutheranism as well as from that in Catholicism (Stjernø 2004: 249). Within Puritanism, salvation was an individual responsibility, not a mediated one.[8] The individual's duty was directly to 'God' and her/himself, not to fellow human beings. What ascetically driven Christianity celebrated, as proof of God's calling, was 'rational legal acquisition by virtue of one's own ability and initiative' (Weber 1930: 179). The exercise of 'personal responsibility, discipline and asceticism' in this life was proof of one's election to the heavenly kingdom in the next (Tawney 1972: 121). As poverty was a sign of moral failing, punishment and correction could be imposed on the poor quite legitimately (Kahl 2005: 117).

Although the route to salvation was less individualistic in Catholic social teaching than in Protestantism, as Catholic social teaching was focused on realizing the 'common good' through 'integrating individuals and separate parts of society into an organic totality' (Stjernø 2004: 212), Catholicism also endorsed a concept of personal responsibility that aligned its socio-political concept of subsidiarity with family, voluntary and local solutions to society's injustices, rather than collective, state-led solutions (Stjernø 2004: 62–73). Moreover, both Catholic principles of subsidiarity and the individualism of Reformed Protestantism attributed a negative role to the state in the securing of welfare (Kahl 2005: 120). These beliefs found expression in secularized Christian democratic traditions where there was 'reluctance towards public engagement in social services' and a belief in using 'tax policy to stimulate personal initiative and responsibility' (Stjernø 2011: 169).

While there are significant differences in how the moral individual is construed within the various Christian traditions, in each one, and for different reasons and at different times, there is an assumption of self-responsibility expressed in the idea of sin and sinfulness (a concept that is also central to Judaism). Although there has also been a parallel if lower-order expectation of doing charitable works, and/or serving the common good within Christian individualism, and these values were resurrected at community level in many countries as people worked to support each other during the Covid-19 pandemic, much of the moral requirement to be altruistic or show concern for needy others has been lost under the neoliberal capitalist pressures to compete and succeed at all costs; there is a focus on personal responsibility for one's own health and economic well-being rather than achieving salvation through serving others. The Christian ideal of creating 'God's kingdom' on Earth is subordinated to making money as proof of one's moral worthiness.

The belief that economic poverty was a personal responsibility was exemplified in the austerity era, post-2008, with the institutionalization of forms of 'active' and 'responsible' citizenship (Frericks 2010, 2014; Frericks, Maier and De Graff, 2009; Van Gerven and Ossewaarde 2012). The unemployed and 'the poor' were subjected to moral appraisal and punishment when they failed to be active and become valuable employed citizens (Boland and Griffin 2018). The judgement of the unemployed paralleled the judgement of the 'ungodly' in religious times; they changed from being citizens with rights to welfare and became customers who were disciplined for failing to follow the moral coda of their professional welfare-state overseers (Sowa, Staples and Zapfel 2018). Moreover, the principle of self-responsibilization was not confined to individuals. While there were frequent references to the 'moral hazards' arising from supporting profligate and 'irresponsible' citizens (who took out banks loans and were now unable to pay them) during the financial crisis commencing in 2007, 'irresponsible countries' were also admonished, with Greece being punished particularly for assumed profligacy (Eriksen 2017). What neoliberal capitalism is doing is stripping moral individualism of its moral responsibilities to the needy other, though, as the experience of managing Covid-19 shows, this narrative also can be and is being contested.

The Individual as Human Capital

While there is no causal relationship between the development of individualism as a psychic structure and the development of capitalism as a political-economic system, nevertheless, the promotion of the concept of the individual as a distinctive moral figure from the eighteenth century onwards both facilitated and enabled individuals to think and act as separate entities in their own interest. Individualized salvation and individualized self-realization were easily aligned with a free-enterprise concept of the self, especially when the latter ideal was successfully marketed globally.

The globalization and deregulation of trade from the 1980s, aligned with the globalization of communication, higher education and transport, enabled the widespread diffusion of neoliberal policies and ideals, not only in the so-called developed worlds but also in 'developing' countries within a relatively short time. The diffusion occurred through a variety of processes, including the relatively clandestine norm-substitution policies pursued by global institutions such as the International Monetary Fund and the World Bank (Kentikelenis and Babb 2019), the dissemination of neoliberal management discourses in the 1990s (Boltanski and Chiapello 2005: 57–101) and the neoliberalizing of both the theory and practice of education (Peters 2016).

The free-enterprise concept of the person found institutionalized expression in education in particular through the promotion of the idea of the individual as human capital (Becker 1964): the individual was to become a repository of potential capitals to be developed for the economy. Human capital principles were systematically promoted by multilateral agencies, such as the OECD and the World Bank (both of which made education for human capital a central theme of policy), and by national governments,[9] so that it became deeply integrated into the lexicon of global education (Mundy, Green, Lingard and Verger 2016). Gary Becker's (1964) human-capital thesis had profound implications not only for the state's understanding of an individual as *homo economicus*, but also for the individual's understanding of her/himself. The individual was no longer just a partner in a commercial exchange in the economy; *homo economicus* was an entrepreneur of the self (Foucault 2010). The person was a source of earnings, creating her or his own project by building a house of capitals from within. Each human was defined as a wealth-producing machine, governed by the logics of the market, an actuarial subject, governed by a belief in self-realization as a consumer citizen (Peters 2016: 298–301).

Within this frame, self-responsibility is key, choice is an obligation, and the obligation is to choose well and insure yourself against unforeseen risks. But as the neoliberal subject is created by the market, it is controlled by it, and in this regard she or he is 'governable' from the inside out (Foucault 2010). Allegiance to the market-defined model of the self makes the individual into a capitalist 'subject'. In enhancing their human capital, especially through expensive investment in higher education, individuals can create a new self, though it is also often an indebted self, controlled directly or indirectly by financial capitalism (Soederberg 2014; Peters 2016).

The human-capitalized individual takes time, effort and investment to produce. It comes at a price, including a care-price: the time and money devoted to capitalizing the self must take place at the expense of time and money spent with and for others, as both human time and money are finite.

Capital's mobile individual

Beck (1992) and Beck and Beck-Gernsheim (2002) claim that individualization is a defining feature of reflexive modernity, operating at two interrelated levels. On the one hand, it is a normative and institutional framework that severs and frees people from predetermined roles and norms. On the other hand, each person's biography is placed in their own hands and the focus is on creating one's own 'life culture' or 'self-culture' (Beck and Beck-Gernsheim 2002: 42–53).[10] The concept of fate or a pre-given destiny is replaced with the ideal of having a' life project' that one creates for oneself; the individual is not bound by a fixed nature as they are architects of their own destiny (Bauman 2001: 142).

Beck (1992) and Beck and Beck-Gernsheim (2002) suggest that the autonomy and choice that individualistic cultures offer come with risks,[11] not only in terms of economic security but also in personal relationships and family structures. Individualization brings an ambivalent freedom, a freedom to fail as well as to achieve, not only financially and in labour market terms but also in terms of relationships and intimate life. The definition of the family mutates and becomes fluid and flexible, so that 'the basic figure of fully *developed modernity* is the *single person*' (emphasis in the original; Beck 1992: 122).

Since Beck published *Risk Society* in 1992, the global economic order has been characterized by increasing market liberalization, with largely unhindered flows of information and of capital, especially financial capital, in almost instant time. Following the flow of capital is the flow of labour; transnational migrations are enabled and encouraged, though the latter do not move in instant time, nor can labour move in an unregulated way. While labour migrations and people fleeing war and persecution are not a new phenomenon, the scale and scope of mobility in the late twentieth and twenty-first century are unprecedented (UN Population Division 2019).[12]

Labour migrations are disproportionately from poorer regions and poorer countries to richer ones, with much of the employment being precarious (Sassen 2001).[13] And, although there are employment opportunities for those whose skills are in demand, especially in technological and professional fields, migrant workers are frequently hired to do the work natives do not want to do: domestic, cleaning and care work (Ehrenreich and Hochschild 2003; Yeates 2009) and work in the construction and service industries (Afsar 2009; Fernandez 2010). Many of those who migrate carry heavy debt, which, in turn, makes them extremely vulnerable to exploitation (O'Connell Davidson 2013).

But not all labour migrations are the same. The business and professional elite who migrate do so as 'super'-citizens moving quickly, securely and comfortably across borders, with business-class flights, segregated lounges, fast-track tickets and good food. As the fast-moving businessman or businesswoman (though it is mostly men) embody the values of the entrepreneurial individualism required of capitalism, their comforts and privileges are not in question (Mitchell 2016: 121). Nor is elite mobility confined to the labour market, as there is also a global market for higher education, with steadily growing numbers of elite students moving transnationally (Hazelkorn 2011; Ball 2012).

While mobility is a lifestyle choice for a tiny minority, for most it is driven by necessity, either by forced displacement or by economic survival. What the longer-term implications of forced mobilities (on a hitherto unforeseen scale) will be for care relations is not yet fully known. What is known is that care migrations per se are creating care deficits in poorer sending countries (Hochschild 2002; Yeates 2009; Mahadevan 2020). While remittances do benefit left-behind families financially, the health impact of migrations is not beneficial for such households: a meta-analysis of 111 studies involving over 250,000 children and adolescents shows that, with a small number of exceptions, parental migration had an adverse impact on the children left behind (Parreñas 2005; Fellmeth, Rose-Clarke, Zhao, Busert, Zheng et al. 2018). A major *Child Health and Migrant Parents in South-East Asia* study found that left-behind mothers and carers in transnational migrant households were more likely to have poor mental health than carers in non-migrant households (Graham, Jordan and Yeoh 2015).

While research on intra-European immigrants shows that immigrants can and do create new attachments, new relations of love and care, in their destination countries, when and if economic security and the cultural context enable them to live grounded and stable rather than 'liquid' lives (Bygnes and Bivand Erdal 2017), this is not inevitable. Those who migrate are at risk of losing life-sustaining love and care relations, especially if they lack face-to-face encounters over extended periods of time, and if they cannot integrate as equals within destination states for cultural, economic, language or political reasons. This risk does not just apply to low-paid workers, as research on migratory labour in elite areas such as higher education shows that love and care precarity is one of the unforeseen costs of regular (often unwanted) migrations even in academia (Ivancheva, Lynch and Keating 2019; O'Keefe and Courtois 2019).

While global communication networks (Facebook, FaceTime, Skype and WhatsApp) enable immigrants to maintain linkages and attachments via social media in a virtual reality, such intimacies are cold in that they lack the physical presence of one another's bodies (Illouz 2007: 97–8). The mutuality of understanding that comes with co-presence is missing in abstract, virtual meetings over the internet; there is no possibility of touching or feeling one another's bodies. Internet relationships are disembodied encounters relying on visual representations, speech and text. In that sense, they rely on cognitive knowledge, not practical embodied knowledge. Though valuable, they are relationships in which hands-on loving and caring cannot be undertaken due to the distances of time and space.

The Political Imaginary of Homo Economicus in Education

Cartesian rationalism, encapsulated in the phrase *Cogito ergo sum* ('I think, therefore I am'), is deeply embedded in Western political thinking and educational practice. Contemporary education has inherited from classical liberalism an indifference to the affective domain, and an allegiance to the education of the rational autonomous subject (Noddings 1984, 2001). Education for doing love, care and solidarity work is generally not part of the formal educational curriculum (Lynch, Lyons and Cantillon 2007). Young people are not educated systematically and formally for a relational life as interdependent, caring and solidaristic human beings.

To the contrary, education draws heavily on Bloom's (1964) taxonomy of cognitive objectives, emphasizing the development of logical, mathematical intelligence and abstract reasoning in measuring educational capacity and success (merit). Interpersonal and intrapersonal capabilities are largely ignored, though emotional intelligences are now known to be discrete domains of human intelligence

(Gardner 1983; Goleman 1995). Moreover, the very institutions of higher education that legitimate what is valid knowledge are deeply disrespectful of care, in ways that are highly gendered (Lynch 2010; Henderson and Moreau 2019).

Even the growing recognition of emotional and personal intelligence within developmental psychology has not unsettled the focus of education on the development of the individualized market citizen. In many respects, it has advanced it; research on emotional intelligence focuses on its relevance for measurable achievement; it is generally defined as a capability that enhances and supplements other marketable capabilities including academic attainment.

While Cartesian rationalism lies at the heart of liberal education, the way in which education in the neoliberal era is officially defined as a preparation for employment is a more recent phenomenon, exemplified in increasing references in OECD country reports and EU policy documents promoting education for a knowledge-based economy.[14] The knowledge-based economy model is basically a new political imaginary devised by governments to manage the population in the service of the market (Jessop 2008; Hay and Kapitzke 2009; Lolich 2011).[15] Education is repurposed in terms of personalized human capital acquisition: one 'is expected to develop a productive and entrepreneurial relationship towards oneself' (Masschelein and Simons 2002: 594).

Within the knowledge-based economy frame, no serious account is taken of the reality of dependency for all human beings, both in childhood and at times of illness and infirmity. When the citizen carer and the care-recipient individual are recognized in the educational arena, this generally only happens when professionals are being trained 'to manage' those in need of care. The inter/dependent citizen is left to the side (Lolich and Lynch 2016).

What neoliberalism does, which classical liberalism did not do, is glorify *homo economicus* above the cultural or politically engaged citizen. While classical liberal thinking extolled the virtues of rationality, and actively promoted the arts and humanities for the cultivation of the mind (Newman 1875), within the neoliberal frame, the ideal type citizen is the cosmopolitan worker built around a calculating entrepreneurial self, servicing the economy (Giroux 2002; Masschelein and Simons 2002; Peters 2005, 2016). Neoliberalism has deepened the disrespect for the relationally engaged, caring and cared-for citizen by attributing supremacy to the economic citizen. Competitive economic individualism is no longer seen as an amoral necessity; rather it is a desirable and necessary attribute for a constantly reinventing entrepreneur (Apple 2013a; Ball 2003). Consumption has replaced friendships and intimate relationships as a way of 'nurturing' the self, be it through so-called 'retail therapy' or through the multiple psychological therapies that are traded on the market (Nehring and Kerrigan 2019).

What is surprising is that education largely ignores developments in social cognitive neuroscience showing that humans are not isolated rational actors but are strongly driven by the desire for social connection. Human brains are made for social connection, not just for thinking (Lieberman, Schreiber and Ochsner 2003). And knowing is not confined to reason only, even if Western thinking assumes it to be (Nussbaum 2001). Studies of infants show that 'the desire for relationship, pleasure in connection and the ability to make and maintain relationship are present at the onset of development' (Gilligan 1995: 123), while a 'neurobiology of attachment' is emerging that is helping to illuminate the importance of love (Damasio 1994). Even when people are rational economic actors and consumers, neither their rationality nor their economic and consumer choices can be presumed to be devoid of relationality (Gilligan 1982, 1995).

Care-Free and Technologically Assisted

One of the purported dividends of capitalism is that it allows individuals to be valued 'on merit' in the market rather than by birth, rank or other market-irrelevant status. This positive celebration of the individual as a potential producer of goods and services of market value has enabled carers, women (and other despised groups) to be incorporated into the capitalist nexus. Women gradually moved out of *nature*, to which they had been assigned historically in pre-capitalist (Lerner 1986) and colonial (Patel and Moore 2018) times, into *society*, as productive workers. Women's care work had a market value, even if it was not a high one. What capitalism offered in addition to this was an opportunity for women and other lower-status groups to be 'saved' from religion and old-fashioned capitalism by migrating and moving in the service of capital (Beck 1992).

In outlining the implications of individualization for gender equality, Beck and Beck-Gernsheim (2002: 54–8) suggest that it now means that women are freed from traditional ideals of living 'a life for others'. They are 'free' to live a life of their own; in many respects the life story of a woman is coming closer to that of a man. Beck and Beck-Gernsheim do not deny that women are still constrained by their gender, but rather claim that individualization, especially as expressed through education, frees women publicly from being defined by living simply for others.

While the growing autonomy and empowerment of women in public and occupational life testify to their relative economic independence, especially in those Western countries where they have access to secure and stable childcare supports and employment (ILO 2019), this does not take away from the fact that women remain the primary unpaid carers throughout the world and that most women have no choice but to do this work, as there is no one else to do it (Oxfam 2020). Nor does it change the fact that care work must continue to be done, in all its messy forms, and that it is women, generally those who are poorer, less educated, from ethnic minority backgrounds and/or are forced to migrate for work, who do this work (Ehrenreich and Hochschild 2003; Duffy 2005, 2011).

Care work is not revalued in the neoliberal era; rather carers are incentivized to manage care and reproductive work in a consumerist manner: middle-class professional workers can pay for care, while migrating mothers and fathers are given the chance to send back 'remittances' to educate their children and/or feed their parents while living at a distance and without the intimacy of presence. In some globalized corporations, professional mothers and potential mothers are given 'job perks' through egg freezing, so they can time pregnancies to fit in with the commercial goals of their employers,[16] while free breast-pumps are offered with health insurance packages to enable new mothers in the US to prepare milk outside work hours; in that way they need not miss work.

For those receiving end-of-life care, there are also market-led initiatives. Care of those who are sick and/or old and alone is being digitalized and technologized in a way that attempts to replace personalized caring. Assistive technologies are now part of the way older adults pursue, maintain and negotiate life, especially in technology-centred societies (Joyce and Loe 2010), be it through personalized alarm systems, motorized wheelchairs, use of e-health care, robotic lifts and/or robotic pets and carers. While assistive technologies can enhance older people's independence, the belief that one *should be independent* in one's old age is also actively promoted by service providers and by commercial technology producers to increase the demand for their services (Long 2012). Although older people can and do welcome certain technological assistances, these are not necessarily a substitute for personalized care, for a host of practical operational reasons that are becoming increasingly evident with new research (Wright 2019). Moreover, older people desire face-to-face care services where that is a widely expected and accepted type of care (Lolich, Riccò, Deusdad and Timonen 2019; Müller 2019).

While capitalism offers opportunities, especially for privileged women and men, to be care-free by hiring others to care, care work still needs to be done when paid carers are not available. People are born dependent and needy, they get ill, get old and often cannot care for themselves. Moreover, caring, be it in hospitals or schools, is an essential part of the public welfare systems of most societies. While technology can provide care assistance, it cannot substitute for the personal and engaged dimension of care relations. Care cannot be reduced 'to bare functionality or mere necessity ... Hence, caring affects are not optional, they are not an added bonus or a luxury that can be siphoned off' (Dowling 2021: 46).

The Independent Citizen

The individuality that was celebrated from the Renaissance onwards was that of creativity and developed personality, the creator of arts and other public goods. Humboldt believed that the full and harmonious development of the 'individual personality' represented a high point of cultural development for humanity (Lukes 1973: 58). Weber equated individual citizenship with being a public persona, an economic and political actor (Barbalet 2010). For Weber, the political individual is above all a rational actor, with political rights vindicated by the state, in return for which they must be ready to defend the state (Weber 1994). Marshall's (1973) influential concept of citizenship followed a similar trajectory to Weber's. It centred on the idea of the citizen as an individual who held civil, political and socio-economic rights, in that historical order, under the protection of the state.

The concept of the citizen with rights was that of the male, employed, most often White citizen (Lister 2003).[17] Social rights were registered for those who were employed in the formal economy, and this excluded most carers. This position was reflected in early European Economic Community and later European Union legislation (the EU Charter of Fundamental Rights and the Lisbon Treaty, both 2007), where the promotion of employee rights is the primary focus.

The work involved in coproducing humanity as relational beings has not been regarded historically as individuality-defining or citizenship-defining. The inevitable dependencies that were endemic to the human condition, and which are necessary at times of infancy, illness or disablement, were treated as secondary considerations. Although there were cultural variations in how dependency was defined, it generally signalled a citizen's 'incompleteness', especially in the post-industrial era. Dependency was not seen as a human inevitability at certain times in life, but as a signal of individual weakness, 'an incomplete state in life: normal in the child, abnormal in the adult' (Moynihan 1973: 17). There was 'no good adult dependency' because 'independence [was] enjoined upon everyone' (Fraser and Gordon 1997: 135). Being employed and 'self-supporting' was once the ideal for adult men, but it became a universal expectation of all adults regardless of their social positioning.

The shift from the acceptance of some inevitable dependencies to the conditioning of dependency is now reflected in the changing welfare systems across Europe, where there is an increasing demand for self-responsibility. Life is framed in the neoliberal logic of individual choice. Increasingly, it is only those who have behaved 'responsibly' who are deemed entitled to solidarity/welfare through the social security system (Taylor-Gooby 2005, 2011; Frericks 2014: 523–4; Mau 2015). The economically independent individual is idealized. Adult dependency, even for those with significant disabilities, is increasingly called into question regardless of impairment (Roulstone 2015; Shefer, Henderson, Frost-Gaskin and Pacitti 2016), while older people are expected to be 'useful', even after retirement (Muehlebach 2012).

The Care Contradictions of Capitalism

The denial of dependency and interdependency has led to the care contradictions of capitalism being exposed. In the early twenty-first century, neoliberal capitalism is facing a care crisis not only in the wealthy dual-earner households of Western capitalist states (Fraser 2016; Dowling 2021), but also in the so-called peripheral economic zones where the sale of migratory care labour is undermining the care infrastructure of poorer sending countries (Hochschild 2002; Gutiérrez-Rodríguez 2014).

While there has always been a tension between care and capitalist values, hitherto this has been accommodated in Western countries, be it through the creating of a bourgeois imaginary of domesticity or housewifery whereby women were assigned a 'duty' or 'calling' to care at home (Mies 1998), or by the patriarchal ideology of the 'family wage', both of which assigned women to inferior statuses and economically subordinated roles in heterosexual marriage (Dalla Costa and James 1972; Delphy and Leonard 1992; Fraser 1997). While the dual-earner family purported to resolve the care/capital contradiction, the gender division of care labour persisted, with all its attendant negative consequences for women, especially with changing family forms; the feminization of poverty became a distinct reality across the life course (Schaffner Goldberg 2010). The most recent care crisis in Western countries has been addressed by hiring migrant workers, generally low-paid, as carers both within care homes and within families (Ehrenreich and Hochschild 2003; Yeates 2009; Lutz 2011; Gutiérrez-Rodríguez 2014; Oxfam 2020). Not only do these resolutions create care deficits in the sending countries, they are often unaffordable in the receiver countries (Pearson 2019). There are also unsatisfactory in care-receiver terms, as profit-making norms begin to dictate the care ethos (Farris and Marchetti 2017). Because care is a process, a way of living relationships (Mol 2008), it cannot be contained or packaged in a clearly defined time, as it is a response to a need that keeps on changing – something older people have made clear when they are asked about what they want in care terms (McDonald, Lolich, Timonen and Warters 2019; Müller 2019).

The ascendancy of neoliberal concepts of caring is evident in the increasing corporatization of care, especially the care of older people, in very different types of welfare state regimes, from strongly liberal states such as the UK (Dowling 2021) to slightly less (but increasingly) liberal regimes such as Ireland (Mercille and O'Neill 2020), and in the more social democratic Nordic states such as Sweden (Szebehely and Meagher 2018). When care is commercialized, it is increasingly reduced to pre-packaged units of 'service delivery' meted out in time slots. The time required to provide the relational and emotional dimension of care is increasingly left out of the 'package', making it a unit of supervision rather than a unit of care (Badgett and Folbre 1999).

Conclusion

Although women and their care labour were seen as exploitable goods for hundreds of years prior to capitalism (Lerner 1986:

212–29), the ideological binaries of Cartesian rationalism, distinguishing ontologically between man and nature (with women being equated with nature), provided a moral legitimation for the cheapening and exploitation of care; it made care an exploitable *thing*, like the women who did it (Patel and Moore 2018: 111–37).

As rationality was regarded as a defining feature of being human in the Cartesian frame, feeling and caring were subordinated as human practices. The ideal of self-realization, an extension of the ideal of individual salvation, was deeply embedded in rationalism, and became closely aligned with possessive individualism over time. Religious beliefs gave individualism a moral imprimatur, as the legal acquisition of goods by one's own efforts and abilities was seen as virtuous, and proof of God's calling (Weber 1930). Both the religious-informed individualism of doing God's calling and being seen to do so, and the secularized individualism of self-realization as a rational economic actor, carried through over time, impacting on contemporary cultural life and beliefs (Kahl 2005; Kapeller and Wolkenstein 2013), albeit in a non-religious political form (Stjernø 2004; Brunkhorst 2009).

Whether individualism is construed positively as individuality, promoting uniqueness, originality and capacity for self-realization, or negatively as indicative of self-preoccupation and self-interest, it is deeply implicated with neoliberal capitalism (Eagleton-Pierce 2016). While capitalism has facilitated creativity, imagination and innovation by enabling and funding the expression of individuality in the academy, the arts, architecture, literature and science, especially in core capitalist states, expressive individuality has simultaneously been incorporated and commodified into the architecture of capitalism. The anti-modernist and anti-Enlightenment perspective that is central to artistic and social critique is also its Achilles heel. Capitalism takes on the critique and 'disarms' it, strengthening some of its 'mechanisms of justice', in such a way that it can claim to be serving the 'common good', thereby incorporating dissent and immunizing itself from artistic and intellectual resistance. The artists' critique has itself been commodified and incorporated into the market (Boltanski and Chiapello 2005: 40–2).

The growing commercialization of higher education globally, not only in terms of marketing education itself as a 'product' (Slaughter and Leslie 2001; Ball 2012), but in terms of changing its internal culture (Shore and Wright 2015; Wright and Shore 2017) so that career-making and stardom (Burawoy 2016) are increasingly rewarded, exemplifies the rise of neoliberalism in academia. The tenured academic is no longer a critical outsider to the capitalist project; they are central to its success. Not only are they funded directly or indirectly by capitalism (most science funding now comes directly from commercial sponsors, and if not, then via state grants that are expected to meet the needs of industry/business); they are heavily rewarded for their compliance with patents and global recognition.

At the global level, the market in creative individualism remains structured along colonial lines, with the major powerhouses of scientific research, publishing, fashion, music, art and architecture still centrally located in powerful Western capitalist states (Connell 2007; Mignolo 2007, 2009). In the academy, it is the Northern metropolises (former colonizing states) that write the theory that the South is expected to read (Alatas 2003). And while the creative artists and scholars in the metropolis can sell their critiques as art, literature, science and so forth, the impoverishment of much of humanity that neoliberal capitalism has produced since the 1980s does not enable or facilitate creative individualism for most of humanity; rather it generates relations of conflict and violence (Springer 2016).

The everyday individual of neoliberalism is a market persona, *homo economicus*, an entrepreneur of the self, comprising a bundle of capitals with market potential, both as a producer and as a potential consumer. As a kind of wealth-producing machine, the individual is governed by the logics of the market: self-realization as a producer/consumer citizen is life's project (Peters 2016: 301). Should they lack spending power, the individual can supplant it through debt, be it via payday loans, credit card debt, student debt and/or mortgage debt. Their indebtedness embeds them deeply into the capitalist financial system, especially if they are poor: through debt they can buy what they have learned to want but cannot afford (Soederberg 2014). The neoliberal individual is also mobile, literally and metaphorically. They are expected to be care-free, independent and responsible for the self. As dependency is denigrated as a sign of immaturity, a failure to grow up, those who are inevitably dependent due to age or infirmity are not regarded as full citizens.[18] The vulnerability and neediness of the human condition are misrecognized as a sign of weakness rather than a social and corporeal inevitability.

Yet vulnerability is not the preserve of any one group, but a primary human experience that not only limits but can also enable. Given this, the solution is not so much to try to master it, but to recognize it for its ubiquity (Butler 2004), and to appreciate how it helps us to know and understand the world better (Gilson 2011: 310).

Though the independent, unattached model of *homo economicus* is a powerful neoliberal individual political imaginary, it is a contested one. *Homo curans* is also a living reality (Tronto 2017). Affective relations have not been and cannot be fully incorporated under capitalism, not only because corporeal relations resist incorporation (Hoppania and Vaittinen 2015), but because there is a moral dimension to human relations that drives people to think otherwise (Archer 2000; Sayer 2011; Vandenberghe 2018). People are aware that the incessant pursuit of individual ends is harmful to the security of humanity, and that it will ultimately rebound adversely on themselves (Mauss 1954).

Care commitments matter to people and influence individual choices even in capitalist societies (Midgley 1991; Barnes 2006; Lynch, Baker and Lyons 2009: 78–92; Lynch, Ivancheva, Keating, O'Flynn and O'Connor 2020; Stets and McCaffree 2014). There is an invisible heart as well as an invisible hand in social and economic life (Folbre 2001). Hence, care relations are a residual political space (Williams 1977); they offer the potential for mobilization and resistance, as they are governed by different logic and values from those of the market (Mol 2008). The challenge is to enable affective care relations to find an intellectual and political voice, to resuscitate them politically and intellectually. The *Care Manifesto* (Care Collective 2020) is an important initiative in this respect. It highlights the importance of universal caring as a model of global governance. Because we live interconnectedly with all other humans and non-human beings, we are individuals-in-relation 'dependent upon the systems and networks, animate and inanimate, that sustain life across the planet' (2020: 94).

7

Care-Harming Ideologies of Capitalism: Competition, Measurement and Meritocratic Myths

This chapter focuses on the role that competitiveness, measurement and meritocratic evaluation play in framing social life in ways that harm people by defining them as failures and holding them responsible for not competing successfully in competitions they cannot win. It opens with a brief comment on ideology, and the issues of comparing and ordering people. It then examines the ways in which the ideology of incessant and unrelenting competitiveness creates harms socially, morally and psychically. Analysis of the role that metrics play in exacerbating and enabling competitiveness, and in hierarchically ordering people in care-harming ways, follows. The chapter highlights the ways in which the metricization of value undermines the immeasurable, including much caring work. This means that care's value is discounted in the very care-related services where it is the foundational ethic of good practice.

The role that the twin ideologies of equality of opportunity and meritocratic selection play in consolidating classed, raced and related inequalities is then examined. The emergence of a new type of eugenics-related thinking, propagating the myth of the talented few, is explored in terms of how it can create a rationale for blaming those who fail in occupational and educational contests they cannot win. Those defined as 'failing' are disproportionately people who are poor, working-class, disabled and/or from ethnic minority backgrounds.

Ideology

Though violence and the threat of violence lie at the root of power, the use of violence alone is generally not sufficient to maintain long-term compliance with inequalities, especially in democratically organized capitalist societies where the use of physical violence[1] for political ends has been delegitimized (Malešević 2010a: 9–10). The violence-based state apparatuses of the military, police and imprisonment need to be supplemented by ideological state apparatuses, including the media, religion and education (Althusser 1971), to give moral and political legitimacy to inequality. Although the power of capitalism is definitively materially based, it is also deeply ideological; it exercises influence through controlling the means of understanding (Gramsci 1971), increasingly through advertising and social media (McGuigan 2010; Zuboff 2019).

The history of capitalist ideologies shows that different phases of capitalism generate new ideologies that manage and incorporate resistances with an appropriate 'logic of justification', thereby perpetuating capitalism's legitimacy over time (Boltanski and Chiapello 2005). Although they are contradictory and volatile, ideologies operate like maps guiding the way to action in the social and political world (Freeden 2003; Malešević 2006). Thus, while capitalism is harmful in multiple ways (Wright 2010: 37),[2] and while it is replete with contradictions and is currently in turmoil (Streeck 2016), its injustices are accepted passively by much of humanity as either inevitable and/or legitimate.

All social actions are mediated through the realm of ideas, and through ideologies,[3] but ideologies are not neutral mediators; they operate on two levels, both as representation and as distortion (Ricoeur 1986). While they represent the world and its institutions, they also distort what is known about social relations, especially power relations: ideologies legitimate power through both representation and deception. Not only do ideologies offset the legitimacy deficits in the abuse of power in social life (Marx and Engels 1974), they also ensure the voluntary appreciation of these deceptions in praxis by those dominated. Ideology moves from functioning as distortion to functioning as acceptance and legitimation (Ricoeur 1986).

One of the most striking ideological features of European societies is that while many profess disquiet about extreme inequalities (such as the growing wealth and power of the super-rich 1 per cent), they remain silent, and even complicit in accepting everyday class (and other) inequalities. Discontent with generalized inequalities does not necessarily translate into action to challenge these; it is more often associated with a 'practical passivity' in the face of specific injustices (Rosanvallon 2013: 5–6). A survey in France in 2009 found that while 90 per cent believed that income inequalities should be reduced, 57 per cent believed that they were inevitable in a 'dynamic economy', and 85 per cent believed income inequalities were acceptable when they rewarded the meritorious.[4] The lack of serious political dissent regarding institutionalized wage and income inequalities across occupations, inequalities that are frequently substantial and increasingly polarizing (Albertini, Ballarino and De Luca 2020), also demonstrates the political acceptance of deep forms of class-based income inequality. Given the widespread dissemination of neoliberal ideologies in Western countries, especially, the acceptance of inequalities is not surprising. Those born from the 1980s onwards have been constantly exposed to a media diet of neoliberalism promoting values of consumption, self-interest and competitiveness (Leyva 2019); being rewarded for outcompeting others is expected.

While data from the International Social Survey Programme in 2009 (involving thirty-nine countries) show that it is those who have the highest social positions that are most likely to support income inequality, a finding confirmed in more recent literature reviews (Mau 2015), the types of in/egalitarian ideologies that are at play in a given society also impact on attitudes to social injustice and inequality. The stronger the belief in meritocracy, the more people generally are likely to accept income inequality (Roex, Huijdts and Sieben 2019). Thus, though there is considerable ambivalence about social injustice and harms that neoliberal capitalism produces, not only do countries vary in their interpretations as to what is socially just, so too do different social classes within them.

Adherence to anti-egalitarian values is undoubtedly related to the active promotion and normalization of neoliberal ideologies from the early 1980s (Harvey 2005), though this is only a partial explanation. Neoliberal capitalism also makes inequality appealing by offering enticements (O'Flynn and Petersen 2007; Konings 2015): it promotes opportunities for excitement, principles of fairness in competitions, and security for the successful (Boltanski and Chiapello 2005). Political indifference to social injustices is also fuelled by disillusionment and weariness with the way parliamentary democracy is operating, and its inability to deliver its promises in a socially just manner (Rosanvallon 2013: 239). While disillusionment with democracy is arguably the result of how the political economy of neoliberal capitalism undermines strong forms of democracy and solidarity (Lynch and Kalaitzake 2018), the causal link between the deep and persistent inequalities, democratic dysfunctions and neoliberal capitalism is neither fully recognized nor fully understood. Ideologies play into invisibilizing and distorting the power relations underpinning these interrelated institutions and processes, thereby enabling inequalities and related social harms to persist.

It is the contradictions and incoherence of ideologies that make challenging them all the more difficult. They proclaim credible principles that few could discount (including efficiency, equality of opportunity and rewarding effort), while concealing the institutional and structural processes and practices that undermine the very principles they profess.

Comparing and Ordering

As humans are social animals, comparisons are inevitable. We define ourselves by our differences and similarities, be it in terms of height, age, gender, wealth or other contextually relevant variables. Comparisons inevitably lead to judgements and evaluations, though most of these are nominal, privately stored and undisclosed. Our personal view on someone's abilities, or their age or weight, is just that, a subjective view; it has no publicly legitimatized signifier.

However, in a capitalist society where economic inequality is endemic, there are visible winners and losers, leading to the public polarization of wealth, resources and statuses over time (Piketty 2014). In a global order of instant online communication, hierarchical orderings are easily made public; they are visible in lifestyles, consumer choices, life and health expectancy, and geographical locations. Moreover, market-determined and market-determining stratifications are constantly consolidated and refined under the capitalist gaze enabled by advanced digital technologies (Fourcade and Healy 2017).

While collecting data and comparing individuals are not new – *les misérables* ('the wretched poor') were the subject of both political and research interest from the eighteenth century onwards (Foucault 1980; Hacking 1986), what makes comparisons significant currently is that they are ubiquitous, are multifaceted and apply to the general population. Comparisons take place with or without consent through the widespread use of digitalized tracking (Mau 2019).

Individualized data collection takes place systematically and can follow people indefinitely (Fourcade and Healy 2017: 11).

Differences are recorded not only nominally, in terms of types of differences, but ordinally, in terms of the highest and the lowest, the best and the worst, the lesser and the greater. Given that nominal evaluations are qualitative, elusive and open to dispute and dissent, it is easier for large bureaucratic institutions of the state and of capitalist enterprises to use ordinal rankings to rate and classify people, as these can be translated into a credible record, through numbers. Ordinal judgements expressed in numerical form (1st class, top 1 per cent, bottom 10 per cent) give the impression of objectivity, while ordinal technology (online tracking of social networks, credit ratings, consumer choices) enables this information to be processed swiftly, cheaply and effectively for the purposes of discriminating between individuals, and between groups (Fourcade 2016: 178).

The divide between rich and poor, the privileged and the destitute, the potentially valuable and the potentially valueless in market terms, translates into hierarchically organized rankings based on a variety of scoring, grading and ranking methodologies. An individual's cumulative capital value, their 'uber-capital',[5] is then available in digitalized, traceable form (Fourcade and Healy 2017: 14). The person's composite market value, their 'uber- capitalization', occurs algorithmically, often without their knowledge or their consent. The tracing and recording of consumer choices, social contacts and/or spending patterns are then deployed by insurance firms, banks and credit institutions to determine the market value of different types of customers or potential customers, with profoundly inequitable outcomes in social class and racial terms (O'Neil 2016). Tracing and ranking without consent are also undertaken by state institutions of very different political persuasions, and with as yet unknown consequences (Snowden 2013; Shahin and Zheng 2020).

Under neoliberal capitalism, comparisons are corporatized and monetized. Those who are poorest and/or vulnerable due to age, disability or other market-limiting criteria become a risk. They are classified by their cumulative negative profile both individually and collectively. Whether they are applying for social housing or for a job, there is artificial intelligence technology available, such as Clearview's facial recognition app,[6] that enables their profile to be drawn up quickly and accurately without their consent. Not only does this undermine people's right to privacy (though these practices are now being contested in the courts),[7] it also undermines many people's chances of getting a job (if they have a criminal or even a civil offence on record) or getting health insurance or a loan for a house (if they have a poor credit rating). It can be used as a means to impoverish and harm the already impoverished.

Competition

Comparisons lead to competition, and the more extensive the range of comparators the greater the competition. Institutionalized comparisons produce competitive relations even in fields that are outside the market nexus. Assessments that were once inconsequential and private mutate to become public and competitive. This is evident in the way the boundaries between the private sphere and the market, between the amateur and the professional, are regularly breached. Amateur sports, cultural and musical activities, spheres of life that are outside the market nexus, are increasingly drawn into the market, often unwittingly. Recruiters and scouts working for professional and business organizations can and do attend amateur events with the intention of locating future 'stars' with market potential; the amateurs can and do enter the market,[8] though they may never have intended to do so.

Neoliberalism deviates from classical liberalism in that it regards competition as both an integral element and a virtue of capitalist markets. Competition is ubiquitous, no longer separable from daily routines; it is a defining feature of everyday living (Mau 2019: 115–18, 168–70). Grading is valorized, with everything from a simple household utensil to a meal, a public utility or a hotel being hierarchically evaluated, while ranking of institutions such as schools, universities, cities and even hospitals is normalized and framed as a responsibility to others. Whether organizations are public service-led or charitable, private or profiteering, is incidental; the norms of evaluation apply to all. Furthermore, competition applies within and without organizations: units and departments within public service bodies (such as publicly funded universities) must compete in their own internal market over resources. Competition at the transnational level is institutionalized and protected as a value by powerful institutions such as the European Commission and the OECD.[9]

An individual's worth is defined by their place in a series of hierarchies, be it in terms of achievements recorded, wins and losses, or their place on the rungs of the work/career and/or fitness ladder. As creativity and uniqueness are defining features of new capitalism, 'the economics of permanent innovation' requires individuals to be 'singular', to stand out (Rosanvallon 2013: 221); they must display multiple, unique 'selling points', something that greatly incentivizes and accelerates competition. Competitiveness is not confined to business, work or education; it is endemic to everyday cultural practices including socializing, leisure and shopping (Streeck 2016: 41–5).

While competition is an outer imperative, a regulatory norm, it also takes an internalized form: it becomes a way of being human (Mau 2019: 168–70). A binary mindset of rating and competing for coveted positions is hardwired into everyday thinking, as choices from buying groceries to opting for a leisure pursuit are mapped out on a road of ratings and rankings. Your choices mirror your own value, while competition with others is complemented by competition with oneself. Regular self-evaluation is actively promoted as an act of self-responsibilization, be it in terms of body mass index, sleep rate, heart rate, ergonomic rates or lifestyle patterns. Competing within your own body is a project, a way of displaying personal responsibility in health terms.

Judgement and harm

A society governed by competition must have losers as well as winners. For everyone who comes first, there is someone who comes last. For all those in the top 10 per cent of privilege, success or wealth, there must be a bottom 10 per cent; winning and losing are reciprocally related.

The price paid for failing relative to others is high. While its most immediate impact is economic, determining an individual's level of housing, transport, educational and food security, it also impacts on health, both physically and mentally. Not only do those who are poorest live in poorer-quality housing and have lower access to quality education, they also experience poorer physical health and more mental illness (Wilkinson and Pickett 2009, 2018).[10] Incessant and ubiquitous competition leaves no place to rest, just *to be*, without achieving.

Given that shame, the fear of being judged as insignificant, lesser or inadequate, is one of the most powerful human emotions (Cooley 1992; Goffman, 1963; Scheff 2000), it is inevitable that very unequal societies, where rich and poor live in each other's presence, produce status anxieties, the fear of not being respected. While the burden of classed inequality is deeply material, it is more than that: it invades people's sense of who they are, leading to 'a feeling of not getting anywhere despite one's efforts, the feeling of vulnerability in contrasting oneself to others at a higher social level, that buried sense of inadequacy that one resents oneself for feeling' (Sennett and Cobb 1972: 58). In a society where winning is what matters, those who know they are not on the winning side feel ashamed, vulnerable and even humiliated and mistrustful (Sennett 1998: 142).

Capitalism undermines human flourishing and harms people in multiple ways, including psychosocially (Wright 2010: 33–85). By institutionalizing hierarchical ordering, it produces *socially evaluative threats* and psychosocial anxieties (Wilkinson and Pickett 2018: 61–87). The negative impact of hierarchical ordering was confirmed in a major European study involving thirty countries and 35,000 people in 2007: it found a link between poorer mental health and income inequality. Status competition in the most economically unequal countries had 'a corrosive effect on social relationships' by undermining the trust that underpins them (Layte 2012: 509).[11]

Excessive competition also has a negative propelling effect. To offset the initial status anxieties stemming from a sense of inferiority, it accelerates risky, and often harmful, behaviours. To avoid negative evaluations, many people engage in ineffectual, and even harmful, social actions to boost their status or sense of well-being. These involve anything from entering into excessive indebtedness, addictive betting, or taking excessive amounts of alcohol or prescribed psychoactive drugs to help boost one's sense of importance and offset the sense of being a 'failure' (Wilkinson and Pickett 2018: 28–9).

Competition: the moral and psychic impact

Intense competitiveness also has a moral impact. It creates an economy of moral judgement whereby some are deemed more trustworthy, more reliable and more accountable than others (Fourcade and Healy 2017). Those with high grades, high credit ratings, socially approved addresses and valuable social networks are not only granted higher financial rewards, they are propelled into a different future by virtue of their moral-economic standing. They are defined as a good investment, promising a better return over time, thereby being deemed worthy of further investment, and having their life chances and opportunities enhanced.

Because economic class distinctions find expression in cultural forms in a hierarchically organized manner, those designated as morally superior, by virtue of their assumed trustworthiness and accountability, feel superior and act accordingly (Bourdieu 1984).

The dress, style, disposition and bearing of 'elite' bodies display the confidence and authority of their class positioning. These dispositions do not emerge accidentally; they are learned, becoming habitual and naturalized over time (Bourdieu 1990: 52–64). They are fostered from a young age, often in socially selective (Lynch and Lodge 2002: 37–63) or elite schools (Courtois 2018).

Competition has negative consequences for those who are lesser, whose bodies are not or cannot be toned, whose age makes them less marketable, whose clothes are out of fashion – an experience that is keenly felt by poor women particularly (Skeggs 1997). Working-class people's class distinctions do not display in a valued marketable form. Their experience of being evaluated culturally is one of being pathologized and judged (Sayer 2005; Walkerdine 2016; Crean 2018). Consequently, they try to become respectable in embodied ways (Skeggs 1997, 2004). But in trying to do so they often make their class of origin even more conspicuous. Because class is performed, it is marked on bodies and in minds. 'We can "spot it a mile off" even in the midst of our wish for it no longer to be there' (Walkderdine, Lucey and Melody 2001: 215).

As the ideology of competition is driven by the promise that only those with the best 'selling points' will reap success on the market (Bröckling 2015), the fear of failure, of being a 'loser', is there for all classes. Making competition a virtue not only impoverishes those who fail financially and socially, but incentivizes the winners to consolidate their wealth and to immunize themselves from responsibility to their fellow citizens. In the upper echelons of wealth, it leads to the development of an oligarchic elite, those not bound to any nation state but with wealth and power that could easily undermine most smaller nation states. These people's global wealth allows them to secede from the societies in which they live, spatially, socially and financially (by being a tax exile in many cases). Their fate and that of their families is detached from the countries where they reside (Streeck 2016: 28–30).

A highly specialist professional and managerial elite (Sklair 2000) services the oligarchic rich in complex ways.[12] The specialist elite's technical legal, financial and economic expertise enables them to be rewarded, not only with high salaries and bonuses, but also with significant share options that allow them to benefit substantially from the wealth-making of the oligarchic elite.

The general middle-classes (and skilled working-class) salariat, who live primarily on earned income, lack sufficient unearned wealth, be it from shares, investments or inheritances, to provide themselves or their families with long-term security (Mau 2015). Like the semi-skilled and unskilled working class, they are vulnerable to economic downturns in capitalism, being one or two months rather than one or two weeks away from poverty. The property-less, share-less and un-inheriting 'anxious' middle classes are increasingly concerned about protecting themselves and their families. Their insecurity finds expression in the weak forms of calculative solidarity that are now prevalent in Europe (Van Gerven and Ossewaarde 2012; Frericks 2014), and in middle-class allegiance to neoliberal values (Mau 2015). Middle-class anxieties are also reflected in how that class increasingly attributes a person's socio-economic impoverishment to individual shortcomings and personal responsibility, rather than oppressive and/or unequal external circumstances (Mau 2015: 18–21).

Though the middle classes of all strata feel and present dispositions of social superiority by displaying their class distinction (Bourdieu 1984), the road they are on is an internally competitive one too. The competition bar is set at different levels and is classed accordingly. The psychic and economic investment involved in creating the successful middle-class professional is high; in this context, failure is often not an option that is countenanced by parents, teachers or even the young middle class themselves (Walkerdine, Lucey and Melody 2001: 172–86)[13]. While exceptional performances are praised in families where they are not familiar, that is not true of professional middle-class families where they are the norm. High grades are expected, not exceptional events, with all the emotional and health pressures that these place on what Walkerdine, Lucey and Melody call 'the bourgeois' girl; she is expected to supress anxiety about failure while also balancing her 'cleverness' with her 'femininity' within a gendered social order (2001: 184–5).

Comparisons lead to competitions, which, in turn, undermine cooperation. They emphasize differences rather than commonalities, hierarchies over equality (Mau 2019: 27–8). As winning is a zero-sum game, why share what you have, or what you know, if you want to be the winner? The incentive at both individual and corporate levels is to consolidate, to conceal, and to protect and defend your own interest even if this comes at a high price to others.

Numbering enabling competition

The practice of counting, measuring and classifying populations is not new. It began in a systematic way almost two hundred years ago when there were systematic attempts to classify (and often to incarcerate) those who were deemed to be deviant, be it in terms of poverty, mental illness or vagrancy. *Les misérables* were the subject of great political and research interest, and over time, statistical tools provided not only a means of documenting their perceived 'deviancy' but also the necessary information to manage and control them (Hacking 1986).

The deviants multiplied with every new classification. They were 'constituted' as 'subjects' 'gradually, progressively, really and materially through a multiplicity of organisms, forces, energies, materials, desires, thoughts' (Foucault 1980: 97). As every new classification brings a new means and rationale for control, those who were defined as 'handicapped' or 'feeble-minded' were not only assigned an inferior and suspect status by virtue of their impairments, they were also defined as morally suspect, deemed culpable and blameworthy for their differences (McDonnell 2007).

While classifying populations focused originally on the deviant, the intensification and elaboration of competitions for privilege under neoliberal capitalism provided a demand for new and more elaborate forms of classification. Comparisons that were once based on nominal differences would not suffice, given their subjectivity and indivisibility. Qualitative evaluations were transformed into gradational, hierarchically ordered differences, not only of individuals but of all types of institutions, including financial institutions, economies and, indirectly, nation states (Mau 2019).

For competitions to have legitimacy they had to be systematic, organized and non-contestable. They had to have the appearance of neutrality in judging competitors. The quantification of evaluations provided such reassurances. Numbers brought an aura of objectivity, absoluteness and certainty, leaving competition results largely uncontested outside 'expert' algorithm programmers and psychometricians. Metrics provided a cognitive summary mechanism for judging individuals and organizations.

Metrics Undermining Care, an Immeasurable

In political and policy terms, metrics simplify governance and control by precluding conflicts over ranking and grading with a seemingly unassailable objectivity (Lingard 2011). The fear of numbers, of being found 'wrong' in challenging the veracity of the grade or rank, silences the outsider dissenter in the face of the expert. Nowhere has this been more obvious than in the misuse of intelligence quotient (IQ) test scores to assign someone a 'general intelligence' or g score on a scale that is itself an artefact of highly selective test construction procedures (Gould 1997). But because numbers such as Standard Assessment Test (SAT), IQ or PISA scores are internationally .intelligible, they can be interpreted cross-culturally without much translation. No matter how arbitrary the evaluation or grading criteria may be, quantification allows for the communication of scores and ranks beyond borders in a way that narrative-laden evaluations do not.

Truth expressed in numbers is perceived to be non-contestable, granting metrics an unwarranted truth status that has been exacerbated by the issue of algorithms, automated decision-making, in calculating grades.[14] By being ostensibly 'objective' in their judgement, metrics create a common cognitive space in which the value of individuals, units and organizations can be appraised, enabling them to be labelled and stratified. Metrics reinforce a myth that what can be ranked hierarchically can be incontrovertibly judged. Yet numbers are neither neutral nor innocent. Metrics are built on a set of values and priorities that are far from obvious and can be arbitrary and harmful on both social class and racial grounds (O'Neil 2016). The means of achieving the rank or the rating is always selective and can be problematic in scientific terms (Borer and Lawn 2013: 49).

Metrics do not just represent the world, however; they create it – they are inscription devices that constitute what they appear to represent (Rose 1999). At both individual and corporate levels[15] they produce and reproduce what they purport to measure (Espeland and Sauder 2007; Sauder and Espeland 2009). Moreover, when performance is judged by a few select measures, this generates 'goal displacement' as people focus on meeting the target (for the sake of promotion or holding/getting a job or getting a grade), often at the expense of other, more important organizational/educational goals that are not measured (Muller 2018). What tends to be ignored in a metrics-led system of appraisal is that 'the measurable and actual contribution' of people are not the same. (Muller 2018: 61). People can and do become what they are measured to be, even if this is not aligned with the core mission of organizations, especially those that are public service-led.

Although numerically recorded ranked evaluations may not be market specific or directly market relevant, they are generated from a market-led morality of efficiency, effectiveness and output evaluation. They discipline people's behaviour by requiring them to operate under market-generated organizational norms where increased outputs, allied to time and resource efficiencies, are prioritized over other values (Taylor 1911). This is profoundly problematic in public service organizations where the mission is to take care of others, by promoting good health, welfare and education, rather than profit-making or gain. Caring in these contexts is not just a mode of action with a goal or purpose, it is also a disposition in action. It is a way of relating ethically through attentiveness, responsiveness, cooperation and informed other-centredness (Tronto 1993). The quality of the hospital, education, housing or welfare service depends as much on the care, consideration and thoughtfulness of its employees as it does on their technical knowledge and skills (Mol 2008). The logic of being *homo curans* (Tronto 2017) is in direct conflict with the instrumental, exploitative, *homo economicus* logic of capitalism. To exercise care-led qualities, staff must be able to exercise good will, collegiality, consideration and respect, and feel rewarded for doing so; but metrics cannot measure these, as they are individualized, relational qualities.

Caring relations are relational goods, in the sense that they can only exist if shared or lived with others (Donati 2010); they are examples of reciprocal relations that are 'produced and consumed simultaneously' (Rosanvallon 2013: 272). Because of this, they cannot be measured with a numerical score, as their outcome is intangible, living and ending in the moment of caring. While there are long-term positive benefits from good care relations, including good mental, physical and emotional health (Wilkinson and Pickett 2018), these are very difficult to decipher and measure in the lifetime of a professional care relationship. Moreover, when metrics are used to evaluate care-related professional work, the very qualities that matter organizationally are undermined by their immeasurability (Mol 2008).

In sum, the quantification of evaluations greatly enables the intensification and sophistication of all manner of competitive comparisons, and these comparisons have negative psychic and moral returns. They override and weaken first-order social and moral values for the sake of realizing second-order principles: trust, integrity, care, compassion and solidarity are subordinated to regulation, control and competition.

In a competitively ordered society there is no moral imperative to care for anyone other than oneself (Mau 2019: 169). Rather, rewards based on measured performances promote a never-ending cycle of competition while undermining cooperation. When winning or losing is what defines the individual, it fosters the desire for the best of everything, be it the best grade or the best school, the best teacher, the best house or even the nicest seat in the café. Being in constant competition changes the way people see themselves and what they desire and value. It creates a culture where *to be* is *to win*. People 'strive to maximize their own metrics, ignoring, or even sabotaging, their fellows' (Muller 2018: 172).

The sanctification of productivity and outputs leads to the amoral becoming the necessary: documenting scores, grades, indices, ranks and attainments becomes an industry in itself, with a very high economic cost.[16] Care-led service relationships become defined in transactional terms, a means to an end, to a better score or a higher rank. And even if care were measurable metrically, the very doing of this would force people into the calculation of other-centeredness that would undermine the very principle of relatedness and mutuality that is at the heart of both primary care relations and public service care work.

Equality of Opportunity and Meritocracy

While the glorification of competition is central to neoliberal capitalism, with all competitions there are rules to the game, so the criteria for determining success/failure, high and low status, relative wealth and poverty have to have political legitimacy. There has to be some mechanism to make unequal outcomes morally justifiable and socially acceptable.

Moral justification for unequal outcomes is provided through widespread allegiance to a liberal code of equality of opportunity and an accompanying ideology of meritocracy (Sandel 2020). This is a belief that all positions in society are open to talent regardless of origin, and that everyone should, in some sense, have an equal chance to compete for social advantages. No one is legally excluded from competing,[17] even though many do not have much chance of 'winning' due to unequal starting points or resources. The principle of equality of opportunity is encoded in EU treaties, and advanced within member states by a variety of legally binding directives. Its legal status adds to its legitimacy as a mechanism for distributing social goods, including education.

Equality of opportunity is formally operationalized as the governing equality principle in education and employment through the practice of meritocratic selection. The most 'meritorious' are those who are assumed to be intelligent and hardworking (IQ + Effort = Merit; Young 1971)[18] and are subsequently awarded high grades or high-status jobs. In theory, in a meritocratic society, social selection for each stage of education and, ultimately, for the labour market is determined on merit.

Because credentialized education is a positional good, its value is always relative; to succeed one must have more of the valued credentials than one's competitors. To acquire the most valued credentials, one must be in a position to outcompete others. Given the relationship between educational success, income, wealth and other forms of social and cultural capital, meritocratic selection is simply unattainable in contemporary capitalist societies (Brown, Lauder and Ashton 2011). Those who hold privileged positions protect them, through social closure and opportunity hoarding to their own group advantage (Weber 1978; Tilly 1999). They alter the rules of the competition in ways that protect their own privilege by increasing the cost, time and social and cultural capital required to get the best qualifications or experience. Those who are least well-resourced or capitalized cannot win, as the rules of the game are set in ways that ensures this does not happen (Duncan and Murnane 2011).[19] The classed achievement gap is matched by the persistent raced achievement gap, and both are related to income differentials and economic inequality (Magnuson and Waldfogel 2008; Reardon 2011). The fabled level playing field is a chimera, as the history of selection into elite higher education institutions demonstrates (Karabel 2005).

There is a dark side to meritocratic ideology (Sandel 2020). Not only does it presume that social hierarchies will persist, it creates a deception that all that is required to rise to the top of this hierarchy is to work hard and have ability; the promised outcome is good educational credentials and occupational success. But meritocratic outcomes are unrealizable for the majority because the abilities and opportunities to be meritorious, to rise to the top, are based on non-meritocratic factors, including inherited wealth, social networks and cultural capital (Bourdieu and Passeron 1977). Furthermore, what is defined as worthy of merit recognition in a given time and culture is quite arbitrary and, by definition, excludes some groups (Mijs 2016), something Black and ethnic minority groups (Bhopal 2018) and women have found to their cost in the academy (Thornton 2013; Montes López and O'Connor 2019). The key question always remains: who has the power to define which abilities are of merit and how does a society know and measure abilities (intelligences) and/

or effort? There is no clear formula for measuring these that is not deeply subjective: what are defined as meritocratic traits in education have changed over time and can be quite arbitrary (Karabel 2005).[20] Moreover, those who have the power to define 'merit' will always do so in a way that will ensure their own kind, in particular their own children, are meritorious (Mijs, 2016: 21).

As the amoral principle of competition becomes the necessary in a meritocratic system, documenting scores, educational attainments and ranks becomes an industry in itself (Muller 2018). Student and staff idealism for working in 'the public interest' is diminished, as energy and time must be devoted to documenting institutional and/or personal achievements (Lynch 2015). Prioritizing the educationally disadvantaged is given less importance, not only because the already privileged actively resist any regulation that would disadvantage their children in class terms (Courtois 2018), but because educational organizations themselves try to protect their own competitive advantage in a market-led system. When the least competitive/most disadvantaged students are a threat to a good performance appraisal for a given school or university, having as few of these students as possible allows resources to be deployed for the use of those who offer a better return on 'investment' in terms of profiling the school or college.

Creating a culture of arrogance and blame

A further problem with the principle of meritocracy is that it overrides and weakens other values; it 'crowds out' debates about equality and need (Mijs 2016: 23–6). This is, as Mijs suggests, perhaps its most dangerous characteristic. It fosters a belief that only a minority of talented (market-valuable) people exist, propelling the so-called 'global war for talent' (Brown and Tannock 2009). Resources and research are redirected towards the so-called 'bright', 'gifted', 'smart', 'able' students. They are hothoused 'as if they were a rare natural resource', something that is profoundly untrue (Wilkinson and Pickett 2018: 170). The myth of exceptional talent also provides a rationale for unjustifiably high salaries, bonuses and rewards for a small number of already privileged people.

On the other hand, those who are defined as failures, many from a very young age, starting in the 'weak' reading group, the 'low' stream, the so-called 'bad' school, are held individually responsible for their own failure. Credentialism has become a very acceptable prejudice (Sandel 2020). Education stamps people publicly as lesser and greater, successful or failing, by streams, grades, examination scores and their lack of diplomas/degrees (Bourdieu 1996; Lareau 2011; Vincent and Maxwell 2016). Later in life, it holds them to account for their subsequent lowly social positioning (Taylor-Gooby 2011; Frericks 2014).

The principle of meritocracy is therefore an ideology that justifies inequality, not a means of overcoming it. What emerges is a twenty-first-century educational manifestation of eugenics-related logic, declaring that only a minority are worthy of investment. The rise of elite academies, centres for so-called gifted children in schools and merit scholarships in universities is indicative of this trend.

There is, as Young (1971) predicted, a new type of arrogance that comes with the myth of meritocracy: those who achieve are told they 'deserve it' due to their high grades, their first-class degrees; they see themselves as a caste apart.[21] A form of state-endorsed nobility is established, with educational grades and degrees replacing royal titles (Bourdieu 1996). The ideology of meritocracy conceals a wealth of classed strategies and resources that favour the already privileged (Reay 1998; Lynch and Lodge 2002: 37–63; Ball 2003).

Conclusion

When market-led relations prevail culturally, they do more than divide people along the lines of income and wealth, polarizing the oligarchic elite and the average waged/salaried workers; they also normalize and valorize hierarchical social relations. Everyone is forced into competitive relations with others, as social goods are distributed by winning or buying (and the two are not unrelated), rather than by need. Ranking and grading normalizes judgement-making;[22] people are subject to constant grading.

The intensification and sophistication of competition are further exacerbated by the quantification of evaluation and use of metrics. Comparisons that were once based on nominal differences are transformed into gradational, hierarchically ordered differences (Mau 2019: 28) that exacerbate status anxieties and generate distrust. Metric-based comparisons heighten awareness of differences and relative deficits, while artificial intelligence enables highly individualized profiling to take place, leading inevitably to ever-increasing comparisons, competitions and hierarchies (Zuboff 2019).

A society of generalized competition also embeds a culture and politics of risk and autonomy, establishing the consumer as sovereign and sacred, while it glorifies competition as the proper way of relating (Rosanvallon 2013: 237–8). Risk is seen as enabling and incentivizing autonomy, creativity and independence; autonomy and risk-taking become mandatory rather than elective, as they are regarded as ways of expressing individuality and a source of productive innovation.

Consumption is an indicator of 'success', the touchstone for measuring worth, and is epitomized in the realization of choice, be it in the choice and display of goods and/or the use of services. The ever-increasing expansion of market choices is promoted as compensating for the loss of meaningful political engagement and the loss of social equality (Rosanvallon 2013: 38). The ideology of choice creates a social gloss concealing the classed and raced constraints on choosing, and the political de-culturation that ensues from time spent in consumption. While participating in society through buying and selling, being part of 'a community of money', provides a sense of living in a 'commons' (Soederberg 2014), it is a commons that is largely built around competitive hedonism (Streeck 2016: 41–5). Participation in the money 'commons', for those who are poor, generally involves increasing indebtedness and further impoverishment (Soederberg 2014).

With the prevalence of the twin ideological myths of equality of opportunity and meritocratic selection, social injustices are normalized. Those who are poor or unproductive are held responsible for their own misfortunes; they are blamed for their 'poor showing', their failure to make the grade. The normative ideology of self-responsibility flourishes within the sphere of meritocratic myths (Frericks 2010, 2014; Van Gerven and Ossewaarde 2012). Meanwhile the successful feel morally righteous in their indifference to the suffering created by the perpetuation of their own privileges. The principles of equality of opportunity work as an ideological mask concealing their own false promises (Rosanvallon 2013: 111). This is especially true in societies that lack equality of condition, where few can realistically achieve their full potential (Tawney 1964). The meritocratic myth compounds the deception. Rather than celebrate meritocracy, we should despise a system where equality is only about changing the faces on top of a hierarchically ordered society (Sandel 2020).

Part III
Violence – the Nemesis of Care

8

The Violation of Non-Human Animals

As life on planet Earth is relational and highly interdependent, care is not only an issue for human relations; it concerns relationships with all species, human and non-human, and the natural environment.[1] The ways in which capitalism undermines these inevitable interdependencies can no longer be denied (Klein 2014). If for no other reason than self-interest, especially given the experience of climate change and the coronavirus health crisis in 2020–1, there is an urgent need to review humans' relationship with other species, especially non-human animals.[2]

To care is to live and feel relationally, and to recognize the suffering other. Non-human animals are sentient beings that have interests of their own; they have feelings and suffer, and because of this it is important to address their care concerns, insofar as these can be known by humans.

When the disposition to care is neither developed nor supported, the practices of empathy, care and concern go rusty through lack of use (Shapiro 2007). This holds true of human relations with each other and with non-human animals, not least because sympathy for non-human animals[3] is a deep primary disposition that is only obscured and repressed by prolonged social conditioning (Luke 2007). Humans have to learn to 'turn off' compassion in order not to sensibly feel the pain and anxieties in animal suffering. Humans have to learn to disregard animals' sensibilities and feelings, and to regard caring as futile or morally irrelevant, to suppress feeling of care. Learned indifference leads to a political passivity to injustices, including injustices against non-human animals (Adams 2007: 21–34).

This chapter examines the many ways in which we learn to be care-indifferent to non-human animals, and how national and international trading in animals as commodities promotes and accelerates their harm and suffering. The chapter highlights in particular the need for social justice theorists to recognize the moral status of non-human animals as sentient beings that can and do experience intense and prolonged suffering at human hands. Although we like to distinguish morally between the killing and abuse of human and non-human animals, it is a short step from seeing non-human animals as disposable objects, a 'mass' of things to be used or abused at will, to seeing certain categories of people as disposable.

Violation

Worldwide meat production has trebled since the 1980s, increasing by 20 per cent in the ten years up to 2011, according to the Worldwatch Institute. The annual increase in consumption consistently outpaces population growth, with meat consumption predicted to rise continuously up to 2050 (OECD–FAO 2011, 2020; Weis 2014; Arcari 2017).

While killing occurs between non-human animals in their natural habitats, it is individualized and driven by the need for basic survival. The killing and exploitation of other species by humans is organized, systematic, and increasingly globalized and large-scale in a world driven by contemporary capitalist ethics where the exploitation and expropriation of nature are a normalized feature of life (Shukin 2009). Moreover, it is not necessary for survival, as is evident from the millions of people who live on meat-free diets throughout the world, most notably in India. There are multiple sources of plant foods available for those who want to live well and healthily, especially in rich countries. However, there is little formal education in most countries on how to plan for a plant-based diet or indeed how to cook plant foods in an appetizing way. Contrarily, cheap meat from non-human animals, especially industrially farmed meat such as chicken and pig, is widely available and extensively promoted.

The killing and eating of other animals would not be acceptable politically and socially without being legitimated. Sophisticated and organized ideological rationalizations and justifications are provided by the 'meat' and food industries, and by recreational interest groups (such as deer hunters and fox hunters) to justify killing, while scientists provide rationalizations for painful experimentation on live

animals (vivisection). In ways similar to the use of ideology justifying the killing of other humans in organized warfare and genocide
(Malešević 2010a), animals are objectified, othered and (in the case
of wild animals) demonized to justify their killing, use and abuse.
Though the Enlightenment promulgated ideals of rights to life,
liberty and freedom, and these ideals found expression in various
international covenants and conventions (such as the Universal
Declaration of Human Rights, prohibiting 'cruel and degrading
treatment of persons' and endorsing 'freedom from torture'), these
principles only applied to humans. There has been no Enlightenment
for non-human animals and there is no global protection system for
animals to date.[4]

The belief that non-human animals are there to service human
animals is both widely held and virtually unassailable in political
terms. This is especially true in countries where the economy is
heavily reliant on the sale of non-human-animal products, including
Ireland, New Zealand, and Australia. In Australia alone, 88 per cent
of the total 405 million hectares of agricultural holdings are used
for livestock grazing (Arcari 2017). What is so pernicious about
the normalization of violence against animals is that it is insinuated
into everyday thinking in a way that makes it invisible. Most people
who eat meat do not think about the suffering that underpinned the
raising of the creature that they are eating (increasingly in factory-
style settings), or about the suffering that was caused in transporting
them, often for thousands of miles, or about the means used for
killing them. When people grill their beef steak, enjoy roast chicken,
lamb or ham sandwiches, they do not think of how the mammals and
birds they are eating are kept in effective captivity and confinement;
nor do they consider their lifelong deprivations of simple life
pleasures like feeding, eating and walking around in the open air,
a fate that is especially true of chickens/hens worldwide (Josephson
2020). A deep anthropocentrism[5] lies at the root of this thinking.
Social thinking focused on self-interest places the enjoyment of
food as morally separated from the sources of that food. There has
been little public debate either about how animals suffer in being
objectified and commodified for food and use, or about the ways
industrialized farming is harmful to human health, although the
Covid-19 pandemic of 2020–1 has focused some attention on this.[6]

While the killing of animals by humans has a long history, the
bureaucratization of coercion that has enabled and secured the
systematic use of organized violence and war to oppress peoples
(Malešević 2010a: 5–7) is also fundamental to the organized killing

of non-human animals. The incarceration of non-human animals in highly centralized feeding operations where they live much of their lives imprisoned in sheds (calves, steers, cows) or in cages (hens, rabbits, mink, foxes and racoons), and their systematic killing daily in slaughterhouses in hundreds of thousands (Nibert 2013), are prime examples of bureaucratized violence.

Despite their known cruelty to animals and dangers to human health, concentrated animal feeding operations (CAFOs) are being established at an accelerated rate (Nibert 2013: 236–40). A report funded by the Pew Charitable Trusts, based on research undertaken at the Johns Hopkins Bloomberg School of Public Health, examined the problems created by CAFOs in four primary areas: public health, the environment, animal welfare and rural communities. Aside from the cruelty of keeping animals and birds in extremely confined spaces, where they are unable to walk around and lie in comfort, and the harm done by concentrated animal manure to water supplies, the widespread use of antibiotics and growth hormones in CAFOs has significant, long-term, harmful implications for human health. The scientists undertaking the research expressed particular concern about humans' ability to fight infections due to the increase in antimicrobial-resistant bacteria arising from the way meat is produced in industrialized settings: 'A World Health Organization (WHO) Report on Infectious Diseases published in 2000 expressed alarm at the spread of multidrug-resistant infectious disease agents and pointed to food as a major source of antimicrobial-resistant bacteria' (Pew Commission 2008: 5). In addition, the scientists cited extensive research that industrial food animal production is a serious threat to public health, including the health of workers in the plants and those living near industrialized facilities. The high level of respiratory problems among workers in industrialized animal production facilities, and the fact that the diseased workers 'can serve as a bridging population, transmitting animal-borne diseases to a wider population' (ibid.: 5), are a major public health concern.

The Anthropocentrism of Language

Language not only defines the world; it also creates the world in terms of how we understand and relate to it and each other. One of the ways in which the suffering and pain of non-human sentient beings are invisibilized is through the use of neutralizing language. The language used about non-human animals generally creates them as objects of use; they are defined as property (and protected as such legally). Most are classified as products, located on the 'food pyramid' as sources of protein (chicken, lean meat) or calcium (dairy products), or fashion accessories (mink coats). They are objectified as things available as a means to human ends. Such language plays a key role in creating and maintaining hierarchical relations between humans and non-human animals (Arcari 2017).

Concepts such as 'meat' or 'poultry' help distance the non-human animals from the consumer's consciousness. These words create a detachment psychologically from the violence underpinning animals' translation from living sentient creatures to cooked flesh. The use of sanitized language reifies the non-human animal or bird as a thing. The suffering of the sentient living creature is invisibilized: the force-fed goose's liver becomes *foie gras*, the bull or heifer's back and sides are divided into *ribeye* and *sirloin steaks*, young calves become anonymized as *veal*, the top of the lamb's back is *a rack*, pigs are classified as *pork or bacon*, bulls and cows as cattle (*red meat*) (Colby and Punda 2009).

While these classifications are neither new nor capitalism-specific, the nomenclature helps serve capitalist purposes by concealing the violence of the act of killing and abusing animals for profit on a vast scale from the act of consuming 'meat' (Shukin 2009). Animals become 'absent-referents' (Adams 2000) in the supermarket and the fashion house when they are reified as products. Defining animals as *meat* or *fur* detaches them from their sentient individuality and persona. Those who consume/display them are desensitized to their lived existence through the moral neutralization of language.[7]

The normalization of the violence meted out to non-human animals is not new. Humankind's transition from foraging and nomadic pastoralism, to hunting, to ranching, and the development of agricultural societies were deeply involved in the use and abuse of non-human animals not just for food but as weapons of war (Salter 2015). However, violence against non-human animals has multiplied exponentially with the industrialization of animal-based food production. The development of CAFOs, originally associated with commercial farming in the US, is now a global phenomenon. The objectification and oppression of animals, and the utilitarianism that underpins human relations with them, are ubiquitous (Francione 1995) and accelerating in the twenty-first century (Nibert 2013; Torres 2007).

Care of Non-Human Animals and Social Justice

This is not to say that the treatment of animals has been unregulated and devoid of concerns for their welfare. There are multiple laws, national and international, governing humans' relations with other animals, but these are generally based on anthropocentric assumptions: they focus on avoiding harm where humans regard avoiding harm as necessary (Hayry 2020). Despite regulations, there are numerous ways in which humans harm animals that are not prohibited by law, in food production, in scientific laboratories, in entertainment and in the wild. The practice of locking cows, pigs and calves into confined concrete sheds for months on end, with little room to walk around (with some never being let out to roam or eat naturally), would be regarded as evil and morally reprehensible if done to humans. Yet humans do this to non-human animals to make them fat quickly for human consumption, without regard to their feelings or needs as unique species. The gratuitous shooting of wild birds and deer for entertainment, the common practices of castrating young bull calves (often without anaesthetic) or spaying or neutering domestic cats and dogs, are all normalized as acceptable in moral terms. Because non-human animals are defined as objects of human utility, much harm can be rationalized and justified.

The lack of human appreciation, understanding and concern[8] for non-human animal suffering exonerates those who organize and benefit from their production and killing for fashion or for food. Heifer, bull, calf, pig or sheep farmers are not subjected to moral opprobrium. Neither are the people who benefit greatly from the industrialized killing of animals, the meat-factory owners (known as *beef barons* in Ireland due to their wealth)[9].

Likewise, scientific experimentation on living animals is defined as 'necessary' for the advancement of human health or science (a debatable proposition in itself) even when non-human animals suffer great pain in the process (Slicer 2007). While there are extensive regulations governing the use of animals in scientific research in many countries, the animals are still defined as objects of use, as their interests are subordinated to those of the researcher. Animals are violated through invasive surgery and the practice of toxicological and disease research that causes them pain and suffering. Research also involves holding animals in captivity in ways that make them suffer; social animals are kept in isolation, while burrowing animals, such as rabbits, are kept in cages where they cannot burrow. More recently, the use of genetic engineering technology for manipulating animals to create 'models' for researching severe human diseases has also led to much pain and suffering among animals in scientific laboratories (Rollin 2017). The animals' feelings as sentient beings that experience pain, suffering, anguish and anxiety are often not named or claimed publicly as a matter of moral concern in the laboratory.

More generally, very little attention is paid to animals' species-specific preferences for living and, in the case of mammals that have the psychological properties of persons (such as apes, monkeys, pigs, elephants and dogs), as beings who are aware of themselves 'as separate entities in space and time', with 'memories, expectations, hopes, and fears' (Hayry 2020: 248).

Distributive Justice, Missing Animals

While it may appear normal that research on *social* justice is human-specific and without much reference to animals, this reflects the absence of a comprehensive relational framework of analysis about the human condition. As non-human animals are part of the human-relational world, there is every reason to include them in our care-maps and mind-maps when examining matters of social and ecological justice. They need to be part of the 'who' of political justice.

Theories of social justice have been dominated on the left by the political economic theories of Marxism and neo-Marxism, and within liberalism by the work of Rawls, over the past fifty or so years. Neither the liberal-distributive models of justice nor the Marxist political-economy model provide a challenge to the practices of using non-human animals as sources of food or in scientific experimentation (Garner 2013: 21).

Hayry (2020) suggests that a shift in philosophical positions, from 'simple ethics' to 'complex politics' in philosophical debates about justice from the 1980s onwards, is one reason why non-human animals have not been taken seriously as species with moral standing in their own right. The prioritization of the *human-social* dimension of social justice has produced a situation where the politics of winners and losers has led to the marginalization of non-distributive concerns.

As the domination and exploitation of non-human animals are, in the first instance, a non-distributive matter, the focus of the social justice debates on re/distributive issues in the human-social world has contributed to the neglect of concerns about non-human animals. As is well recognized in the literature, not least by leading scholars such as Axel Honneth (1995) and Iris Marion Young (1990), there are many injustices that are not distributive in character. These include injustices arising from the need for self-determination, respect, affiliation and companionship, and correlatively, freedom from oppression and domination.[10] Animals are not an organized interest group that can initiate recognition and respect-based movements on their own behalf, not least because they lack the capacity to organize against human brutality (though they do self-organize; Shukin 2009), as indeed do vulnerable humans including most children, the very ill and those with severe intellectual disabilities. The distributive paradigm is limiting, therefore, in terms of its understanding of the complexities of oppressions (Young 1990: 15–38), as many deep injustices arise in the first instance through non-recognition and misrecognition.

Even though economic gain drives much of the harm non-human animals experience, the generative site of their injustices originates in the non-recognition of their status as individual subjects with species-specific needs and rights. Relying on an economic-distributive justice paradigm makes their well-being contingent on the good will and moral motivations of human beings. It is derived from a concept of charity and forbearance, rather than principles of justice that recognize non-human animals' inherent value in their own right (Garner 2013). Once questions of respect and recognition for the uniqueness of non-human subjects are not defined as matters of moral concern, there is no avenue for incorporating them into the political justice frame.

As the distributive paradigm, within the liberal tradition, is also characterized by individualism, it fails to put structural and institutional injustices under the microscope (Young 1990: 18–24), thereby underestimating the importance of the political economy of injustices.[11] The failure to put established structures and institutions under critical analysis leads to silence around the systematic abuse of non-human animals in profit-led industrialized farming and scientific laboratories.

The distributive paradigm also fails to address the property problem in terms of animal rights and welfare. Many animals live a life of captivity, be it in private homes, sanctuaries or zoos. No matter how well treated animals living in confinement are, they remain ultimately the property of those who care for them, and can be disposed of at the will of their owners when they become a 'burden' due to age, illness or disability (Gruen 2014; Cudworth 2015). Keeping animals in captivity as 'pets', though caring for them in a paternalistic manner, raises other questions about animals' rights. Donaldson and Kymlicka (2011) argue that sentient animals brought into our homes as pets have rights as *co-citizens*, including the positive right to mobility and a negative right not to be restrained and confined. Whether they should have the freedom to exercise such rights without some constraints is the subject of further debate, as the freedom to roam and hunt unrestrained can cause unnecessary harm to other species (nesting birds in the case of cats, while wandering dogs can cause car or bicycle accidents), especially in places with limited natural habitats and safe spaces, such as cities (Palmer and Sandoe 2014).

Ethicists, Welfarists and Animal Rights

While there has been a tradition contesting the abuse of non-human animals, instigated especially by Singer's (1975) original book *Animal Liberation*, and there is now an extensive literature on animal rights emanating from different disciplines (Regan 1983; Adams 2000; Plumwood 2000; Francione 2009; Donaldson and Kymlicka 2011; Cochrane 2012; Gruen 2014; Kalof 2017[12]) including within feminism (Adams 2007),[13] the dominant academic perspective on non-human animals within the academy is an anthropocentric one in justice terms. Non-human animals are generally not considered as key subjects in debates about social justice. They are not defined as having capacities and capabilities that grant them rights and interests as independent moral subjects. Moreover, the case for engaging with non-human animals in egalitarian and social justice terms has, in many respects, receded from public discourse in recent decades.

Peter Singer's concept of practical ethics (1993) promoted the idea of treating animals equally by having their 'interests' considered. However, the 'equal consideration of interests' principle does not grant all humans or non-human animals the same moral standing. While Singer claims that non-human animals' interests must be considered, he distinguishes between moral valence, or significance, and moral considerability. Considerability does not mean equal treatment; it means treating like interests in a comparable fashion.[14]

While it advanced thinking about the moral significance of animal use and abuse, Singer's approach is largely utilitarian, allowing as it does for the instrumental use of animals in particular circumstances (Regan 1983; Torres 2007). Singer morally endorses human actions that prioritize human interests above those of animals on the grounds of maximizing values and outcomes (Jones 2015: 469–70). In contrast, Regan (1983) and especially Garner (2013) claim that non-human animals have *moral entitlements*; they must not be judged in terms of their utility or how they relate to humans. If non-human animals possess an inherent value, they possess it on equal terms with human animals, and as such they cannot be treated as a means to a human end.

Animal ethicists, unlike Singer, recognize that non-human animals are sentient beings with a life of their own (Francione 1995, 2009), creatures that have their own capabilities, to grow, to mate and to provide companionship for each other. They are recognized as unique, differing in temperament and in their taste and food preferences from other animal species.[15] Non-human animals also have interests in their own well-being; they have a life to be lived, independent of humans, and they experience pain, suffering, anxiety and loss, all of which signify their unique moral standing (Jones 2015). Moreover, they are creatures of uniqueness in their own right that contribute to the beauty of the natural world.

While welfarism has gone some way towards advancing the protection and welfare of non-human animals, it does not address the problem of treating animals as human property (Francione 1995, 2009). It focuses primarily on the minimization or elimination of suffering as the primary goal. Welfarists use the rhetoric of rights in their advocacy for non-human animals while rejecting rights-based theory in favour of utilitarianism, in so far as they regard non-human animals as property (Torres 2007). The right not to be regarded as property or a simple 'resource' for humans is in many respects the moral baseline for an effective animal rights movement for non-human animals (Francione 2009).[16]

Moral Indifference to Violence against Non-Human Animals

Throughout the world, tens of billions of non-human animals are farmed and slaughtered for food each year, with data from Worldwatch showing that meat production has tripled in the late twentieth and early twenty-first century (Petrovic, Djordjevic, Milicevic, Nastasijevic and Parunovic 2015). An estimated 70–75 per cent of agricultural land is given over to the production of animals for food (Arcari 2017: 70–1), and an estimated 80 per cent of growth in the non-human animals bred for meat (what the FAO calls 'livestock') now comes from highly industrialized production systems (FAO 2006).

Even 'companion' animals such as dogs and cats are systematically killed, usually by being euthanized, if they are not wanted or defined as 'strays' or 'feral' (Cudworth 2015). Non-human animals who are defined and used as a source of food often experience great pain and deprivation before they are transported, killed and eaten by humans (Mitchell 2011). Animals that live in natural habitats, including elephant, deer, birds and rabbits, are hunted and killed, sometimes for food, but often for pleasure; they are defined as 'game', killed for amusement. When they are not killed for fun or for fur, or eaten for food, non-human animals remain major players in agricultural production in the less-industrialized areas of the world, and are widely used as instruments of scientific, including military, research, and in organized warfare (Salter 2015).

Although the 'domestication' of animals is represented as a 'partnership', a benign and welcome engagement between humans and animals, such is not the case. Puppy farming and pet farming are big business and relatively unregulated in many countries. When non-human animals are domesticated, they become the property of those who have them. They are owned, controlled and, whether bought or taken in voluntarily, disposed of (what is euphemistically called 'put to sleep' or 'put down') at the will of their owners. Even those living with non-human animals as companions rarely see them as being independent subjects of life. They live by the will of their owners.

The multiple ways in which human beings control, biologically manipulate, capture and kill other animals violate the sanctity of their life as sentient beings, and are a form of desecration – what Nibert calls 'domesecration' (2013: 12).[17] What is astonishing is that it is permissible for humans to treat sentient animals in a way that would be considered profoundly unjust and immoral if the same treatment were meted out to human beings, no matter how reviled (Jones 2015). This attitude reflects what Francione (2000) terms a type of 'moral schizophrenia'[18] at the core of humans' perspective on non-human animals; by this he means that humans have deluded and confused moral attitudes to other sentient species. Humans' benign and caring attitude to their companion animals (cats and dogs especially) runs in parallel with indifference to the violence and abuse meted out to equally sensitive animals, such as calves, pigs, lambs or cows, in their rearing, transporting and killing (Torres 2007). The pleasure of eating the meat of non-human animals trumps humans' moral concern for non-companion animals.

Guilt

Humans, though generally remaining silent on the cruelty meted out to non-human animals, also experience guilt. They hide away from becoming informed and are very defensive when asked about their meat eating by vegetarians or vegans. They do not visit slaughterhouses (most are kept well hidden from view), nor do they examine or query the conditions in which animals are managed on industrialized farms. For their part, the media does not report on the mass killing of sentient beings in abattoirs. So-called 'meat plants' only became known or named in media reports in the EU and US during the coronavirus crisis when relatively high proportions of the workers in these plants contracted the Covid-19 virus.[19] Although working conditions in slaughterhouses are crowded, stressful and intense, what happens in them is rarely brought to public attention. This reflects the fact that 'meat' factories are staffed by relatively low-paid, poorly educated, often migrant workers, many of whom are working in precarious working circumstances and are afraid to speak about their poor working conditions for fear of losing their jobs.[20] Not only does the lack of interest in animal killing reflect animals' low moral standing, it also reflects the low status and relative powerlessness of workers in this sector throughout Europe (Hansen 2018). There is a conflation between the exploitation of non-human animals and of humans.

Capitalism and the Abuse of Animals

Defining animals as property, deployed for human pleasure and utility, is not new in historical terms, nor is it unique to capitalism, having predated it by hundreds of years. Nomadic pastoralists relied on non-human animals for food, water and wealth. They gradually expanded their territory from the Eurasian steppes into Eastern Europe and Northern China to graze their flocks several hundred years ago, displacing sedentary agriculturalists in the process (Harris 2004). Nomadic pastoralists lived in patriarchal societies in which power and status was largely determined by the number of 'stock' (cows, horses, sheep etc.) a man (*sic*) owned. Men without herds became the 'hired hands' of those who owned the herds. To increase one's wealth, and the capacity to exercise power and control over others, one had to increase the herd. This meant nomadic pastoralists were always in need of fresh grazing and pastures, and these were generally acquired forcefully from others, most often agriculturalists and farmers who were less powerful. With the rise in pastoralism, non-human animals were deployed as sources of food and materials, while also being used for work (pulling ploughs and transporting goods) in times of peace and war, and as a resource in maintaining and holding the lands seized (Nibert 2013: 15–18).

But the rise of pastoral nomads in Eurasia does not explain the globalization of non-human animal production for food on a vast scale in North and South America, Africa, Asia and Europe. These developments were much more closely linked to the marauding powers of the elite within their own territories, and, more significantly, to the colonization of places as diverse as Ireland, Mexico, Rwanda, Brazil, Guatemala, New Zealand, North America and Australia by globalizing, powerful, European elites. People were evicted, threatened, terrorized, killed and even deceived (in the case of the Maori in New Zealand) into giving up the lands on which they lived and survived. Ranching violence was the norm (Nibert 2013: 126–95) and killing indigenous people who interfered with the development of the business of 'ranching', or the *great plantations* as they were known in Ireland (McCarthy-McMorrow 1986; Bardon 2011),[21] has been ubiquitous throughout human history.

While violence against animals has a long history, neither marauding pastoralists nor colonizers explain the rise of the massification of chicken factories where thousands of birds are reared in confined cages and/or sheds for their entire lives, or the fact that half the egg-laying hens of the world are now intensively farmed in wired battery cages in windowless sheds with little room to move so they will fatten quickly (Greger 2009). The animal-industrial complex of contemporary capitalism (Twine 2012) has greatly extended, intensified and exacerbated human domination over other-than-human animals and the natural world (Torres 2007: 11). The employment of industrialized technologies and scientific knowledge has enabled the maximizing of profit from the ranching and killing of animals and birds in factory-style farms for intensified meat and dairy production (Nibert 2013; Josephson 2020).

While killing and eating non-human animals for food is not unique to capitalism, the scale and intensification of animal production have been greatly exacerbated by capitalism. Nowhere is this more evident than in South America in recent decades. Brazil is now the world's largest exporter of 'beef' and a leading supplier of feed grain and meat to China, Russia and Europe. To establish itself in this position, it has created ranches on a vast scale, often forcing people off their ancestral lands and depriving them of their livelihood. The practice of planting lands (as was done in Ireland in the sixteenth and seventeenth centuries) is undertaken not by governments but by commercial interests. In Paraguay, Venezuela, Mexico and much of Central America, forcing people off their ancestral lands is common. The murder of indigenous people, farmers and activists who resist the takeover of lands is not infrequent. While some of those killed are well known, such as Sister Dorothy Stang, a seventy-three-year-old Catholic nun who was shot and killed by gunmen hired by ranchers in Brazil in 2005, most are not; they are ordinary farmers and community organizers who are murdered for resisting loggers and ranchers taking over their lands (Nibert 2013: 224–8). Those who lose their lands face impoverishment due to lack of education and forced labouring on ranches for negligible or no wages. Ironically, others are forced to migrate to find work for low wages under poor working conditions in slaughterhouses in the US (ibid.: 228), and in countries as far away as Ireland (MRCI 2020), undertaking difficult and distressing work (Dillard 2008) that native people in recruiting countries do not want to do.

Increases in the rearing and killing of non-human animals for meat does not happen accidentally; meat eating is normalized and actively promoted through trade missions and financial incentives from governments. Within Europe, approximately 20 per cent of funding from the Common Agricultural Policy (CAP) is given in the form of 'livestock' farming supports (Greenpeace 2019).[22] Income support benefits nearly 6.3 million farms throughout the EU and represents a significant share of agricultural income: on average, from 2010 to 2021, income support represented nearly half of farmers' income.[23] In many countries, including Ireland, beef and sheep farming would not be viable for most households without subsidies.[24] Given the reliance of small farmers especially (and relatedly their local economies) on subsidies for economic survival, it is not surprising that there is huge resistance among them to any cut to supports to the 'meat' industry; it would bring an end to their livelihood. But rather than enabling small farmers to survive and live well by producing other plant-based agricultural food, or by offering new services, governments continue to subsidize them to produce animals for food.

Subsidizing farmers who produce animals for food is not unique to Europe. In the US, where farms are multiple times (over ten times on average) the size they are in Europe,[25] they are also heavily subsidized. During the pandemic in 2020–21, the US Food and Agriculture Coronavirus Food Assistance Program provided approximately US$16 billion in direct payments to America's farmers and ranchers impacted by the Covid-19 crisis.[26]

Given the scientific evidence that eating large amounts of meat is bad for your health, contributing to heart disease, strokes, obesity and some cancers (Nibert 2013: 252–3), making it appear moral and healthy to eat meat required official endorsement. State endorsements of meat eating are widespread globally, especially in big meat-producing countries like Brazil, where 70 per cent of the land available for agriculture is given over to ranching, and Australia, where 88 per cent of land in agricultural holdings is used for livestock grazing (Arcari 2017: 71).[27] Even in small agricultural countries like Ireland, the Irish National Food Agency, Bord Bia, actively monitors and promotes meat eating.[28]

Conclusion: Learning Not to Care for Non-Human Animals

The key question posed by Bentham, in terms of how we relate to non-human animals, is not whether they can think, reason or talk, but rather whether they can suffer (Derrida 2002: 396). Two hundred years later, we know from science that non-human animals can and do suffer greatly. Yet, as Derrida (2002) observes, for the last few centuries we have 'waged a war against compassion' and concern for the suffering of animals, both human and non-human. This war is a compelling one; it obliges us not to be pitiful or to recognize the suffering our actions impose on others. It allows, even obliges, us to suppress feelings of revulsion in the face of abuse and violence, to deny it is happening, or even to see it as necessary for some nefarious reason.

The war against concern for suffering operates 'not only as a duty, a responsibility, an obligation, it is also ... a constraint that, like it or not, directly or indirectly, everyone is held to' (Derrida 2002: 397). It is the denial of suffering that allows us to tolerate factory farms (CAFOs) where animals are systematically treated as a 'mass' of things (Adams 2007), objects of human utility whose deprivations and sufferings are collateral damage in the service of human pleasure. It is lack of compassion that stymies public articulation about the fear and suffering of the frightened lambs, calves, pigs and cows that pass us by on the roads, packed into lorries on the way to their death, often suffering painful journeys in overcrowded transport in intense heat or cold. While abuses and injustices against non-human animals are pervasive and overwhelming, people have to learn not to see these; they have to learn to be indifferent.

Massifying non-human animals (or people) is one way of concealing their individuality and their suffering. By being grouped as a category, a *mass* of *things*, they are transformed from non-human subjects with feelings and desires into non-human objects lacking individual feelings and suffering (Adams 2007). Defining young calves that are prematurely fattened and killed in mass terms as 'veal' is one way of making them absent from the table where they are being eaten. This is what Adams (2000: 51) calls the 'absent referent': 'Behind every meal of meat is an absence; the death of the nonhuman animal whose place the meat takes' (Adams 2007: 23).

A further reason why people lack care and concern is that the killing and abuse of animals is physically removed from most people, especially when they are enjoying the pleasures of eating. The polished wine glasses, the linen tablecloths and sparking cutlery keep the violence of the killing that brought the beef Wellington, liver paté or pork belly to the table far out of sight, both literally and morally. It is regarded as 'bad manners' to raise such matters at the dinner table.

Animal laboratories are secret places, the preserve of those doing experiments, with strict rules for entry. Abattoirs are located out of sight and sound, generally placed far outside towns and cities so that the bawling, bleating and terror of the cows, pigs, lambs and calves on their way to being killed cannot be seen or heard. Families visit farms to pick strawberries or fresh fruits in summer; they do not take their children to see young calves being killed for veal, or lambs being butchered. There are no organized visits to 'pet the animals' or 'feed the ducks or chickens' in windowless sheds, slatted houses or cages made of concrete, wire and steel. Care for non-human animals is also discouraged by not proactively developing and supporting empathy and caring in others through education, or by trivializing and denigrating care, often by feminizing it (only women feel that way; Adams 2007).

There is a long and well-established literature suggesting that the dominance of Cartesian rationalism in Western thought contributes to a suppression of our moral sensibilities to suffering, including the suffering of animals (Midgley 1983). Once ontological distinctions were simplified in binary terms between mind and body, between nature and society, between what was fully human and what was not, it was morally justifiable to exploit those things that were natural, or non-human. Non-human animals were objectified, becoming 'things' available for cruel scientific experimentation, such as vivisection (Luke 2007). Opposition to the slaughter of animals was also seen historically as a sign of superstition and being 'womanish', rather than exercising reason. While some feminist care ethicists attribute this attitude to animals to the rationalist masculine bias of political theory generally, including even among animal rights theorists (Donovan 2007a), Bordo (1986) claims that Cartesian thought is foundationally masculinizing in its disregard for the logic of emotions and feelings for the relational other, leading ultimately to the objectification and abuse of those who are 'othered', including women and nature, and animals as part of nature.

A survey undertaken of animal rights/welfare activists some years ago indicated that the majority of activists are women, an estimated 75 per cent (Shapiro 2007: 159). Why this is the case is a matter of considerable debate. One suggested reason is that women have been involved historically in the production of *use* value goods that are directly care-focused[29] more than in *exchange* labour, especially with the division of labour between the public and family spheres. It is claimed that their daily provisioning socializes women to be care-aware, working close to the human (vulnerable) body where a lack of care is always evident, while men are not *socialized*[30] in the same way (Mies and Shiva 1993). The gendered division between *use* and *exchange* labour, between care and market-led work, would seem to be accompanied by a division of moral labour in care terms, which, in turn, encourages women to be more care-oriented through practice than men (Bubeck 1995; Donovan 2007b: 186–7). What this literature suggests is that taking responsibility for caring and being careless are learned, practised dispositions. They are not prede-termined in some essentialist gendered manner.

Because non-human animals lack the means of collective violence to retaliate against human harm (they do not have guns, bombs or weapons), and especially because they cannot organize bureau-cratically to resist their oppression, they are forced to live, like many totally subordinated people, at the mercy of powerful humans. Given their powerlessness and inability to systematically resist domination, the brutal treatment of non-human animals makes such action immoral in ways that are different from but just as serious as the abuse of other humans.

If we regard non-human animals as disposable objects, things to be used and/or abused at will for human ends, it is all too easy to apply a similar logic to categories of human persons. As Theodor Adorno observed, 'Auschwitz begins wherever someone looks at a slaughterhouse and thinks: They're only animals' (cited in Adams 2007: 28). The Holocaust happened because ordinary people chose to ignore the extraordinary oppression and abuse being inflicted on innocents by the Nazis. Millions of people went about their daily lives, knowingly disregarding the suffering of those they did not know or relate to, those who were deemed unworthy of life. And perhaps it is the acceptance of a hierarchical world in which killing is normalized that led to the failure to respond in time to the genocides of the twentieth century, be it those in Nazi Germany, or in Rwanda and Bosnia (Adams 2007: 31).

But there is also resistance to the abuse and use of animals, reflected in the movements towards vegetarian and vegan foods. Not only are there growing numbers of people attempting to move towards a plant-based diet, but there is more intellectual and political engagement with the issues arising from awareness of the adverse impact of industrialized animal farming on the environment and human health.[31] There are also popular initiatives to address the fear and ignorance about veganism by guiding people about how to change to a plant-based diet (Leenaert 2017), as well as attempts by scholars like Haraway (2007, 2016) and Meijer (2019) to model ways in which humans and non-humans can develop more egalitarian inter-species relationships.

9

Violence and Capitalism

To ignore violence when speaking about love, care and solidarity is to ignore what lives in their shadows. Humans' capacities for love and care are paralleled by their capacities to be care-indifferent, neglectful, abusive, hateful and violent. Which capacities are developed, enabled and legitimated culturally and politically is not accidental; it is a matter of choice for humanity. It depends on what values are prioritized, especially whether domination and gain are prioritized over cooperation, mutual care and concern for all of humanity, other species and the environment.

The practice of violence is not unique to capitalism; it long preceded it in both public and personal forms. But capitalism, enabled and facilitated by the state and geopolitical interests, created new means and mechanisms of violation, especially new institutional means through which violence could be practised and legitimated, bureaucratically organized and resourced (Malešević 2010a, 2014; Tyner 2016).

Although we tend to associate violence with direct physical violence and war, these are but some of its manifestations (Kilby 2013). Violence can also be institutional and systemic, built into the fabric of organizations, in terms of both their internal structures and/or the outcomes of their policies and practices (Gerth and Wright Mills 1958; Hearn and Parkin 2001; Scheper-Hughes and Bourgois 2004). Violence is also often highly personalized and gendered (Lerner 1986; Walby 2009) and racialized (Melamed 2015). Those involved in both unpaid and paid care, mostly women, are especially susceptible to violence, due to their exposure to poverty, austerity and the negative impact of climate changes (Nellemann, Verma and Hislop 2011; Oxfam 2020).

This chapter opens with a short commentary on the way debates about violence and care occupy separate academic spaces in sociology, briefly examining the implications of this for understanding the interface between care and violence. After highlighting the complexity of violence, it comments on the violations arising from enforced poverty, exploring how capitalism and the state are active agents in its precipitation, both separately and conjointly, especially in institutional terms. The racialized and gendered character of the violence that underpins profiteering in trafficking, in the care industry and in the sex industry is then briefly reviewed.

The chapter concludes by noting how unregulated profiteering can deprive people of a livelihood, health care, clean water and/or clean air, but is not registered in the calculation of costs of capitalism: it is regarded as an unaccountable externality. The violence of letting people die, which is endemic to a capitalist value system (Tyner 2016), is not seen for what it is, a violent action through inaction.

Many aspects of what is admired in capitalism – its sophisticated technology, elaborate financial systems, means of communication and legal institutions – are misrecognized as wholly positive, though they also create 'expulsions' for many people from the basic securities of life, not least because of the concentration of power, control and ownership-related wealth in the hands of so few (Sassen 2014).

Violence, Care and the Separation of Spheres

Those who write about love, care and, to a lesser degree, solidarity work in a very different research space from those who write on violence. While there is some overlap among those writing about domestic and sexual violence and the dark side of care (the violence and abuse of women and children especially), scholars in the care field do not generally write about violence, and those who research violence tend not to write about care. Being a specialist on the subject of care or of violence does not compel one to research its opposite. Yet to violate a person or persons is to demonstrate a lack of care for them; love, care and solidarity operate on the flip side of violence, abuse and neglect, even if the intersections between these social processes are not overtly addressed.

Those who write on care tend to be feminist, and their work is mostly published in anthologies and journals that are not in the sociological mainstream (Lynch, Kalaitzake and Crean 2021).[1] A brief perusal of Malešević's major text (2010a) on the sociology of war and violence, or the special issue of the *European Journal of Social Theory*[2] devoted to 'Theorizing Violence' in 2013, shows that scholarship on violence is largely undertaken by men. Thus, not only are men more engaged in war and violence than women, while women carry the primary responsibility for care work, but the study of the respective subject matters is also gendered. Academic scholarship about love and care is undertaken disproportionately by women, while much of the work on the sociology of war and violence (with the exception of domestic and sexual violence) is written by men.[3]

One reason for this separation of spheres appears to be the impact of gender-essentialist preferences, even among those who are highly educated. Women and men remain strongly socialized to follow idealized gender-stereotypical choices, and their preferences are reflected in curricular and research choices (Charles and Bradley 2009).

What the subjects of love and violence have in common, however, is their sociological peripheralization historically. Violence is a relatively 'new' theme of sociological investigation (Malešević 2010a), although it is slowly gaining traction in mainstream publications (Kilby 2013). Equally, the study of care has not been a mainstream research topic in the sociological field (Aulenbacher, Lutz and Riegraf 2018).

There is a strange irony, therefore, that two matters that are so central to social life, namely care and violence, have both been neglected in sociology, though the social and political processes that engender both are undoubtedly related. It is almost impossible to analyse care without addressing its nemesis, neglect, abuse and violence, and vice versa. And, as one of the leading scholars on violence has observed, people are as prone to solidarity and care for others as they are to selfishness (Malešević 2010a: 3). The dispositions that are activated at a given time depend on a host of sociological, political, economic, cultural and ideological factors.

Another reason for the peripheralization of the interrelated subjects of care and violence lies deep within rationalist ontological assumptions in social scientific thinking as to what is central to social life and the human condition. War and violence were regarded by the male founders of sociology (the so-called, 'founding fathers') as irrational and anachronistic features of social life that would ultimately disappear with the onset of modernity (Malešević 2010b). Although Sorokin (2002) did try to place matters of love as central questions in sociology, he had little success in this endeavour; as noted above, he was forced out of his post in Harvard and replaced by Talcott Parsons.

The misrecognition of emotions as irrational and incidental in determining patterns in social life and politics (Ahmed 2004; Nussbaum 2013) was not confined to sociologists. It was also evident among utilitarian scholars in law, politics and economics, a number of whom assumed that humans were 'rational maximizers of satisfactions', and that emotions were distinct from rationality (Becker 1965; Posner 1997).

The denial of the importance of emotions such as fear and hate, as well as emotions such as those of altruism and solidarity, in political and economic life has deep roots in Western and Eastern philosophy, where emotions were seen as feminine and, by association, as irrational (Nussbaum 1995a). The emotional and care work involved in producing human beings through nurturing was regarded as instinctual, something women did 'naturally', a pre-given disposition, not a fit subject for scholarly investigation. The expression of emotions such as compassion signified weakness, a lack of wholeness, 'sources of softness, holes, so to speak, in the walls of the self' (Nussbaum 1995a: 367).

Because caring and loving were defined as an instinctual (feminine) disposition, they were effectively defined as a-sociological, actions that did not require research investigation. The understanding of care as instinctual and pre-social was further consolidated by an ontological understanding of the human subject as an autonomous individual rather than an individual-in-relation (Archer 2000; Donati and Archer 2015).

The scope, meaning and normative promise of social actions were framed in a way that forestalled analysis and debate about the generative power of inter/dependencies for promoting solidarity, on the one hand (Mooney 2014: 36–8), and conflicts and violence, on the other, especially when solidarity actions become exclusionary. Despite its peripheralization in sociology, violence is endemic to social life, and deeply embedded in institutions and regimes of inequality (Walby 2009).

Forms of Violence

The common-sense understanding of violence is that it is a subjective experience of violation, especially in terms of physical abuse, and an objective phenomenon expressed through organized war and brutality that entails the systematic injuring and killing of large groups of people using bombing, shooting, poisoning and/or terrorizing. It is tacitly assumed the violence is intentional and deliberate, that it is motivated by a will to do harm. This common-sense view of violence is widely adhered to within the social sciences and informs much of its historical conceptualization (Schinkel 2013). While violence is all of the above, it is a complex social practice with different manifestations. At times it is material and symbolic, organized and incidental, legal and illegal, visible and invisible, and both collective and individual (Kilby 2013: 263). Just as care is a slippery concept, multivocal in both its academic and colloquial expressions (Martin, Myers and Viseu 2015), so too with violence; it has no clear boundaries (Scheper-Hughes and Bourgois 2004); it varies greatly in terms of scope, scale, agency, time and place.

Violence finds expression in very different contexts through different means depending on whether it is exercised in private or in public, in institutions or at an individual level. There are different 'regimes of violence', some of which are the explicit and state-endorsed, such as the regimes of violence enacted by the military and the police (Schinkel 2013). Other regimes of violence are less explicit but still operate at a structural and institutional level, including organizational violence such as verbal abuse and bullying, and the violence of being subjected to poverty and homelessness. Violence can also operate covertly or even with explicit approval, such as family violence (slapping, verbally abusing and threatening children).

While physical violence is widely recognized for what it is, be it enacted by the state or by an individual, and while there is some appreciation of how violence can also operate through psychological processes such as bullying and harassment, the ways in which structural practices can exercise violence at institutional levels are less well appreciated. The problem arises from the ways in which violence is framed, especially the implicit assumption that violence is deliberate and intentional. Not only is much of the harm and violence to which people are exposed not deliberate in any direct sense, but the agents that precipitate it are not visible and accountable. The structural violence arising from poverty, hunger, humiliation and exclusion has no singular visible agent (Scheper-Hughes and Bourgois 2004), though it does produce outcomes that are similar to physical violence, including fear, anxiety, shame, isolation, trauma and both physical and mental illness.

The foundational violence that underpins the authority of the state (Gerth and Wright Mills 1958) and is operationalized through bureaucratic means including laws, policies and practices, is generally exercised to protect the wealthiest and most powerful, though this violence is not seen for what it is: violence legitimated through 'democratic' mandate. The structural violence that forces people into homelessness, begging, alcohol and/or drug abuse due to poverty and hopelessness is misrecognized as the outcome of individual choices and personal responsibilities (Tyner 2016). Mothers surviving on precarious incomes and wages, without adequate childcare supports, are often forced into what Dodson (2010) terms 'moral disobedi- ences' in order to protect themselves and their children, although such disobediences carry an 'illegal' price tag. Those who engage in poverty-induced transgressions are often met with severe sanctions, and even imprisonment (Wacquant 2009), yet they continue to care even in the face of adverse judgements (Luttrell 2020).

Violating the Impoverished

One of the most obvious outcomes of classed inequalities is how they are encoded on people's bodies; those who are poorest look older and more worn for their age. The size and shape of their bodies and the lines on their faces display their impoverished class positioning (Skeggs 2004; Adair, Brown, Clark, Perez-Cotrich and Stanfield 2007). On the other hand, the faces and bodies of the super-rich are refined, polished, pleasing and polite;[4] yet the pleasing countenance, the honed body and dispositions, the designer clothes and luxurious ways of living are always underpinned by the exercise, or threat of the exercise, of force, no matter how far removed and invisible the form of that force may be. Wealth and land that are acquired, including that which is illegitimately acquired, are secured, protected and handed on intergenerationally by legal means that are ultimately built on the threat or the use of violence (imprisonment, punishment or, in many cases, death).[5]

Though social inequality is both habitual and widely legitimated in many societies, it always has 'a coercive coating' to protect it (Malešević 2010a: 274). Violence is never far from the policy or political table. It sits in the corner of the political room, waiting to intervene should it be required. The use of violence as a means of controlling the poor is evident in the most mundane practices, such as the daily imprisonment of those who steal (without using violence, such as in shoplifting) and the criminalization of begging in several countries, including European countries such as England and Wales, Denmark, Ireland,[6] Norway (some counties) and Hungary. While crimes of violence against the person, including sexual crimes, remain the principal reasons why people (mostly men) are imprisoned, theft remains one of the major reasons for imprisonment[7] (Sturge 2019). Notwithstanding the fact that the increasingly high rates of incarceration globally (Walmsley 2018) are related to the imprisonment of political dissidents, prisons in most parts of the world are disproportionately full of poor people, mostly poor men. This holds true in societies with such radically different rates of incarceration as Ireland and the US[8] (Taibbi 2014). The growing imprisonment of the poor, especially in rich countries, is proof of how state-legitimated violence is deployed to control the impoverished in highly unequal capitalist societies (Wacquant 2009; Sassen 2014).

Capitalism and Violence

Capitalism is built around the principles of accumulation, for to be a capitalist is to accumulate. Accumulation relies on the exploitation of classes created by the hierarchies within capitalism itself, and the related expropriation of wealth, if necessary through the use of violence. The expropriation of wealth occurs between those who own the means of production and workers without the means of subsistence, between creditors and debtors, and between conquerors of land, which is then translated into legitimated property, and those who are dispossessed and removed (Melamed 2015: 77). Even if the violence is historical, the appropriation and reappropriation of people's land and labour do involve violence.

Powerful capitalists do not generally have to engage in direct violence to protect their interests, as their wealth is protected by private property laws, constitutional provisions and an international legal infrastructure that is framed in terms of their interests (Monbiot 2000; Allen 2007; Klein 2007). Corporatized capitalists employ the violence-based bureaucratized machinery of the state (especially the police and the army) to defend their interests. While the history of slavery is an extreme example of state-endorsed violence enacted in the interest of capital, there are also many more contemporary and local examples. The interface between state and capitalist violence was evident in the Shell to Sea campaign in the West of Ireland, where local peaceful protests (against bringing a dangerous gas pipeline close to people's homes) were broken up with excessive force by private security forces, aided by the police, to protect the interests of Shell Oil.[9] While workers have a right to strike in many countries, if they seek to exercise that right in a way that is not approved by the state, blocking entrances to a work site or factory, this is generally treated as an act of violence with which the state engages in a violent response by physically removing them. More extreme forms of violence are also employed directly by capitalists: the murder by hired gunmen of indigenous people, mostly farmers and activists who resisted the takeover of lands by loggers and ranchers, occurred for many years from the early 1990s in Brazil (Heil 2010). Similarly, in Guatemala violence was deployed by those controlling the drugs industry to hunt people off their lands in rainforests and set up ranches to launder drugs' money (Nibert 2013: 227).

Capitalism is a mode of production in which producers and consumers depend on the market for their basic needs. It is a mode of production that is heavily protected and endorsed by most nation states. Although people are formally or nominally free to participate in the market or not, in reality they are forced by material circumstances to sell their labour power to capitalists who own the means of production. The market is anything but free; it is built on coercion, compulsion and, ultimately, force (Tyner 2016: 45–6). Even where a political majority objects to protecting capitalist interests, the majority interest can be overruled, as was seen in the financial crisis when the democratic wishes of the Greek people were disregarded in the interests of financial-capital Europe in 2010–12 (Kalaitzake 2017). In the everyday world of politics, the global oligarchical elite have the power to circumvent democratic institutions by buying political majorities and social legitimacy (Streeck 2016: 228–30); and they can violate the health and dignity of people by imposing austerity and poverty on millions in the interests of capitalism, as happened after the financial crash that began in 2007 (Tooze 2018).

The Violence of Allowing People to Die

Because capitalist logic and ethics prevail in the social as well as the economic and political realms, the value of a given life is subjected to an economic analysis and assessed according to its *exchange value* (Cacho 2012). The loving, caring, companionship, community and solidarity work that people undertake on a voluntary basis does not count in the metrics of the market. Neither do the lives of people who are defined as 'unproductive' in *exchange* terms. Work that produces products that are marketable is what matters.

Capitalism's indifference to *use values* can and does result in indifference to life itself, and to the quality of life for 'unproductive' people. As independence and autonomy are socio-cultural imperatives under neoliberalism, there are no morally approved dependencies for adults. Being unemployed is seen as a personal responsibility (Frericks 2014; Boland and Griffin 2018), not an inevitable outcome of economic policies and capitalist practices. Consequently, *workfare* has replaced welfare throughout much of Europe: those who are unemployed are forced to take up employment, no matter how low-paid or how inappropriate it is relative to their skills (Sowa, Staples and Zapfel 2018).

Policy changes governing welfare supports for people with disabilities indicate that they too are expected to be active, productive citizens, even if their disability is heavily demanding on their time and energy in and of itself (Parker Harris, Owen and Gould 2012). Everyone is expected to be an 'active economic agent', including people with disabilities (Barnes and Mercer 2005; Van Aswegen 2020).

While capitalism may not initiate a chain of events that directly leads to killing people (although capitalists have hired people to kill those who undermine their profits, as is well known from history), capitalism can create conditions that allow people to die. It can kill people slowly and indirectly through pollution, or by undermining their livelihoods by destroying natural resources and habitats in highly racialized ways (Pulido 2017). People can also be allowed to die by being slowly poisoned due to lack of health and safety protections in dangerous industries (Tironi and Rodríguez-Giralt 2017). Or capitalism can allow people to die younger and earlier by employing them under conditions that adversely impact on their health due to low wages, precarity and insecurity (Berlant 2007), or, in the case of people with disabilities, by expecting them to work at a pace that is unrealistic given their impairments (Goodley, Lawthom and Runswick Cole 2014). Those in power can permit 'an already existing causal sequence' to culminate in someone's death. The act of letting die can be due to not doing something to prevent death where a harm is already known. Letting people die when a harm is known is killing by active or deliberate inaction (Tyner 2016: 206). A prime example of action through inaction is the failure of most countries in the European Union to respond to the major refugee crisis in 2015, which, in turn, led to death and displacement, both at sea and on land.[10]

Death through indifference and inaction is not confined to those seeking asylum. It also happens at national levels, even if this is not recorded in the global media. The failure of the Irish state to provide adequate health care and housing for Travellers (an indigenous nomadic ethnic minority) has contributed significantly to Travellers' low life expectancy.[11] State inaction means Travellers live shorter lives because their lives matter less. It is violation through inaction.

Indifference to the lives of those who are less powerful, poorer and ethnically different is also evident in relation to the management of pollution. Chemical and pharmaceutical companies, pesticide manufacturers and electronics manufacturers, as well as the companies that process and produce the many technologies that create the hardware for our very technologized world,[12] have to get rid of their waste. They 'sink' it in air, water or land, with all the long-term problems that arise from landfill and air and water pollution. But waste is not disposed of at random; companies generally 'sink' it in geographical areas that are well removed from privileged populations (Park and Pellow 2011). The transnational movement of waste and its associated pollution, to poorer communities and countries from richer ones, is a global pattern that comes at health and quality-of-life risks to those where it is located, albeit one that is increasingly being resisted transnationally by global environmental justice movements (Pellow 2007).

The belief that exporting toxic waste to where the poor live is not an outlier policy position. It is a widespread practice, one that was endorsed by the chief economist of the World Bank, Lawrence Summers, in 1992. He proposed that the World Bank should encourage the poorest societies to accept the world's most toxic industries: 'shouldn't the World Bank be encouraging more migration of the dirty industries to the LCDs [less developed countries]? ... The economic logic behind dumping a load of toxic waste in the lowest wage country is impeccable and we should face up to that.'[13] The callous 'efficiency' logic here was that the poorest have least to lose by pollution as their health, life expectancy and quality of life are already inferior to those of the rich: earlier death, arising from living too close to toxic waste, is deemed efficient in simple cost–benefit terms. Given the racial dynamics between the rich North and the poorer Global South, this is also a deeply racialized environmental policy, as it is the poorest and most vulnerable within the Global South who will suffer most (Pulido 2017).

Capitalism is not just a way of organizing people; it is also a way of organizing nature (Moore 2015), and people within nature, in a way that is deeply racialized (Melamed 2015). The history of slavery illustrates how much of the wealth that has accrued to the White Global North has been accumulated from the lands of the Global South, and on the backs of Black bodies forcibly removed from the South to the North, be it to the US (Coates 2015) or to Europe (Patel and Moore 2018). What made this permissible was the deep hierarchical differentiations that capitalism fostered, though it did not always initiate them; by separating, ordering and isolating people in classed/racial/gender terms, capitalism encouraged a sense of community and belonging through the market in a highly individualized way that was also deeply stratified and ranked. People were defined by their customer status as individuals in market relations, coming together through a technology of anti-relationality (Melamed 2015).

In a market-led society, collective life is lived to a large degree through collective consumption, fuelled by debt (Soederberg 2014). Belonging operates through buying and selling, through being a customer. 'Customership' is sold and endorsed as a value system, undermining collegiality and collective action in the face of capitalist power (Streeck 2016: 95–112). As participation in the commons of incessant consumerism is costly, it promotes indebtedness, and in the case of those who are already poor, impoverishment (Soederberg 2014).

As capitalism accumulates by producing and moving through relations of severe inequality among human groups, it literally capitalizes on pre-existing racial and gender hierarchies, consolidating them in prefigured identities that undermine collaborative collective actions, including political actions. By distinguishing between those who are valued and the devalued, groups are made incommensurable with one another. They are defined by their differences and kept apart. It is for this reason that Robinson (2000) recognized the imperative for people of African origins and descent to preserve their 'collective being, their ontological totality'; they needed to reconstitute collectives for collective resistance to racism within capitalism.

The State and Violence

Having a monopoly on the use of physical violence is a defining feature of nation states. While states must engage in trade and have political legitimacy, most of all 'a state is a human community that (successfully) claims the *monopoly of the legitimate use of physical force* within a given territory' (Gerth and Wright Mills 1958: 78; italics in the original). But the state does not only deploy physical force to protect its national borders and interests; it can and does deploy it to protect the interests of capital.[14]

While capitalism gains directly from violence, most obviously through the production and export of arms and the machinery of war, it does not gain from the business of violence by acting alone. It acts in collaboration with state bodies that frequently benefit from the trade in violence, most notably through the sale of arms.[15] In the field of violence, the interests of nation states are generally aligned directly with capitalism, through their need and use of weapons of violence to maintain control internally and, if necessary, internationally, and, in some cases, through the sale of weapons. For their part, institutions of capitalism are protected through state violence, or the threat of state (police and army) violence, as well as by legal, ideological and political actions.

This is not to suggest that organized violence is a new phenomenon or that it is capitalism-specific; organized violence long preceded capitalism, as exemplified in the brutal imperialism of the Roman and Ottoman empires prior to the institutionalization of capitalism as a politico-economic form. However, the bureaucratization that was endemic to the success of capitalism both facilitated and exacerbated the use of bureaucratized violence for political ends, especially when operating in parallel with the rise of nation states and the technologization of warfare. Rather than being mutually exclusive forces, 'neo-liberal capitalism and bureaucratization often underpin one other' (Malešević 2014: 77), and both are aligned with the state machinery and its use of violence.

It was bureaucracy and discipline that underpinned the success of armed forces, from the ancient Romans to the armies led by the famous European generals Maurice of Nassau, Gustavus Adolphus and Oliver Cromwell. These generals 'planted the institutional seeds of military social organization that eventually gave birth to the modern bureaucratic nation-state' (Malešević 2010a: 112). The disciplinary learning derived from military operations also informed both the organization of capitalist institutions and the institutions of the state, from prisons to schools (Foucault 1977: 135–94). A dialogical relationship operated between capitalism, bureaucratization and military forms of organization in terms of how to control, regulate and maximize the efficient use of resources.

Frederick Taylor exemplified this deployment of bureaucracy, discipline and control in the interests of accumulation.[16] The disciplinary logic of Taylorism, whereby factory workers were treated as machines (interchangeable parts) subject to surveillance and control to increase their productivity through measurement and sanctions (Taylor 1911), was widely deployed in factory-type settings and now operates across the service industries. The use of time wristbands in Amazon for tracking employees' rate of productivity, and the use of GPS tracking of couriers and care assistants, both operate on a quasi-military disciplinary logic in the interests of capital. The rise of managerialism in the post-1980s era also heralded a revival of Taylorist ideals, exercised within the civil bureaucratic machinery of the state (Clarke and Newman 1997). Surveillance capitalism (Zuboff 2019), whereby digital technology not only tracks online preferences but actively works to shape them, is a further example of the interface between the military and capitalist technology, and is only moderately regulated by the state.

Capitalist businesses, and organizations modelled on their bureaucratic logic, do not generally need to be openly violent, or to employ state-backed violence to protect their interests, because the means of violence are already institutionalized in their seemingly neutral, rational business practices (Hearn and Parkin 2001). Control and compliance rely on both explicit and implicit violence, though they do not present as such. The threat of removal from one's post or job (and thereby from the means to earn a livelihood) is at the heart of employment relations. Organizational rules can be deployed to discipline, control and punish those who deviate, in a way that can be experienced as dominating and violating.

Capital is also mobile; it moves, leaving people without a means of survival, through downsizing or by moving production from one low-wage location to another. The language of 'letting people go', making the company 'lean and agile' because it is 'good for business', is derived from accounting and strategic planning. It conceals the violence involved in forcing people out of employment: 'no human bodies appear on the books, thus such violences are accomplished as gender neutral and abstracted from actual human consequences' (Acker 2004: 31).

The state–capitalist nexus is underpinned by violence and the threat of violence. Whether explicit physical violence is exercised in the interests of national or capitalist interests depends on the context, though the interests of the two frequently overlap.

Capitalism Building on Other Injustices: Race and Violence

Although capitalism is intrinsically violent, in that it pursues its goal of accumulation regardless of the human or environmental costs (Žižek 2008: 10), it builds on and exploits pre-existing hierarchies and systems of violation. Pre-capitalist stratifications of gender and race and of disability/ability (the latter frequently coded as intelligent/lacking intelligence) are relied on to provide normative, quasi-legal and moral justification for ongoing inequalities in social outcomes, and to justify the exploitation, expropriation and accumulation that capitalism requires.

The politically and economically driven violence that preceded capitalism was often justified on the grounds of racial superiority alone. The ideologies of racial superiority underpinning slavery were rooted in the idea that those whose skin was coloured Black or Brown were lesser humans than those who were White. The origins of this thinking are multiple and complex, but they have deep roots in European thought. Throughout much ancient Graeco-Roman literature and philosophy, and in key Christian texts such as the Bible, whiteness is represented as the colour of purity and goodness and blackness as evil, objectionable and barbarian (Tsri 2016). Those whose skin was Black were defined in early Graeco-Roman literature as 'Ethiopian' ('people with burnt faces') and were geographically located as African (south of Egypt). Their racialized designations had negative associations that 'intimately tied African peoples to the term "black" and its objectionable characteristics' (Tsri 2016: 40). A whole continent of people, with different histories, languages and cultural, economic and political traditions, were reified as one: Black and or Ethiopian. They became singular in identity terms, subjected to 'conceptual and semantic structures' over which they lacked control, and that were intended to denigrate them (Tsri 2016: 174).

But it was not only religious teaching that was used to rationalize violence; so too was 'science'. The social binaries of mind/body and nature/society emanating from the time of Descartes were aligned with the claims of influential scientists, such as Francis Bacon, distinguishing between those who were part of 'nature', and not fully human, and those who were part of 'society'. To the European colonizer, the world was divided between those who were human and non-human, between *society* and *nature*. Most women, indigenous peoples and those whose skin was Black or dark were defined as part of nature, and thereby available for use and exploitation (Patel and Moore 2018: 92–5, 185–92).

The attribution of a lower human value to indigenous peoples, or to those who are Black or female, mutated easily into assertions of lower ability and capability that justified their exclusions, losses and dispossession over time (Patel and Moore 2018). While devaluation of the feminine on the grounds of capability has been eroded for women[17] in much of the world, it is still operational for those who are working-class, Black and/or indigenous, and for people with disabilities. The fiction of different talents and capabilities based on race and class continues to conceal the myth of meritocracy in racial, class terms and ability terms (Mijs 2016). The relative 'under-performance' of working-class, Black or other minority children in education is explained away as a lack of cultural capital, or so-called 'intelligence', rather than being seen for what it is: an inevitable outcome of economic inequality due to classed/raced positioning and differential resourcing (Marsh 2011). As it is the White, well-educated middle and upper classes who also exercise cultural power, it is they who determine the definition of what it means to be 'intel-ligent', 'educated', 'qualified', 'capable' (Bourdieu and Passeron 1977) and 'distinguished', in Bourdieu's (1984) sense of that term.

The financial wealth of the world is now concentrated in very few hands, with the new oligarchic rich controlling both financial wealth and political power in many countries (Streeck 2016: 28–30). The largely unearned wealth of the oligarchic elite has its historical origins in the organized violence of colonialism, enclosures and slavery, and in the expanded trade systems that paralleled these developments, greatly facilitating the accumulation of wealth in the Global North (Tyner 2016: 50–1). It was a deep and prolonged violence against indigenous peoples that contributed most to the accumulation of wealth, a violence that was deeply racialized and rationalized through ideologies of racial superiority (Robinson 2000).

Capitalism and Gender-Based Violence

Physical violence against women is a global phenomenon. It is widespread across all classes and cultures. Yet gender-based violence has not been a subject that has been mainstreamed in the social sciences. Why this is so in sociology is, no doubt, related to the neglect of violence more generally (Kilby 2013). However, it is also connected to the ways in which domain assumptions within disci-plines impact on paradigmatic assumptions (Gouldner 1970). The male leaders of disciplines like political philosophy, sociology and criminology, including those who write about violence, are unlikely to be primary carers and/or living in states of economic dependency. This has meant that the ways in which economic dependency and isolation in private households can leave one susceptible to harm are not generally within these writers' personal experience, as senior male scholars operate at the pinnacle of academic power (Misra, Lundquist and Templer 2012; Lynch, Ivancheva, Keating, O'Flynn and O'Connor 2020). Senior (mostly White) men's distance from interpersonal physical violence, allied to liberal assumptions in the social sciences more generally that what happens in the household is a private matter (Smith 1990; Okin 1994), have also contributed to the neglect of research on domestic violence, and of gender-based violence in the academy (Kavanagh and Brown 2020).

In their critique of both Slavoj Žižek's (2008), Bourdieu's (1990) and Bourdieu and Passeron's (1977) ways of defining violence abstractly, as deriving from systems of classed inequality in an undifferentiated way, Walby, Towers and Francis (2014: 189–91) observe how this obscures the direct physical harms and physical violence that men inflict on women. While some male sociologists do examine the gendered dimension of physical violence (Malešević 2010a), in criminology, a field of study that is closely allied to sociology, and one that undertakes extensive research on interpersonal violence, the subject of gender 'is remarkable by its absence' from the main schools of thought (Walby, Towers and Francis 2014: 191–3).

While rape as a weapon of war is systematic and bureaucratized, as is the trafficking of girls and women for sexual exploitation, much violence against women and girls is not organized; it is individualized, and even culturally condoned. Individualized gender-based violence preceded capitalism by a few thousand years, not least because patriarchy, as a social system of norms, values, customs and roles, has provided a moral rationale for the domination of women for centuries (Lerner 1986: 212–29). The deeply gendered perception of care work as 'naturally women's work' globally means that women are morally sanctioned if they fail to meet what are seen to be their obligatory care duties within families (Hays 1996), and within particular cultural contexts these sanctions include violence (Maina and Kimani 2019).

Although the violence to which women are subject is not capitalism-specific, capitalism operates in ways that indirectly produce violence against women, not least by failing to recognize and pay for the millions of hours spent on human reproductive and caring work globally (Oxfam 2020; Folbre 2020), work that is a direct subsidy to capital. While lack of economic independence does not generate intimate partner-related violence per se,[18] when women are confined to unpaid domestic work and care work, and left without a secure income and independence, they are not only impoverished but also driven to taking up dangerous employment for survival. They migrate out of economic desperation, working in low-wage, poorly renumerated, unregulated employment, including the domestic sector and in the hospitality sectors, where they are susceptible to trafficking and violation (IOM 2020).

When women work in paid care, they are poorly protected in domestic settings. A lack of adequate regulation and social protection means family care workers are highly vulnerable, and subject to unfair and unreasonable working conditions (Da Roit, González Ferrer and Moreno-Fuentes 2013); as they often lack legal status and the right to collective bargaining. Violence and harassment are commonplace, including within the formal care sector, with health workers across the world reporting particularly high levels of violence (Lippel 2016). Carers are also subject to a serious wage penalty relative to their skills and qualifications, which is a further violation (England, Budwig and Folbre 2002; Dowling 2021).

Sex industry violence

The many ways in which capitalism exacerbates the conditions and forms of male-on-female violence are a major study in themselves, and for that reason cannot be addressed in detail here. Where capitalism has a direct and visible presence in perpetuating violence against women is in the commercial sex industry. The commercial sex trade is a multibillion-dollar industry worldwide, mostly involving women and young girls (Coy 2012; O'Connor 2019). Jeffries (2010) estimated the value of the strip-club/lap-dancing industry in the USA in 2010 to be US\$75 billion. The legalization of the sex trade in certain Australian states (documented by the economics monitor IBIS) led to a wider culture where prostitution has thrived. In 2015, the sex trade in Australia was ranked the highest of all personal services in terms of market returns (O'Connor 2019: 103).

Human trafficking, especially for sexual exploitation in pornography and prostitution, is widespread and, even though illegal, it is highly profitable (O'Connor 2019) and highly gendered: 'Women and girls are overwhelmingly (96 %) the victims of trafficking for purposes of sexual exploitation and [they are] the majority (75 %) of victims of trafficking for all purposes' (European Commission 2016: 3). As trafficking is also deeply integrated with other criminal activities such as migrant smuggling, drug, arms and tobacco trafficking, document fraud and currency falsification, it inevitably involves physical violence, although there is a growing use of psychological and emotional violence (European Commission 2018: 5).

Gender is a social division that is stratifying, and like racial divisions it is exploited within capitalism for profit. While women, like indigenous peoples, were exploited prior to capitalism, capitalism offers new avenues for exploitation through what are historically seen as women's 'natural' attributes, their caring roles and their roles as providers of sexual pleasure for men. For those women whose skin is Black or Brown and who are working-class, there is the intersecting burden of exploitation based on gender, race and class.

Conclusion

The practice of violence is not unique to capitalism, but capitalism, enabled and facilitated by the state and geopolitical interests, created new means and mechanisms of violation, especially new institutional and technological means through which violence could be practised and legitimated, bureaucratically organized and resourced. The industrial production of arms that could kill people without seeing them was enabled by capital *and* state investment, especially the investment of powerful nation states that both produce and deploy arms on a vast scale. 'Capitalism is not just the sum of "economic" transactions that turn money into commodities and back again; it's inseparable from the modern state and from governments' dominions and transformations of natures, human and otherwise' (Patel and Moore 2018: 28). Given that so many nation states are beholden to powerful capitalist firms – corporations that have disposable wealth that frequently far exceeds that of national governments – these businesses can determine the rules of engagement. They can threaten direct violence, or more likely indirect violence by withdrawing investment, leading ultimately to unemployment and civil unrest that can threaten the integrity and security of the state itself.

Although the deployment, or threat of deployment, of arms can achieve capitalist/state interests, its use is not simply capitalist-driven. Some wars are quite clearly driven by overlapping economic-capitalist-political interests, such as the Gulf War of 1991, but others are not.[19] Whatever the reason for war, modern collective violence is enacted at a distance; those who violate do not have to witness the suffering of those with dismembered and burned bodies writhing in pain. Bureaucratically orchestrated violence 'is the psychological opposite of the ceremonial ferocity of patrimonial society' (Collins 1974: 433). New technologies of war enable killing, maiming and terrorizing to occur at a safe distance from its perpetrators. It is remote cruelty and without feeling, and this allows it to be all the more pervasive and perverse in its impact: the suffering inflicted is not witnessed sensually and bodily by the perpetrators.

While the impact of physical violence is highly visible in its painful imprint on people's bodies and their livelihoods, and in the destruction of buildings, land and other living creatures, it has impacts beyond these in the longer term. It impacts on memories and creates future fears of what might happen again. It destroys trust and hope as well as destroying bodies and nature. Its harms carry into the future. People inherit a culture of abandonment, fear and related anxieties intergenerationally when they have experienced mass murder as in the Holocaust (Lichtman 1984; Gangi, Talamo and Ferracuti 2009), or death through starvation as in the Irish famine (Kelly 2014). Persistent gender-based violence and racialized violence have similar effects, forcing women and girls, and those who are Black and/or from ethnic minorities, to live in fear of violation, violations that are habitual and normalized across cultures.

But direct physical violence is only one manifestation of violence. Violence can also be institutional and systemic where it is built into the fabric of organizations, in terms of both their internal structures and/or the outcomes of their policies and practices. 'Callous violence', the cruelty that 'people may inflict on others without a special intent to hurt', is endemic to bureaucratic organizations (Collins 1974: 432). As the machineries of the state and of capitalism both rely heavily on bureaucracy to exercise power, they are both institutions that are potentially violating, no matter what their declarations to the contrary.

Because capitalist businesses are bureaucratically organized, and money is the medium through which its bureaucracies exercise power, their primary unit of value is what can be counted in monetary terms. Externalities stemming from internal violations due to profit-making do not register in the calculation of costs. If people die early due to the lack of a living wage or due to poor health or lack of care, or if they suffer lifelong illnesses that arise from the pollution of air, water or food, these are not matters that concern businesses directly. Nor are businesses held directly responsible for them. The violence of letting people die, which is endemic to a capitalist value system (Tyner 2016), is not seen for what it is: a violent action through inaction.

While violence is resisted, as numerous uprisings of colonized, impoverished and enslaved people show historically, capitalism exploits pre-existing hierarchies based on race and gender to enhance profit-making, be it through legal or illegal means. Those involved in both unpaid and paid care (mostly poorer women) are especially susceptible to violence due to their exposure to poverty, austerity and the negative impact of climate change (Nellemann, Verma and Hislop 2011; Oxfam 2020).

Given the interface between care and violence as foundational social practices, and the relationship of carelessness, callousness and violence to each other, it is impossible to pursue affective justice without examining its nemesis, violence, in all its forms. Equally, to ignore the salience of love, care and solidarity as political and cultural values, no matter how 'residual' they are construed to be, is to under-estimate their potential as moral and intellectual tools that can be deployed in undermining the normalized and legitimized violences of capitalism.

While violence is a dimension of human reality that can be expected, there is no reason why it cannot be contained. Humans have the capacity for making peace and preventing war as much as they have the capacity for violence (Fry 2007). Although appropriate and proportionate laws are necessary to contain violence, laws are only one way, and not always the most effective way, to reduce the incidents and harms of violence. Mobilizing and educating around an ethic of care could assist in providing a set of standards and ways of relating, personally and politically, that helps pre-empt the conflicts that generate violence, be it personal or political, national or international (Held 2010). Resourcing and enabling economic institutions that are built on principles of non-exploitation and cooperation to grow and develop is also crucial for developing alter-natives to capitalism, such as the cooperative enterprises that are already known to be successful in countries as different as Rwanda, Italy, India, Brazil, Canada and France (Sánchez Bajo and Roelants 2011; Roelants, Eum, Eşim, Novkovic and Katajamäki 2019).

Although those who are most vulnerable are most susceptible to violence, they are not passive agents in political terms. Because people are poor, or because they are women or girls, does not mean they cannot mobilize and organize. The public protests of the Mothers of the Plaza de Mayo against the state-endorsed 'disappearance' (murder) of their adult children under the military dictatorship in Argentina in the 1970s and 1980s is a long-standing emblem of this organized resistance. The paternalistic humanitarian discourse that couples vulnerability and passivity needs to be challenged. It is especially time to challenge the 'masculine ideal of heroism in resistance', in which vulnerability is seen simply as weakness, and where a self-sufficient and sovereign individual subject is lionized as the primary agent of resistance (Butler, Gambetti and Sabsay 2016). It is possible to organize against violence in a systematic way, as women are doing increasingly to challenge gender-based violence. The Ni Una Menos ('Not One Less') movement has mobilized over a million women across Latin America (and Spain and Italy) by taking to the streets to demonstrate their resistance to male sexualized violence against women. Such movements were unimaginable a few decades ago, but they signify a new type of resistance by seemingly 'vulnerable' women (Butler 2020).

Part IV
Conclusions

10
Resisting Intellectually, Politically, Culturally and Educationally

The theories we employ exert great influence over how we think; they put boundaries around what we can see and know and how we come to know (Tronto 1993: 4). In my own experience the boundaries of thinking about social justice and social change were framed in my early years as a sociologist within a male-dominated narrative of Weberian (especially) and Marxist sociological theory, and by the equally male-dominated narrative of political egalitarian theory that I came to know when working with colleagues to establish the Equality Studies Centre at University College Dublin in the 1990s (Lynch 1995, 1999). While the debates about the care-related injustices were well rehearsed in feminist care theory, this work was not given much attention in mainstream political egalitarian or sociological theory. It had a ghostly status and was not part of the canon of either discipline.

As there was very little attention given to nurturing relations of love and care among the so-called founding 'fathers' of sociology, especially Marx and Weber, it was not surprising that the relations of care have not been prioritized in the discipline. While Durkheim and Mauss recognized that interdependency was endemic to the human condition, affective relations have been treated as secondary sociological matters compared with economic, political and cultural relations. Despite the path-breaking work of people such as Arlie Hochschild, to write about what were seen as 'feminized' subjects, care and love, located the speaker/writer on the periphery of the male-dominated discipline of sociology (Aulenbacher, Lutz and Riegraf 2018; Rusu 2018).

What my own empirical research over many years had shown, however, is that while people are habituated and socialized to pursue their economic, power and status interests, they are more than that in sociological terms.[1] Their relationality and interdependency feed into morality within them, and this enables them to identify morally appropriate behaviour in themselves and others that orients and regulates their actions (Vandenberghe 2017). The affective care-relational world runs its life in parallel to the political-economic world; consequently, it is as important to understand it, and find ways of developing and resourcing it, especially if the ethics of care are to help subvert the ethics of capitalism.

The dominant narrative in political egalitarian theory has been a liberal one, in which the master (*sic*) narrative was ideal moral theory. This offered a highly rationalist view of the human condition with scant reference to the sociological reality of human inter/dependency (Okin 1994; Kittay 1999). Furthermore, the lack of reflexivity on the politics and sociology of knowledge within the liberal field led to a lack of appreciation of how the conditions in which political egalitarian theories were created and validated greatly limited their framing of inequality and social injustice (Goodhart 2018; Casalini 2020).

Ideal moral theories of justice seemed to be applying pre-packaged, impersonal and abstract principles to logically calculate what was socially just.[2] While internally coherent and intellectually engaging in logical terms, ideal theory lacked a grounded 'empirically saturated reflective analysis of what is going on in actual moral orders' (Walker 2007: 11). The everyday suffering of injustices, experiences that are 'lived and felt as an intolerable neglect, lack of care and injury', was left outside the frame, as was 'humankind's bodily, relational and pluralistic nature' (Casalini 2020: 60–1). The maxim that 'there is no view from nowhere', that academics cannot be God-like in research terms, became increasingly compelling; to do good research one could not be beyond the body, culture and beliefs (Haraway 1991) in framing theories of justice or developing sociological theories. This meant that one had to engage in dialogue[3] and examine the world as lived by those experiencing injustices, not only in the political, economic and cultural spheres, but also in the affective relational sphere of life, which is what I did with colleagues in a range of studies (Lynch, Baker and Lyons 2009; Lynch, Grummell and Devine 2012; Lynch, Ivancheva, Keating, O'Flynn and O'Connor 2020).

Stepping outside the mainstream theories of justice was liberating intellectually and personally. It created a space to get to know worlds that had been silenced, especially the care world, a world in which I was, like most women, deeply implicated through family, work and other commitments. It allowed us to have our 'voices' recognized, so that what we said was not just background 'noise' to serious thinking. The discovery of feminist and socialist-inspired care scholarship gave a language in which to 'speak and be heard in the public space' (Rancière 1999: 29).

While the desire to proclaim the importance of care and affective relations as matters of justice and politics, and matters of sociological import, was a major motivation for writing this book, so too was the desire to challenge the naturalization of neoliberal capitalism as a way of life, as expressed in both the 'TINA (there is no alternative)' mentality and the 'futility' perspective. The belief that capitalism is so powerful that all resistances will be reincorporated in a way that further consolidates capitalism, on the one hand (Boltanski and Chiapello 2005),[4] and the belief that all resistance is futile unless it involves a comprehensive (violent) communist revolution, on the other, can lead to economic determinism and inaction (Block 2018: 209–13). Neoliberal capitalism is a human creation, and as such it can be contested in a multiplicity of different sites and through different means. It is not an internally sealed system, built on perfect logics and coherence, but rather one where there is an inherent tension between economic liberalism, with its goal of establishing 'a self-regulating market', and 'the principle of social protection', with the aim of ensuring the 'self-protection of society' (Polanyi 2001). How these tensions work out politically, in terms of movements and counter-movements, is by no means guaranteed (Alcock 2020).

Based on the purported ideals of merit-based rewards, choice and personal autonomy, neoliberalism is highly appealing to the successful and those who want to be at the pinnacle of the supposed meritocracy in Western democratic capitalist states. But neoliberal capitalism is also 'inconstant, differentiated, unsystematic, [and] impure' (Brown 2015: 20), and these inconsistencies and incoherencies create potential for resistance.

One of the places in which capitalism's incoherencies and contradictions are most visible currently is in the world of care relations, where care deficits lead to ongoing crises and tensions over the care of children and older persons particularly (Folbre 1994, 2006; Tronto 2013; Fraser 2016; Dowling 2021).What can be learned from these care crises, especially the crises arising from the coronavirus pandemic, is that we are not compelled to live forever in a capitalo-centric world where all meaning and purposes are framed in terms of capitalist inevitabilities (Gibson-Graham 2006; Gibson-Graham, Cameron and Healy 2016). While solidarity was far from perfect during the coronavirus pandemic, the global investment in vaccines

to control the virus, and the numerous displays of care shown at local
levels in different countries, demonstrate that it is possible to arrange
good care when humanity organizes itself to do so.

While it is important to maintain a healthy 'agnosticism' as to what
reforms or strategies will work in advance of action to challenge the
power of neoliberal capitalism, and while the barriers to change are
formidable (Block 2018: 211), which battles are won or lost is not
predetermined by the inherent logic of neoliberal capitalism; it will
depend 'on which side is more successful in mobilising both people
and resources to determine political outcomes' (Block 2018: 209).
While political and economic resource mobilization is required,
cultural action, including educational action, has a central role to
play in this process (Apple 1979, 1982, 2013a, 2013b; Giroux and
McLaren 1993). As Polanyi observed, we need 'a cultural revolution
of economic and political education ... [to] save democracy from
suicidal demise' (Polanyi 1932: 3, cited by Alcock 2020: 6). The
creation and dissemination of new ideas about how to organize and
think about a socially just political, social and economic global order
are part of that revolutionary struggle in education and research.
The challenges in doing this cannot be underestimated given that we
live in a society that bears all the hallmarks of capitalism, in which,
as Erich Fromm observed in *To Have or To Be* in 1976, *having* is
equated with *being*, and knowledge is defined as a possession; the
value of education is commensurate with the amount of property and
social prestige that will accrue in later life from the credentialixed
knowledge accumulated.

While much of contemporary education is domesticating, in the
Freirean sense of that term, simply preparing people to service
the economy with bundles of market-ready human capital at their
disposal (Peters 2016), education also has revolutionary potential in
terms of creating a more socially just and democratic world (Apple
2013a), and a more loving world (Darder 2002). It is for this reason
that it is feared, something Black scholars and human rights activists
recognized over one hundred years ago when confronting the reality
of slavery: 'The] South believed an educated Negro to be a dangerous
Negro. And the South was not wholly wrong, for education among all
kinds of men [*sic*] has had, and always will have, an element of danger
and revolution, of dissatisfaction and discontent' (Du Bois 2009: 27,
cited by Apple 2013b: 36). When critical pedagogies are employed
(Freire 1970, 1971; Asimakopoulos and Gilman-Opalsky 2018), the
subaltern can speak and claim their cultural place in naming the
world. In exercising their voice they open up new windows on the

taken for granted, the hegemonic common sense, thereby contesting the dominant order. When educated to transgress (hooks 1994), people are enabled to challenge the boundaries of racial, classed, gendered, ableist, ageist and other hierarchies. They develop capacities to speak and challenge the silencing of the affective relational world, thereby imagining and creating a different world.

Humans are *homo curans* as well as *homo economicus* (Tronto 2017). The logic of being *homo curans* is governed by cooperative, nurturing, non-exploitative values and ways of relating to other humans and the natural world that contradict the instrumental, exploitative *homo economicus* logic of capitalism (Brown 2005). Because everyone is engaged in affective relations, the nurturing world of social and emotional (re)production is one in which the contradictions of capitalism come into sharp relief on a daily basis. They are sites of tension and contradiction (Fraser 2016), but also of resistance to the overarching hierarchical order (Care Collective 2020; Dowling 2021). When affective relational life's priorities and values are named and opened up to public debate and education, the salience of care ethics both as a challenge to capitalism and as a means of realizing a more socially just, cooperative and care-led social order can become visible. This opening up is happening most recently through the work of Tronto (2013) on creating a caring democracy, Federici (2019) and Gibson-Graham, Cameron and Healy (2013, 2016) on the importance of the commons, and Folbre (2020) on challenging the hegemony of market economics in framing political values.

Rethinking democracy in affective care terms requires rethinking how affect operates within politics itself, not least because affective cultural dynamics play a central role in producing, reproducing and transforming different 'socio-political assemblages' (Coles and Haro 2019: 104). Although the management and manipulation of negative emotions, particularly the politics of fear towards the Other (Ahmed 2004), are widely recognized as central to politics, there is no reason why humans cannot think and feel differently (Lakoff 2008). Even if achieving this rethinking and re-feeling (especially) is a major challenge, it is entirely imaginable that people could learn to think with care and concern for the suffering of others (Puig de la Bellacasa 2012), rather than perceive and construe politics through the lens of fear and/or domination.

The rethinking and re-feeling with care and with mindfulness of the suffering of others is also possible and necessary in terms of human relationships with non-human animals and the environment. This conversation was initiated arising from the global Covid-19 pandemic during 2020–1, as human health and well-being were shown to be intrinsically linked to how human relationships with other animals were operated and managed. While the moral argument regarding the cruelty of warehousing and industrializing the production of birds, pigs, cows and other non-human animals may not have been heard, the compelling scientific evidence that several new viruses, including SARS and Covid-19, have developed through human use and abuse of non-human animals is giving a strong message regarding the cost of treating animals carelessly (Wiebers and Feigin 2020).[5] As Wiebers and Feigin observe: 'What is good for nonhumans and the earth is virtually always in the best interests of humans, given the profound interconnectedness of all life' (2020: 3).

The Contradictions of Care and Capitalism

There are few areas of life where the contradictions of capitalist-governed ways of living and being are more visible than in relations of love, care and solidarity. While care relations are predominantly nurture-centred, market relations are primarily gain-centred; market logic presumes the speeding up and condensing of time on task, to increase efficiencies and financial returns, while care-needs lack boundaries and cannot be time-defined; capitalist logic works through bureaucratic rationalities, operating through explicit hierarchies of power, status and income differentials, while care contradicts scientific and bureaucratic rationalities. Caring work also lacks a career structure and has no identifiable beginning, middle and end. Unlike purely instrumental tasks, relationships are central to caring as a practice. Furthermore, care tasks are governed by the personal needs of others rather than simply applying abstract rules of justice.[6] Even when and where care can be legitimately provided on a paid basis, such as day-care for children, there is a voluntary and affective dimension to the child–carer relations that cannot be supplied to order; it cannot be guaranteed by regulation alone. While regulations are necessary in paid care situations, care for children/adults without the development of voluntary bonding between the child/adult and carer in the care relationship can be arid; it will provide for physical well-being, organized supervision, protection from harm and, in the case of children, informed education and development, but care must go beyond education/supervision/protection to nurture and affirm the child/adult in terms of their emotional and related identities. Human life is 'not reducible to bare functionality or mere necessity. There is a difference between feeding and clothing an elderly person so that they can survive, and the act of doing so carefully, which means taking time, acting attentively, with affection and concern' (Dowling 2021: 45–6).

While the non-substitutable dimension of love labouring distinguishes it from secondary care work (see chapter 3), there is a reciprocal and a voluntary dimension to all care relationships built on a mutuality of recognition, responsibility, giving and taking through time that cannot be supplied to order. This voluntary dimension to paid care is not and cannot be included in the employment contract because it is contingent, built on relational dynamics and a mutuality of engagement that cannot be predetermined; it is a dimension of paid care that resists commodification (Weicht 2019: 267)

As the logics of care are antithetical to the logics of capital, and as capitalism is making ongoing inroads into the lifeworld of caring, imposing an alien market logic on affective relations, it is time to resist this and create a new kind of politics, and not allow capitalism to take over the meaning and making of humanity itself. As neoliberalism appears to be 'the rationality through which capitalism finally swallows humanity' (Brown 2015: 44), an ethics and politics of care and social justice is needed to replace it. To begin this process, recognizing the relationality of life, the interdependency and vulnerability of all of humanity, of all other species and of planet Earth itself is of pre-eminent importance.

Given that affective relations are a site where contradictions between values of care and capitalism meet at multiple intersectional points, be it at home, at work or in community or political life, they can be a site where conflicts are examined, where alternative narratives can be created, and where political platforms for moving towards a more humane, non-exploitative way of organizing the world are established.

Capitalism's Internal Contradictions

Capitalism is neither monolithic nor incontestable; while it has successfully maintained ideological hegemony, as a desirable political-economic system (Leyva 2019), it is not invincible. It operates in dysfunctional, contradictory and illusionary ways. While there remains a widespread belief in the internal coherence and unchangeability of the capitalist system, this belief is built on an illusion that capitalism operates according to unassailable logic and rules (Block

2018). The TINA illusion that the capitalist rules must be obeyed, or we risk losing the material well-being and health outcomes that have been achieved, largely ignores the socio-political reality that the majority of humanity still live in poverty despite several generations of capitalism (Roser and Ortiz-Ospina 2013). A second illusion is the view that capitalism has been largely stable for at least two hundred years (Block 2018: 10). There is a lack of recognition of capitalism's contradictions, including the wars and environmental destruction it generates and funds, and its never-ending economic crises. Yet capitalism's illusions are widely promulgated by a largely capitalist-controlled media, and by the political elite, who are embedded with the financial elite[7] (Kalaitzake 2017, 2019a, 2019b), and frequently 'in thrall' to their capitalist rhetoric (Block 2018: 8).

While the illusions of capitalism help undermine its legitimacy (it never delivers for everyone), there are also structural and environmental constraints on capitalism that can undermine it. There is a limit to growth within a finite and bounded world. In simple spatial terms, globalized capitalism has no 'new world' where it can exploit as yet unknown land and people on Earth; in many respects it has reached the zenith of its exploitative range (if not depth). The futures market has limitations in human and spatial terms; and even if other planets are on capitalist horizons, their accessibility is open to question in the short to medium term. Moreover, the internal contradictions of capitalism between the democratic imperative and the profit imperative propel never-ending cycles of conflict, social disorder and entropy, a world without a clear direction or purpose, all signifying capitalism's lack of coherence and potential decline (Streeck 2016: 13).

Given the contradictions, illusions and dysfunctionality of capitalism, there is a need to move outside the capitalocentric thinking box that puts capitalism at the centre of all meaning-making (Gibson-Graham, Cameron and Healy 2016) and, by extension, at the centre of resistance. Meaning-making and life itself are not only produced on the market; they are also produced and reproduced through affective relational life (and in cultural and political life). Caring is an ever-ongoing social process, involving caring for oneself, for others, for non-human animals and other species, and for the Earth itself (Tronto 2013). The underlying affective logics of care and its moral intent (the focus on the other(s) in need) set it apart from simple social reproduction or welfare in particular. Although what care means as a human activity is highly variable in cultural terms, 'care remains a central trope around which moral conceptions of personhood, social relationships and societies are anchored' across many cultures (Nguyen, Zavoretti and Tronto 2017: 205).

While the contradictions of capitalism can lead to the double movement and counter-movements of which Polanyi (2001) spoke, it is naïve to believe that such movements will necessarily be progressive and lead to a more democratic and socially just society. Resistance to the commodification of the lifeworld and 'society' may take actively ideologically progressive forms, but it can also lead to the development of inchoate forms that are unconscious and regressive, and even fascist (Polanyi 1934). There is a politically unconscious resistance 'which is not against ... the self-regulating market ideology [of capitalism] but the everyday negative material and social effects inherent in that ideology' (Alcock 2020: 2). Consequently, 'certain types of self-protection of society, or countermovements, do not lead to a progressive solution' (Alcock 2020: 6). The rise of new-right movements throughout many countries in Europe in the 2000s,[8] especially after the financial crash that commenced in 2007, shows how counter-movements challenging the negative effects of market capitalism (lack of decent work, declining wages and welfare), rather than taking on a clearly articulated progressive ideological project (of which the anti-capitalist degrowth movement is a good example), can lead to fascist-style rather than progressive politics.

While organizing for decent work matters globally, especially for vulnerable migrant workers (Galotti 2015), relying on organized labour in the economy as the principal site of resistance at all times is problematic, not least because organized labour is so integral to capitalism itself. There are many conflicts over status, power and wages between classes, and conflicts arising from geopolitical interests, that are also racialized, that capitalism can and does exploit successfully to its own advantage, undermining labour mobilizations. While the labour market is a very important site of resistance, it is not the only political and social space for the generation of action or resistance to the social injustices of capitalism, not least because of neoliberal capitalism's 'ubiquitous economization of all features of life' (Brown 2015: 31). Classed, gendered and raced inequalities are produced and reproduced, both inside the market economy and outside it, in other political, cultural and social sites. Meaning-making is not confined to market relations alone; people have affective relational priorities as well as economic and political preoccupations (Folbre 1994, 2001; Nelson 1997; Federici 2012, 2019). Human lives are grounded in moral frameworks that are deeply embedded in their relationality (Sayer 2011; Vandenberghe

2018). People have a care consciousness as well as classed or political consciousness (Crean 2018); this politicized consciousness can be enabled, resourced and endorsed to actively contest the values and practices of neoliberal capitalism (De Chiro 2008; della Porta 2017).

Resisting Capitalism

There are many organized civil society resistances to the globalized injustices of the world, injustices that are generated at the capitalist/ patriarchal/racist interface, though varying in form and cultural specificity. These are exemplified in movements as diverse as the Occupy movements of 2011–12, the climate change movements, the degrowth movement, the vegan movements, and environmental protests over urban spaces and democracy, such as those in Taksim Square, Istanbul, in 2013. The Black Lives Matter movements that began originally in 2013, the MeToo movements that accelerated in 2017, and even the development of community gardens across many Western and Northern cities[9] are all indicative of a global desire for a new and more socially and environmentally just way of organizing the world.

The development of the worker-owner and producer cooperative movements is not recent, but it is significant in both scale and scope, not least given the important role these enterprises play in providing examples of successful, long-standing cooperative (rather than purely capitalist) financial institutions, including Desjardins in Canada and the cooperative businesses and social services in the Basque region of Mondragon (Sánchez Bajo and Roelants 2011). There are now several cooperative enterprises throughout the world, many run by women, including those in Rwanda, Brazil and India (Roelants, Eum, Eşim, Novkovic and Katajamäki 2019). Cooperative and commons-based principles have inspired extensive campaigns throughout Africa by women farmers fighting for their communal lands (Federici 2019: 116–33), and movements throughout much of Latin America, especially by indigenous women working to promote radical change in how the world is organized (Federici 2019: 134–50). These have significant impact, and provide inspiration, even if the resistances begin slowly and locally. The achievements of the Maya women in Ciapas, Mexico, within the Zapatista movement,[10] fighting for indigenous rights, gender rights, control over land and control over their bodies, exemplify the gendered character of important radical egalitarian movements in South America (Klein 2015). Federici even claims that 'Women's activism is currently the main force for social change in Latin America' (2019: 135).[11]

It is not surprising that it is poor people who are leading the struggles over farmland, forests and clean water in South America, Africa and elsewhere; poor, often landless, indigenous women are the people who are most adversely affected by the enclosure of common land, transnational mining, deforestation, commercialization and the destruction of the environment. Indigenous women have seen their expertise in seed stocks, water conservation and herbal medicine, all developed over thousands of years, denigrated and trivialized, and lost to future generations. All of these developments have the potential to undermine carers' food sovereignty, their capacities to feed and look after their families and themselves in societies where there is little or no social welfare infrastructure at times of illness, unemployment or old age. It is for these care-harming reasons, however, that they can generate resistances, as they threaten to undermine the very basis of making and maintaining life itself.

People who are working as paid carers and domestic workers are also increasingly organized. In the USA, the National Domestic Workers Alliance was formed to challenge the lack of legislation to protect domestic workers as employees; it now has extensive membership across twenty states. The International Domestic Workers Federation[12] has half a million members across fifty-four countries. While these movements or organizations of care workers are not anti-capitalist per se, they are challenging a core principle within capitalism, which assumes that care labour (mostly women's labour) is free and exploitable. These movements represent a new development in gender politics, as women as carers have begun to find their voice. Though socialized to be 'good' girls and mothers/sisters/partners by being silent, by 'keeping their voices down', they are finding their voices and resisting (Gilligan 2011) in new and unexpected places.

Newer social movements have several precedents in movements that led, albeit over a long time, to important UN Declarations and Conventions promoting equality and social justice. It was global mobilizations by women that led to the binding UN Convention on the Elimination of All Forms of Discrimination against Women in 1979 (now ratified by 189 states), the UN Convention on the Rights of the Child in 1989 and the UN Declaration on the Elimination of Violence against Women in 1993. People with disabilities have mobilized over many years to create a major social movement leading to the adoption of the UN Convention on the Rights of Persons with

Disabilities in 2006[13] and is now ratified by 166 countries. People also mobilized for the passing of the 1969 International Convention on the Elimination of All Forms of Racial Discrimination, to which 182 nations are now party (albeit many with qualifications). While these are not anti-capitalist movements per se, and while they are not actionable in social justice terms in the courts, they are standard-setting and global-shaming mechanisms. They are proof that progressive change can and does happen, even if it is slow and limited, given the mobilizing powers of those who want to conserve the prevailing politico-economic order (Hochschild 2016).

Affective Relational Resistances and Refusals

Even within the realm of care relations itself, there are resistances to the corporatization of care, albeit in diverse and often silent ways. While there has been an explosion of home care services for older people, increasingly run on a for-profit basis in several countries (Mercille and O'Neill 2020), there is also resistance by older people to spending their final years in nursing homes (Berry and Bell 2017; Aulenbacher and Leiblfinger 2019). Although this may not represent a counter-movement in the Polanyian sense of that term, it is a very important development, and resistance may well be intensified following the high death rates in nursing homes during the Covid-19 pandemic. While the response to this resistance has been the development of home care that is also increasingly profit-led (and provided increasingly by low-paid, female, migrant labour), it does represent a refusal by older people to accept care in the corporatized manner in which it is offered, and over which they lack control within institutions.

The low wages and poor working conditions in the home care sector have also led to resistances among care workers: in the US, Cooperative Home Care Associates is now the largest worker cooperative, with positive results for both those needing home care and the working conditions of carers (Berry and Bell 2017: 385). The resistance of paid carers to low pay and insecurity in Ireland has also led to a cooperative initiative by migrant workers in that sector (MRCI 2020).[14]

The declining birth rates in European, North American and many Asian countries[15] demonstrate women's greater choices in terms of pregnancy, their greater control over their bodies. However, it also signals a refusal to have and rear children on the care-work terms available, especially among women (Balbo, Billari and Mills 2013; Friedman 2013).[16] While the reasons why fertility is declining are complex, there is no doubt that women who have had the experience of being educated and working on equal terms with men are no longer willing to accept the highly unequal gendered division of labour in family care work (McDonald 2000; Cooke and Baxter 2010). The refusal to have children is itself a resistance, an as yet unorganized counter-movement to a socio-political order that does not value the work involved in both the physical and social reproduction of human life. The non-existent and/or diminishing public childcare (and eldercare) services in many countries (especially after the austerity imposed by the financial crisis, beginning in 2007) have left the tiny nuclear family responsible for family care, a task that falls disproportionately to women. This is entirely unsustainable due to lack of capacity. Circles of care have become too narrow, with unrealistic expectations placed on two parents, or just a single parent, or a single person (generally a single woman); one or two individuals are expected to undertake multiple generational caring while simultaneously earning a livelihood and living at a distance from older relatives in need of hands-on (presence-based) caring. This care crisis has not led to a radical, care-oriented counter-movement in Western politics as yet. Instead, it seems to have fed and reinforced a neoliberal ideology of self-care and self-responsibilization. There is a preoccupation with 'family', only caring for your own, which has served as a launch pad for neoconservative, populist, new-right politics built around a naïve political assumption that calling for a return to 'family values' will enable good care to happen with no resources or supports (Care Collective 2020: 17–18). However, there are important initiatives such as the debate that is being opened up in New Zealand by Philip McKibbin (2019) about the importance of love in politics;[17] the biggest ever pre-election march about child care in Dublin, in February 2020;[18] and political mobilizations such as the Società della Cura (Caring Society) movement in Italy, to which 700 associations are affiliated, and the Biden initiative in the US in 2021 calling out and investing in what he named as the essential *caregiving infrastructure* of the country. 'About a fifth of the $2 trillion in the American Jobs Plan was devoted to "caregiving infrastructure"', those 'workers and services that take care of older and disabled Americans' (Voght 2021).[19]

Feminist movements for social justice, including those involving domestic workers and carers, the mobilizations of indigenous peoples, the Black Lives Matter movements, the environmental/

ecological/ justice movements, the animal rights movements and the disability movements, are all indicative of injunctions against the carelessness underpinning capitalocentric, patriarchal, racist and disablist perspectives on the human and natural world. The challenge that now faces humanity is to ensure that these generally quite separate movements can align and cooperate to become a global movement that can unseat capitalocentric and affiliated ways of thinking about humanity and the planet. To do so requires intellectual and ideological, as well as political, work.

While marching, engaging in direct action forms of resistance and profiling issues of injustice on social media are important, these actions need to be complemented by resistance at institutional levels through painstaking organizational and political work against the enduring inequalities (Tilly 1999). These must be built up over time, across social and political institutions, where injustices become bureaucratically embedded and protected by law, precedence and the power of money. This means ensuring that those who could potentially govern and manage the major institutions of society from the inside, and those who are resisting injustices from the outside, have the vision, expertise, commitment and moral courage to do the tedious but essential organizational work involved in realizing radical egalitarian change. Developing a democratic resistance to injustices is a slow process and systematic critical education is central to it (Apple and Beane 2007; Verma and Apple 2020; Tett and Hamilton 2021).

Education and Resistance to Capitalism

Just as dominant ideologies (Althusser 1971) can reinforce and legitimate social injustices, so can the ideological institutions of education, media and religion be sites of resistance. While ideological control is maintained by excluding groups from accessing and controlling symbolic systems, especially in education and cultural institutions, this dominance can also be challenged (Thompson 1984), not least by resurrecting and reclaiming residual values and organizing politically on the basis of these (Williams 1973). The mind is a site of political struggle, so power and control are not only exercised in the market; power is also exercised through controlling the means of understanding (Gramsci 1971). Symbolic systems, including the arts, education and the media, are sites of social practice, replete with contradictions that provide openings for resistance and developing revolutionary reconceptualizations as to how to create a caring world order that is also politically, economically and socially just. To instigate change in these fields of practice means engaging in both informal and formal education and in cultural action and pedagogy (Freire 1970, 1971; Giroux and McLaren 1993).

Since the end of World War II, the direction of education has been strongly influenced by Bloom's (1964) taxonomy of cognitive educational objectives, largely ignoring the affective educational objectives that Bloom also identified (Krathwohl, Bloom and Masia 1964). This rationalist (generally Piagetian-led) tradition focuses on the development of logical-mathematical capabilities and abstract reasoning in assessing educational capacity and merit (Gardner 1983). The student is understood socio-educationally as an autonomous agent living in the public sphere as an economic (largely), political and/or cultural actor. She or he is not educated for a relational life as an interdependent, caring and solidaristic human being (Noddings 1984, 2001). The goal of educating the autonomous rational actor, encapsulated in the Cartesian dictum *Cogito ergo sum*, remains pre-eminent. The person to be educated is defined in a non-relational way, largely ignoring the dynamics of affective life. Most students leave school and college without a paradigm for care and social justice in either intellectual or experiential terms. If care education is included in their education, it is as part of ancillary programmes on health and welfare, sexuality and relationships and/or pastoral care. It is focused on the individual in their private and personal life, not on caring as a way of relating to, thinking about, and acting in the world at community, institutional and political levels. To realize change, students need to unlearn carelessness thinking and acting, and relearn how to think with care (Puig de la Bellacasa 2012).

In the latter part of the twentieth and early twenty-first centuries, the rationalism of the past has taken the form of education as human capital, making oneself productive and entrepreneurial (Masschelein and Simons 2002: 594); the goal is to outcompete others, personally and professionally. A narrow range of metrics (Grade Point Averages, SATs, PISA and IQ scores) frame a given person's educational (and labour market) value. Metricization grossly simplifies the perception of human capabilities to what can be measured in the short term. By simplifying and quantifying people, metricization violates human worth, reducing people to numbers and enhancing the myth of meritocracy, while legitimating classed and raced inequalities in its wake (Lemann 1995; Muller 2018; Mau 2019; Sandel 2020). Within the human-capital-led frame of education, there is little time or space given to think about organizing the world differently, or creating a world led by values other than competitive individualism in a systematic way; there are few rewards or recognition for anything but individual achievements and grades. The banking concept of education rules (Freire 1970), where education is a cultural product from which one can elicit personal gain at its highest level (Peters 2005). It is as if human beings had no relationships, responsibilities or commitments beyond being an economic actor. Their affective relations are invisible within the human-capital-led educational frame.

Creating knowledge is a relational practice with significant consequences for the shaping of possible worlds (Haraway 1991). If we fail to enter into creating new knowledges and understandings of how to care and how to think with care, new epistemic models in which care- and justice-led perspectives prevail, neoliberalism will continue to reign intellectually and socio-culturally. It is necessary to unlearn current ways of thinking about knowledge as primarily a form of capital acquisition, a kind of banking education that Freire (1970) critiqued. If we want a different and better world, it is time to rethink how we do education. As Wendy Brown observed: education needs to focus less on providing a 'career bang for the buck' than on cultivating people that know and understand the 'enormously complex global constellations and powers' that affect them. It needs to develop 'capacities of discernment and judgment' as people read, watch or hear about the world, so that there is some understanding of our shared, interdependent humanity (Brown 2015: 198–200). To do the important work of resisting neoliberal capitalism and the violations that ensue from pursuing it politically, people must be educated not only to think with care (Puig de la Bellacasa 2012) but to live out care, equality and social justice as social practices. This means developing epistemic resistances to overcome the silences imposed on the many who are not part of those who frame knowledge and dominant epistemologies. It means listening to the resistances of students, who, while they recognize the need to survive economically, are also mindful of the affective care relations as a primary value in their everyday lives (Lolich and Lynch 2017). Speaking out about carelessness and affective equality is not easy, as, like women's experience of sexual intimidation, it lacks a name that is claimable and knowable (Fricker 2007). Under neoliberalism the world of care provisioning remains 'divested of a place in language'. It is visually and discursively absent from public consciousness (Brown 2015: 104–7), but this is not inevitable.

For expression and organization to occur, effective communication has to take place, 'publics have to be formed and to become able to express themselves; and social sensibilities of openness have to be cultivated for those publics to be listened to and responded to properly' (Medina 2013: 9).[20] For carers and those in need of care to be heard, providing political spaces, education and resources for group formation and the development of care movements is essential. People need to be given the conceptual and analytical tools to think about and with the world differently, and to be enabled and resourced to organize around this thinking and knowing.

Just as we need to counter hate speech with education (Verma and Apple 2020), so we need to educate people in cooperative, caring ways to create a different world (Noddings 1984; Lynch, Lyons and Cantillon 2007). It will not happen by accident. It has always surprised me that we expect young people leaving school and college to be anything other than self-interested and self-preoccupied. As a study I undertook over thirty years ago showed (*The Hidden Curriculum*; Lynch 1989b), throughout their schooling, students are highly rewarded for engaging successfully in individualized competitions for grades and ranks. They are punished, in status and recognition terms, if they do not play the self-entrepreneurial game. The game in the twenty-first century is much more competitive and intense than in the late 1980s; credentialization has gathered pace, and more and more high-status (expensive) credentials are required, except for those with wealth and social capital, to get employment – credentials that are not always relevant or necessary for the work involved.

An education that does not educate about love, care and solidarity or social justice, and/or that undermines respect for care and cooperation in practice due to its intense competitiveness at formative stages of life, cannot enable or resource young people to think and act with care. Because altruism does not 'fall from the sky' (Folbre 1994: 250), it has to be learned and practised, reinforced culturally and politically, and economically resourced. Education is central to the initiation of that process.

As the logics of care are antithetical to capitalist logic, in order to learn to know them there is a need to step outside the capitalocentric world of thinking as to what matters politically, economically and socially. It is not possible to generate a new care and social justice language and politics within capitalism's toolbox. Governed for centuries by exploitative, racist and sexist values, capitalocentric thinking will not produce a new narrative of justice, as the language of love, care and solidarity exists outside the frame of the master's (capitalist) house (Lorde 2007).

There are many challenges to be overcome. The politically excluding character of high dependency, and the organizational and resource challenges facing carers and those for whom they care in intimate settings, are often overwhelming. Moreover, those who hold power are not only 'hands-free' in care terms, they also have considerable resources to counter any resistance. But given that care ethics and concerns are not confined to intimate relations or care-specific work, it is not impossible to begin to change the narrative. The values of solidarity, collegiality, cooperation and attentiveness to the needs of suffering others are widely adhered to and practised throughout the world; they inform much of public service life and solidarity between peoples globally.

Aligning social justice and care, rights-based with needs/care-based thinking, is a universal concern (Casalini 2020), not just for humanity but for the safety and well-being of the non-human world and the environment; it offers ways of interpreting, managing and organizing the world in a way that challenges the 'greed-is-good' ethic of neoliberal capitalism. The war of position (Gramsci 1971) between neoliberal capitalism, practices of love, care and solidarity, and political, economic and cultural justice needs to be planned, organized, funded and persistent over time in the face of adversity.[21] This will take time, education and new mobilizations, especially by women, carers and those who need care – which is all of humanity at some point in their lives.

Outside of formal education, organic intellectuals have to be resourced and enabled to grow from the ground up, people who will work for a world driven by 'universal care', a world in which we hold joint responsibility for hands-on care work, and for the community, professional and political social-justice-led care work necessary to create a caring world order (Care Collective 2020: 26). Taking leave of the autonomous independence model of humanity, and especially of an idealized masculinity where dominance and its attendant violences are prized, is also necessary. It is not only dangerous for men; it has failed humanity. Relatedly it is vital to 'break the destructive linking of dependency with pathology and recognise that we are all formed, albeit in diverse and uneven ways, through and by our interdependencies' (Care Collective 2020: 30).

History is made, not pre-given, and there is every possibility of creating a world where the wisdom of love is what directs human existence, rather than an ethic of neoliberal capitalism that attempts to commodify all manner of human activity, including the activity of co-creating each other in our relationality.

Postscript: Care Lessons from the Covid-19 Pandemic

Privileged Ignorance

When I started writing this book coronavirus was not a household concept, and millions of people had not died from Covid-19. Although the world had been warned of the dangers of new viruses, especially following the impact of the SARS virus in China in 2002–3, the swine flu pandemic of 2009–10 and the Ebola outbreak in West Africa from 2014 to 2016, these were matters outside the cognitive concerns of many Western academics writing about social injustice. Scholars like myself were part of the epistemically privileged academic world and the geopolitically privileged Northern capitalist world. We were spoilt, not only by enjoying the status of being assumed to know about social justice, but, or more importantly, by 'having the privilege of not knowing and not needing to know' about the on-the-ground sufferings and injustices that were geopolitically removed (Medina 2013: 32).

The problem of living in 'privileged ignorance' is that scholars are mindful of some injustices, but also very distant from major life-threatening health crises and war-related injustices; they are protected and privileged within the boundaries of their own nation state, regional location and social class. Epidemics that led to great suffering outside of Europe, the US, Canada, Australia, Japan and other rich OECD states were not part of the social justice repertoire of most Northern/Western academics. The assumed normalcy of having a long and mostly safe and healthy life has immunized people from recognizing their privileged ignorance. I am among those who has lived with 'epistemologies of ignorance' (Sullivan and Tuana 2007) in terms of pandemics, a state that is not so much a lack of knowledge as a condition in which you 'don't need to know' and simultaneously 'need not to know' (Casalini 2020: 61). As sociology's feminist standpoint theorists have observed (Harding 1986, 1991; Smith 1990), the position of the knower, their standpoint, influences what they can see, know and observe. Like political and economic security, love and care security[1] and health security can be taken for granted when living with them in abundance.

What the Covid-19 pandemic has shown is that people cannot live in 'privileged ignorance' anymore. Our global health inter-dependency compels us to know, not least because it is a matter of life and death. Ignorance can no longer be an excuse for disregarding injustices that do not touch us in the present, as they will touch us sooner if not later. The pandemic has forced people to recognize that they live in a globally inter/dependent world in terms of health and personal security in a way that was unimaginable until 2020: people's physical survival depends from day to day on the cooperation and consideration of unknown others (be it through wearing masks, using hand sanitizers or regular handwashing). The death rates from the virus have shown particularly that few of us are really autonomous, especially if we are ill (Mol 2008). People are born dependent, they age differently and have very different capacities to exercise autonomy throughout life (Lanoix 2007, 2020).

Touch, Presence and the Limits of Technology

The absence of sociation, of friendships, social networking and intimate engagements, that the pandemic enforced on so many people, and on children, people living alone and older people in particular, was a powerful reminder of what is taken for granted in everyday life: the recognition and reassurance that come from being known and affirmed in the presence of others (Honneth 2003). By depriving people of meeting in person, and especially depriving them of *touching* one another, the pandemic eliminated a key means by which we co-create each other in intimate nurturing relations. It generated a global sentient deficit through the lack of touch, as tactility was outsourced to digitalization and eliminated in the process. An affective deficit in terms of physical affection followed under the new regulations of not touching.

The technologies that enable touching virtually and digitally have tried to fill this deficit, and they do have potential to enhance caring over distances and time (Puig de la Bellacasa 2017: 95–122);

they create virtual communities and a sense of belonging that would not be possible without them. They have facilitated forms of virtual care and communication that are profoundly enabling for many people with disabilities who are housebound and/or isolated due to age, illness or infirmity. However, feelings communicated in gesture, movement, voice and touch cannot be expressed fully through technological media. Virtual care is de-physical, literally detached from the body, and from the feelings that go through the body. It relies on the eyes, not on the touch of the skin (Kearney 2021). Text on a mobile phone or computer screen is a mediated means of communication; there is no possibility of affirmative, presence-related, bodily communication. It has a finality, especially in written form, that limits emotional expression and the nuances of feelings. While digital communication is limited as it is not tactile, it does matter, especially across distances of time and space;[2] yet the touching and embodied presence that are integral to hands-on love and caring are missing.

Death in Care Homes: Questions on the Corporatization of Care

While the long-term impact of the pandemic on the world is not yet known, what is known is that the pandemic compounded existing social inequalities. Those who were poorest were most adversely affected by the disease within and between countries. Moreover, the poorest in the world, especially those living in Sub-Saharan Africa, are predicted by the World Bank to be most likely to experience extreme poverty due to the pandemic over time.[3]

Older people were also more likely to die from the pandemic than young people, and in rich countries, of the older people who died, the majority were in nursing homes. More than 50 per cent of *all* Covid-19-related deaths in the early, intense stage of the pandemic occurred in care homes in several European countries (European Centre for Disease Prevention and Control 2020),[4] and 82 per cent of those in Canada. In the UK, some 40 per cent of Covid-19-related deaths were reported as occurring in care homes (Amnesty International 2020).[5] Why so many older people died while in care has not yet been fully explained, though it was evident that both their age and incarceration had been invisible politically until the death toll started to rise (Amnesty International 2020). One of the questions that the high death rates gave rise to is how, and if, the increasing marketization, and especially the corporatization, of care of older people impacted on the death tolls.

While forms of paid care vary depending on the culture, politics and welfare histories of different states, and the role and status of women within them, paying for care is a global and expanding phenomenon, with an estimated 11.5 per cent of total global employment now being in the care sector[6] (ILO 2018). Not only is care a global industry but the marketization of care is increasing throughout Europe, the US and most of the industrialized world (Fine 2007; Aulenbacher, Lutz and Riegraf 2018). Care of older people in particular is moving systematically from family (unpaid, women-led care) and state-provided, voluntary and community care to for-profit provision (Dowling 2021), even in countries like Ireland which did not have a strong tradition of for-profit care until the new millennium (Mercille and O'Neill 2020). The size and spread of the markets in home care are also exponential, reflecting the enormous potential for profit-making (Grand View Research 2020).

The corporatization of care is slowly but radically altering the culture and the terms on which paid care for vulnerable persons is provided, not least because the logics of care are contrary to the logics of the market in several respects (Mol 2008; Mulkeen 2016; Farris and Marchetti 2017; Mercille 2018; Szebehely and Meagher 2018). With corporatization, care is defined as a product. It becomes a 'commodity' like any other in market terms, and the person in need of care becomes a 'consumer'. Care is then driven by a logic of profit, not a logic of nurturing. Because of this, the corporatization of care is neither morally nor care neutral.

As the corporate care sector does not exist in a discrete realm, separate from community, voluntary or state care provision, given its size and wealth, it is redefining the terms on which other non-profit bodies can do care. The concept of care itself is altering under the weight of corporatization. Caring is no longer defined as a needs-based relationship, and the more person-centred perspectives are being pushed aside: 'By turning it [care] into an activity that is ever more codified, less personalized, poorly paid, and less sensitive to the changing needs of the people toward whom it is oriented (children, disabled, and ill or elderly persons)', care work is made a site of capitalist opportunism, albeit a contested one (Farris and Marchetti 2017: 127).

Yet, as Folbre (1994, 2001) and Tronto (1993, 2013) have demonstrated over time, good care work is relational and affective work requiring the intensive deployment of energy in mind and body. It is not infinitely condensable and cannot be done well in less and less time. 'Efficiency gains' in caring are very limited. It is not a 'lucrative industry, unless one is in the business of servicing the luxury market, which, given that everyone needs care, is not an option for society as a whole' (Dowling 2021: 132)

The Pandemic: A Care- and Rights-Based Perspective on Justice

The limited research available at the time of writing on the impact of the pandemic on those living in residential care shows that those who live in institutions had little control over their own lives and were generally not involved in planning their own care (Amnesty International 2020). Not only did older people die in disproportionately large numbers in care homes, but many of those living in these homes also experienced isolation-based pain and suffering, due to lack of social contact with their families/friends, that was significant, if not documented (Amnesty International 2020). Their voices were mediated by others, who, no matter how well intentioned, were not directly experiencing the suffering.[7]

The inability of those in residential care to be heard or noticed during the pandemic has highlighted the dangers of relying solely on a rights-based concept of social justice. Not only are rights-based frameworks removed at times from the lived experiences of those experiencing the injustices (Casalini 2020), rights-based frameworks tend to take insufficient account of how some people are unable to enter into contract to negotiate their rights, due to cognitive, developmental and related impairments, or illness. There are many people who are not able to organize and claim their rights. Consequently, they are excluded from framing the 'who and what' matters of social justice (Lanoix 2020).[8] The pandemic has demonstrated why both a needs-/care-based and a rights-based perspective on justice are necessary, as one is incomplete without the other (Casalini 2020). As Carol Gilligan observed: 'Once the ethic of care is released from its subsidiary position within a justice framework, it can guide us by framing the struggle in a way that clarifies what is at stake and by illuminating a path of resistance grounded not in ideology but in our humanity' (Gilligan 2011: 43).

Notes

Introduction

1 Since the early 1980s, the richest 1 per cent have received more than double the income of the bottom half of the global population, while the richest 1 per cent have consumed twice as much carbon as the bottom 50 per cent since the mid-1990s. The growing gap between rich and poor builds on and exacerbates the existing racial and gender inequalities (Oxfam 2021: 3).

2 Worldwide, billionaires' wealth increased by a staggering US$3.9 trillion between 18 March and 31 December 2020. Their total wealth at the time of writing stands at US$11.95 trillion, which is equivalent to what G20 governments have spent in response to the pandemic. The world's ten richest billionaires have collectively seen their wealth increase by US$540 billion over this period (Oxfam 2021: 11).

3 Capitalocentrism was defined by Gibson-Graham in 1996. It refers to the way that different 'economic relations are positioned as either the same as, a complement to, the opposite of, subordinate to, or contained within "capitalism"' (Gibson-Graham, Cameron and Healy 2016: 193).

4 'No hard-and-fast line can be drawn between our own selves and the selves of others, since our own selves exist and enter as such into our experience only in so far as the selves of others exist and enter as such into our experience also. The individual possesses a self only in relation to the selves of the other members of his social group' (Mead 1934: 164).

5 This was expressed passionately by one of the mothers in the *Affective Equality* research: 'It is something that if you didn't have it to do ... I mean it is part of your life. I mean if someone told me in the morning your job is gone, I would go, I will get another job, so be it! But if someone told me in the morning I didn't have to care for my kids or I didn't have them or something were to happen to them, I would scream, I would go to pieces, I really would!' (Clodagh, a mother of three primary-school children, in Lynch, Baker and Lyons 2009: 65–6).

6 Bearing in mind that millions of people are stateless due to war, displacement and enforced migration.

7 His work in the Harvard Zero project was further enhanced by Goleman's research (1995) on emotional intelligences.

8 I published a paper in *The Sociological Review* (Lynch 1989a) on love labour, the original title of which was 'Love labour: Its nature and marginalisation'. However, both the editor and reviewers at the time thought that the use of 'love' in an academic article was 'over the top' (their words), so it was changed to 'Solidary labour: Its nature and marginalisation' although it was about love rather than solidarity.

9 It is time to name women as 'founding mothers' just as sociology identifies the canon with its 'founding fathers', generally Durkheim, Weber and Marx.

10 Reared on a farm in the West of Ireland, I was keenly aware that women had two jobs: unlike men, they worked both 'inside and outside', a phrase used regularly by women living and working in farm households. Yet their *inside* work was not named as productive. Not only was women's care work and domestic labour not recognized in monetary terms, the work they did on the farm was not fully counted for much of the twentieth century. While men were counted in agricultural surveys as *one unit* of labour, women working on farms counted as *a percentage* of men's labour (equal to that of a young teenage boy). Yet women did equal amounts of farm work and most of the caring and household service work for the family.

1 Care and Capitalism

1 Indeed, all living species, and the Earth itself, cannot survive without care.

2 Doxas are unarticulated assumptions, powerful but hidden from view, because they are taken for granted and accepted. They are 'that undisputed, pre-reflexive, naive, native compliance with the fundamental presuppositions of the field'(Bourdieu 1990: 68).

3 Emphasis in the original.

4 To make the text less cumbersome, the collective noun 'care' will be used regularly to refer to the three different forms of care and the contexts in which care happens, namely primary, intimate, love labouring relations; secondary relations of care, both paid and unpaid, professional and non-professional; and tertiary relations of solidarity at the political level with personally unknown others. For a more detailed discussion on the different forms of care see Lynch (2007) and Lynch, Baker and Lyons (2009).

5 Though the rise of capitalism is commonly associated with the French and American revolutions of the late eighteenth century and the industrial revolution of the late eighteenth and nineteenth centuries, much of the financial and infrastructural apparatus that we associate with

capitalism, in the form of debt, banks, bond markets, shares, brokerage houses and speculative bubbles, preceded factories and wage labour and even the science of economics itself. Capitalism had found very visible expression in the age of European-led capitalist empires from the late fifteenth century onwards (Graeber 2011). European powers, ravaged by plagues, the Black Death and war, sought wealth and the alleviation of war debt through conquest and invasions especially in the Atlantic region (Patel and Moore 2018). The capitalist mantra of 'growth' was realized in the form of profit-led slave trading, arms trading or drugs trading that was (and is) deeply abusive, long before factories were established in the industrial cities of Europe (Graeber 2011: 307–60). I would like to thank my UCD colleague Ruben Flores for bringing Graeber's work to my attention.

6 The reasons for the rise of new-right politics are complex, varying from country to country, and across time. For a review of research on these movements see Mudde (2007, 2014); Golder (2016); Muis and Immerzeel (2017).

7 The EU is a prime example of a political and legal institution that has implemented deep forms of neoliberalization. Since the late 1970s, ongoing welfare-state retrenchment and a decline in redistributive solidarity are a salient European development (Korpi 2003). Social protections are increasingly marketized and outsourced, with an attendant lack of protection for those who are most vulnerable in a pay-as-you-go welfare system (Frericks 2011). What has emerged is a new 'post-industrial welfare support coalition' predominantly rooted within the professional and managerial middle classes (Gingrich and Häusermann 2015; Mau 2015). State supports have shifted from compensating people for income loss and vulnerability towards labour activation policies and human capital investment programmes. Welfare supports are increasingly commodified and social protections are tied to market processes. The individualization of responsibility for one's own welfare is central to this process (Lynch and Kalaitzake 2018).

8 There are now moves at EU and OECD level to introduce some type of global taxation. The finance ministers from the world's seven leading economies (the G7), at their meeting in Cornwall on 5 June 2021, agreed on the principle of introducing a global minimum effective tax rate of at least 15 per cent in each country in which a business operates. How this will be translated into practice is as yet unclear, but it is a hopeful sign in terms of global tax reform. https://www2.deloitte.com/nl/nl/pages/tax/articles/g7-finance-ministers-agree-on-taxation-of-digitalized-economy-global-minimum-rate.html.

9 It has been through such protest movements that progressive and 'left' politics have found expression (De Chiro 2008; Casalini 2017), while the 'right' has organized more through political parties (Hutter 2014).

10 For a full discussion of the similarities and differences between love, care and solidarity see Lynch (2007) and Lynch, Baker and Lyons (2009).

2 Care as Abject

1 Scholz (2009: 129) summarizes this position very well: 'the symbolic order of the commodity-producing patriarchy is characterized by the following assumptions: politics and economics are associated with masculinity; male sexuality, for example, is generally described as individualized, aggressive, or violent, while women often function as pure bodies. The man is therefore regarded as human, man of intellect, and body transcendent, while women are reduced to non-human status, to the body. War carries a masculine connotation, while women are seen as peaceful, passive, devoid of will and spirit. Men must strive for honor, bravery, and immortalizing actions. Men are thought of as heroes and capable of great deeds, which requires them to productively subjugate nature. Men stand at all times in competition with others. Women are responsible for the care for the individual as well as for humanity itself. Yet their actions remain socially undervalued and forgotten in the process of the development of theory, while their sexualization is the source of women's subordination to men and underwrites their social marginalization.'

2 That use value could be enumerated if there was a political commitment to do so (Waring 2004).

3 The demand for carers is growing in rich countries with ageing populations, such as Japan, where there were already 1.71 million paid carers in 2014 (Miyazaki 2019). In December 2018, Japan passed amendments to the Immigration Control and Refugee Recognition Act that took effect in April 2019. This allowed for the immigration of an estimated 60,000 carers from 2019 to 2223, the largest single type of migrant worker being admitted under the new immigration laws. And it is likely that a very large proportion of those will be women, given the overlap between care work and gender globally.

4 Of all nurses immigrating to the UK between 1998 and 2003, the vast majority were from the Philippines (17,329); this was more than three times the number from South Africa and four times the number from India (Brush and Vasupuram 2006).

5 Officially, there were 163.8 million migrants globally in 2017, of whom 58 per cent were men and 42 per cent were women (IOM 2020: 34).

6 And when they migrate due to internal displacement and war, seeking asylum and refuge in other countries, while both women and men are exploited through forced labour, it is women and girls who are most often subject to trafficking for sexual exploitation (UNHCR 2020).

7 https://www.ilo.org/dyn/normlex/en/f?p=NORMLEXPUB:12100:0::NO::P12100_ILO_CODE:C189.

8 An imprimatur from the Catholic Church was sought (and given) for much of the exploitation and enslavement that followed not only from the Crusades, but from the colonization of Africa and the Americas. A

refusal to become Christian was justification for enslavement (Patel and Moore 2018: 92–5).

9 https://www.statista.com/statistics/778577/billionaires-gender-distribu tion.

10 The data for this study came from the 2003–7 American Time Use Survey (ATUS), a nationally representative cross-sectional time use survey organized by the US Bureau of Labor Statistics. Men's time spent on caring for children alone, attending to their physical needs and managing their care rises when wives are working full time (Raley, Bianchi and Wang 2012: table 6). The survey, covering households with children under thirteen years, involved 6,572 fathers and 7,376 mothers.

11 https://ec.europa.eu/eurostat/statistics-explained/index.php?title=How_ do_women_and_men_use_their_time_-_statistics&oldid=463738#.

12 https://www.pwc.com/gx/en/news-room/press-releases/2021/women-in-work-index-2021.html.

13 The caveat is mine.

14 In her book *Object Lessons* (1996) Eavan Boland meditates on how the experiences of women qua women, such as caring for children, were not defined as fit subjects for poetry. While Irish women could write poetry, they were expected to take their subject matter from men's handbook. Through her life's work, Boland created a space, for the first time within modern Ireland, where being a woman and a poet was no longer a contradiction in terms.

15 The vernacular terms reflect their association with disgust and abjection: shit, pee, sputum and vomit.

16 'Well it's basically twenty-four hours a day, seven days a week. I mean you are on call all the time, … you cannot leave them' (Valerie, a daughter, who had taken leave from her job to care for both parents, in Lynch, Baker and Lyons 2009: 59–60).

17 'I think that being a mother is the most thankless task in the world … because it's taken for granted particularly in Ireland in terms of the whole culture and the whole thing. That is just the way it is. It's taken for granted. Nobody really cares at the end of the day … Society doesn't appreciate it; the Government doesn't appreciate it either' (Paula, employed full-time, separated mother of four children, of whom three were adults and one school-going, in Lynch, Baker and Lyons 2009: 80–1).

18 'We [carers] don't exist, we get the usual pat on the head at election time, [we are] patronised. We don't exist. As long as you are prepared to do it, they will wring their hands and say you have done a great job and leave it to that' (Tom, single man, caring full-time for his father, in Lynch, Baker and Lyons 2009: 82).

3 Making Love

1 This chapter does not examine the attempts to sell sex as love. The ways in which the sex trade operates as an abusive multibillion-dollar

industry built on violating (mostly) poor women and young girls globally is discussed briefly in chapter 9.

2 Pitirim Sorokin was professor of sociology at Harvard, where he led a research centre on creative altruism. Sorokin did try to raise the themes of love and relations of caring, attempting, unsuccessfully, to bring them into the centre of sociology. (I would like to thank Kieran Keohane of University College Cork for this observation).

3 Large research programmes, such as Horizon 2020/Horizon Europe, funded by the European Commission, require research teams and research proposals to operate according to gender equality principles. Projects have 'to describe how sex and/or gender analysis is taken into account in the project's content': https://ec.europa.eu/research/partici-pants/docs/h2020-funding-guide/cross-cutting-issues/gender_en.htm. However, there are also ongoing status and gender hierarchies *within* gender research itself. The swift rise in the citation status of the *Men and Masculinities* journal (ranked fourth among the world's 131 gender journals for the three years up to 2018) tells us something about what is valued in gender research terms. Although it was only established in 1998, its citation rates are surpassed by just one women-focused gender journal (the *Psychology of Women Quarterly*, ranked second), a journal that was established twenty-two years previously, in 1976, while *Signs*, a leading journal in feminist theory established in 1975, was ranked sixty-ninth in 2018. The *European Journal of Women's Studies* (established 1994) was ranked fifty-eighth: https://www.scimagojr.com/journalrank.php?category=3318&page=2&total_size=131.

4 See Gouldner (1970) on how domain assumptions influence paradig-matic assumptions in research.

5 Although women in Europe have consistently outperformed men academically, comprising 59 per cent of all graduates in 2010, just 44 per cent of lecturers, 37 per cent of senior lecturers and 20 per cent of professors are women (European Commission 2013: 6). Data from Germany and the US confirm that academia is not child-friendly, especially for women: 75 per cent of the female research fellows and 62 per cent of the female professors in Germany had no children in 2006 (Bomert and Leinfellner 2017: 120). Female research fellows, as well as female professors, are more likely to remain childless than their male colleagues throughout their careers: 62 per cent of the female compared with 33 per cent of the male professoriate had no children in 2006 (ibid.). In North America, academic women are less likely to have children than other highly educated professional women (Reuter 2018).

6 A study led by the author probing women's and men's attitude to caring in the academy reflected a deep gender essentialism in some, though not all, male thinking. An extract from one of the interviews with a senior university professor in the science field reflected this standpoint. Caring for children was seen as women's work, with this professor believing women (not men) 'suffered' if they could not care for their own children;

he recognized, however, that staying out of work was costly for mothers in work and income terms: 'So, she's either going to suffer by parting with her children or by parting with her income and her work, you know … the satisfaction that comes from working.' He believed that most men did not really want to care for children full-time: 'I don't think the men care. I don't think they're interested in paternity leave particularly, but they'll take it if it comes their way. But what will happen then is that the guys who can take leave and work at home will do it' (the interviewee had three adult children and his wife worked at home full-time when they were young). See Lynch, Ivancheva, Keating, O'Flynn and O'Connor (2020); http://irc-equality.ie.

7 The WHO introduced an International Code of Marketing for Breast-Milk Substitutes in 1981, recommending the prohibition of advertising and promoting these products in early infancy. Although point-of-sale promotions of breast milk substitutes are counter to the code, and are prohibited by national legislation in many countries, formula milk and other follow-up formula products continue to be actively promoted in supermarkets and grocery shops in poorer countries (Champeny, Pereira, Sweet, Khin, Ndiaye Coly et al. 2016).

8 Merton (1973) identified four norms or principles that should govern the operation of ethical scholarly research: *disinterestedness*, meaning detachment from vested interests, was a key one of these. *Communism* or common ownership of knowledge, *universalism* and *organized scepticism* were the others.

9 Mulkeen's (2019) in-depth study of thirty-seven carers living with children and young people in residential care gives extensive evidence of the differences between distant, detached care and being engaged in care at a deeper level. Children and young people in state care were highly sensitive to what they lacked in their affective relational lives, notably deep attachments and attentiveness from committed adults. (Mulkeen 2019: 161–2).

10 Adults who experienced neglect (and abuse) in institutional settings in Ireland spoke about how, either in or out of state care, they 'never had someone caring about' them; they could not learn as 'nobody cared' or 'nurtured' them. People came and went from their lives, 'they walked away' (Feeley 2009: 205–10). The lack of love was not confined to institutional care settings, however. Feeley also found that some did not recall their own birth parents either 'saying loving things … or showing love' before they were taken into care.

11 This was confirmed in detail in five volumes of the *Report of the Commission to Inquire into Child Abuse* (Commission to Inquire into Child Abuse 2009). Many witnesses reported an inability to trust and relate in intimate relationships. They believed these difficulties to be a consequence of childhood abuse, including the deprivation of secure emotional attachments and nurturing relationships (ibid.: vol. III, 291).

12 Though it is always potentially a place of abuse and neglect, a site of love's failures.

13 As when a parent dies and there is no one to mind a sick child or a dependent adult sibling, or when a friend or close other person is in need for some unforeseen reason.

14 Each care location is intersectionally connected to the others, moving along a fluid continuum from deep and consistent love, care and solidarity to carelessness, neglect and abuse and violation. (See chapter 1 as well as Lynch 2007; Cantillon and Lynch 2017.)

15 To say this is not to deny that love labouring can become routinized and emotionally disengaged especially when people are tired, stressed or unwell. However, the commitment to engage in the care of another is strongly affectively driven and this prior emotional engagement sets the context and frames the care relations. Even if love labour is undertaken without expressed feeling, that remains implicitly part of the relationship.

16 Love relationships draw from the energy associated with deep feelings, but they do not colonize or co-opt them.

4 Time to Care

1 These include extensive studies of family carers and care receivers (Lynch, Baker and Lyons 2009) and the care experiences of employees across disparate occupations in the higher education sector (see Ivancheva, Lynch and Keating 2019; Lynch, Ivancheva, Keating, O'Flynn and O'Connor 2020).

2 https://www.cso.ie/en/releasesandpublications/er/sic19wm/socialimpact ofcovid-19onwomenandmenapril2020.

3 The power relations between groups – what Mills (2020: 299) terms 'chronopolitics' – exercise control over the interpretation of time and the representations of the relations between groups and the world in their specifically temporal dimension. One obvious way in which power is exercised in the definition of time is in the widespread globalized use of the Western (Gregorian) calendar; within this calendar, time is defined with reference to the birth of Christ (AD 2020).

4 Sasha got a carer's allowance, as two of her children had disabilities. Having a carer's allowance only permitted her to work ten hours per week, but no one would give her work for such a short period. She found it hard to survive on the carer's allowance alone.

5 Usury refers to unreasonably high interest charged over time on borrowed money. Charging interest on loans is forbidden in Islam; it is regarded as a form of excess, or *riba*. Under Jewish law, people are forbidden to change interest to other Jews, though they can charge interest to non-Jews.

6 Those who commanded high interest on loans could not receive the sacraments, nor could they have a Christian burial.

7 Although Polanyi noted that when markets were created historically, they 'grew up' with regulation to ensure they served society (Polanyi 2001: 71), rather than just themselves; the economic order was responsive to and regulated by the social order.

8 It was at the beginning of the nineteenth century that classical economists began to argue that the economy is, and should be, independent of other areas of social life. This perspective led to the development of laissez-faire economics, the idea that the economy is autonomous and should be allowed to self-regulate independent of the state. This view still prevails, especially in conservative economic thinking, having been successfully promulgated in the post-World War II era by the powerful free market theorist Friedrich Hayek (Block 2018: 34–6).

9 Taylorism or scientific management was developed by Frederick Taylor in the late nineteenth and early twentieth century. Taylor held that improving worker productivity involved increased surveillance, monitoring and control under the direction of managers, thereby creating a management class with increased power within work organizations. This created a type of officer class within the factory system who oversaw scientific management (Taylor 1911). Fordism refers to the model of work organization in the car manufacturing plants owned by Henry Ford. Ford's factories represented a new capitalist model for organizing labour in general, using a combination of control and coercion at work, and seduction in the world of consumption. The combination of a tightly, mechanically regulated workplace, relatively high wages and ideological instruction incentivized productivity in the factory and high levels of consumption outside of it. However, it also led to the development of greater worker organization and resistance to the model itself (Watson 2019).

10 The ways in which supermarkets and shops 'reward' their customers with points and money back exemplify how profit times dictate spending times. The €10 off a €50 spend on groceries only applies within narrowly defined targeted dates. The buy-one-get-one-free offers are only for specific times, so one needs to keep this time in mind or 'lose out' on the offer.

11 Families and households are also often closely linked to financial markets without seeing or knowing it: this occurs through their pensions and savings, and in the way their car loans, credit card and house mortgage debts are turned into bonds and sold to global investors (Davis and Kim 2015: 204).

12 The concept of work–life balance is a contested on several grounds, not least of which is that it implicitly implies that there is no work outside of paid work.

13 The European Social Survey investigates key questions about time conflicts between paid work and personal life. There are three key questions for this item, one of which is: 'How often do you feel too tired after work to enjoy the things you would like to do at home?', while

another addresses the problem of having not enough time for loved ones: 'How often do you find that your job prevents you from giving the time you want to your partner or family?' (Schöneck 2018: 12).

14 General service work such as cleaning and catering in public services has increasingly been outsourced to commercial companies, while professional jobs are broken up into 'packages', 'projects' or 'consultancies', all of which are temporary.

15 University College Dublin has an Agility Unit dedicated to 'increasing agility and effectiveness' in the university's processes and procedures. It has a director, a leader and a co-ordinator on the Agility 'team'. To become agile, staff are encouraged to do training. The director has a Lean Six Sigma Green Belt qualification. This qualification is provided by the Acuity Institute (a private business): https://acuityinstitute.com/courses. Over 550 staff had been through various white-belt (half day), yellow-belt (full day) and green-belt (six days) training in summer 2020: https://www.ucd.ie/agile/about.

16 Everything from 'car park barriers, central heating boilers, building security systems, burglar and fire alarms, accounting software, vehicle fleet maintenance systems, [to] local authority revenue systems, child protection registers, benefit systems, emergency service communication systems and medical equipment' is dependent on software (Thrift 2005).

17 The oppressive character of these tracking devices was well documented in the film *Sorry We Missed You* (2019), a British–French–Belgian drama directed by Ken Loach, written by Paul Laverty and produced by Rebecca O'Brien.

18 In Germany, long-term care insurance specifies a time limit for each care task or package of tasks in home care: for example, thirty-seven minutes are allowed for un/dressing, showering, brushing teeth and oral hygiene. Spending social time with older people is not counted as work time (Müller 2019). Similar specifications apply in other European countries, with care tasks with older people designated in minutes (fifteen minutes) by some private providers in Ireland (McDonald, Lolich, Timonen and Warters 2019). Minutes are allocated to tasks rather than care in the social sense of that term. An article in the *Telegraph* newspaper in 2015 reported that 500,000 home care visits lasted less than five minutes each in the UK (*The Telegraph*, 15 February 2015).

19 Artificial intelligence technologies such as the sociometric badges or sociometers devised by Pentland (2014) at MIT are time-regulatory devices designed to record every move and every conversation, while affective computing and software for decoding facial expressions and tones of voice are designed to predict moods and emotions. While all of these devices are fascinating in how they can record human activities and feelings, they also have enormous potential for controlling and regulating behaviour in work settings (Mau 2019: 149–51) and beyond (Zuboff 2019). It is self-evident that social time or care time at work could

be seriously circumscribed by tracking and recording socio-emotional responses through sociometric 'badges', given the potential to abuse this information within or without work settings.

20 My siblings and I had extensive personal experience of this in caring for my very elderly mother in her own home. What she wished for in terms of personal care and attention varied from day to day, even hour to hour.

21 Nursebots are robots designed to provide nursing care.

22 Location data is extracted from smartphones through 'geotags' when the phone embeds personal identity software in photos and videos without people knowing. The embedded tags enable Google, Facebook and other social media platforms to know how, where and when you move. The system is designed to keep those using it ignorant of how their very private behaviour is being mined and used without their permission. People are not told they are being tracked, or where, how and with whom personal information is being shared. Nor is tracking confined to geotags.

23 *Affective Computing Market: Global Industry Analysis, Size, Share, Growth, Trends and Forecast 2015–2023* defines affective computing as 'a technology which helps in recognizing human decision making through analyzing facial expressions, heart rate, voice and other body parameters. … [It] includes use of emotion analytics engine, machine intelligence, big data and sensors such as camera, and head-up display to collect and analyze the customer emotion. It also includes software for speech and facial recognition, gesture recognition and neural analytics. Apart from these segments, affective computing also includes device or software that exhibit emotional capabilities, according to the requirement of human being.' https://www.transparencymarketresearch.com/affective-computing-market.html.

24 The EU Court of Justice delivered a ruling on Thursday 16 July 2020 in the Schrems case that put some limit to the transfer of personal data from Europe to the US (Schrems II (C-3111/18)). The ruling was based on the grounds that US law cannot adequately ensure protection of EU personal data. The landmark decision of the Court struck down the Privacy Shield, one of the most widely used mechanisms allowing US commercial companies to transfer and store EU personal data in the US.

25 The action is being taken by the Department of Justice in the US against Google, but is too little too late, as the Google search engine is the unrivalled gateway to the internet for billions of users to whom advertisers must pay a toll (Karlin Lillington, *Irish Times*, 22 October 2020): https://www.irishtimes.com/business/technology/google-s-incredible-power-is-the-result-of-decades-of-regulatory-failure-1.4387348.

26 Zuboff (2019: 352) defines instrumentarianism as 'the instrumentation and instrumentalization of behavior for the purposes of modification, prediction, monetization and control'.

27 While social media provides people with an opportunity for virtual social connection and a sense of belonging, being under constant

self-scrutiny through inevitable comparisons with others on Facebook leads to envy and anxiety (Chou and Edge 2012). As one is constantly 'on show' online, and subject to evaluation and surveillance, this can undermine rather than enhance one's subjective sense of well-being (Kross, Verduyn, Demiralp, Park, Lee et al. 2013). It is not surprising, therefore, that an experimental study with young adults, reported by Zuboff (2019), found that the more participants used Facebook, the more their life satisfaction levels declined over time. This is the opposite of what happens with supportive offline social networks, where frequent interactions enhance one's sense of well-being. Social media tracking is complemented by self-tracking, whereby people choose to evaluate and monitor their own behaviour digitally, ordering and ranking themselves numerically (Lupton 2020).

28 https://www.dw.com/en/un-68-percent-of-worlds-population-to-live-in-cities-by-2050/a-43818167.

29 Gibson-Graham 'characterise commoning as a relational process – or more often a struggle – of negotiating access, use, benefit, care, and responsibility ... Commoning thus involves establishing rules or protocols for access and use, taking care of and accepting responsibility for a resource, and distributing the benefits in ways that take into account the well-being of others. When these relationships are in place, what results are any number of commons including biophysical commons (e.g. soil, water, air, plant, and animal ecologies), cultural commons (e.g. language, musical heritage, sacred symbols, and artworks), social commons (e.g. educational, health, and political systems), and knowledge commons (e.g. Indigenous ecological knowledge, scientific, and technical knowledge). The resulting commons may also be of varying and overlapping scales from the household and family to the national and international; from the micro (such as a microclimate) to the macro (such as the planet's atmosphere)' (Gibson-Graham, Cameron and Healy 2016: 195).

30 The feminist economic geographers Julie Graham and Katherine Gibson are among those who have been proposing 'a postcapitalist politics' identifying community-engaged action research to recognize and support non-capitalist economic practices that already exist (Gibson-Graham 2006). Gibson-Graham proposed a politics that aims not only to challenge the hegemony of capitalism as an economic system, but also to think about politics in a different way – as a politics of possibility.

31 Degrowth movements are centred on recognizing the limits of the liberal Enlightenment idea of progress. 'They criticise the varieties of capitalism approach and the belief that growth will eradicate poverty through national economic enhancement.' Their aim is to make people aware that the economy 'cannot continue to grow by extracting and exploiting recklessly and haphazardly a world with limited material goods' (Neyra 2019: 566).

32 For information on Transition Networks see https://transitioninitiative.org/.

33 'Degrowth initiatives have given rise to communities with urban gardens and valley gardens, such as CanMasdeu in Barcelona, and have evolved into a network of collectives that reclaimed 35 hectares in the Collserola Natural Park owned by the Hospital de Saint Pau ... By 2015 10% of the Barcelona economy was based on cooperatives, time banks and SCMOs [sustainable community movement organizations], grounded in multistakeholder social pacts working in a non-corporatist manner with NGOs, business and government. Following the Popular Unity victories in the May 2015 local and regional elections, a New Mayors for Change interurban network for solidarity economies was formed' (Neyra 2019: 567).

34 Veltmeyer (2019) lists several countries where there are significant mobilizations and resistances: Argentina, Bolivia, Brazil, Chile, Colombia, Ecuador, Mexico, Peru and Venezuela. Mining and natural resource extraction are leading to much resistance in particular because of their negative socio-environmental consequences. 'Throughout Latin America, out of a total of 184 ongoing resource conflicts 154 of them are mining related ... These conflicts have affected 222 communities (179 of them in South America) and involve 247 companies' (Veltmeyer 2019: 1278).

35 Initiatives such as the Società della Cura (Caring Society) movement in Italy (https://societadellacura.blogspot.com) and the movement for democratizing work (https://democratizingwork.org), both of which have been challenging the neoliberal narrative in recent times.

5 Liberalism, Care and Neoliberalism

1 https://www.oecd.org/gender/data/why-dont-more-girls-choose-stem-careers.htm.

2 The Covid-19 pandemic that took hold in 2020–1 impacted adversely on older people in Sweden due to lack of state investment in their care. See https://www.socialeurope.eu/sweden-the-pandemic-and-precarious-working-cond.

3 Rawls (1971) exemplifies this tradition, claiming that 'In comparison with liberty and equality, the idea of fraternity has had a lesser place in democratic theory' (1971: 105). He effectively claims in *Political Liberalism* that affective relations are not political: 'The political is distinct ... from the personal and the familial, which are affectional, ... in ways the political ... is not' (Rawls 1993: 137).

4 This was evident when appeals to solidarity were gradually dropped from Labour Party policies, initially by Neil Kinnock and especially by Tony Blair.

5 In *What Is Sociology?* (1978), Elias devoted chapter 5 to the subject of affective bonds. Elias spoke of society as interdependent people in the plural, and the individual as interdependent in the singular.

6 Among the many who have contributed are Barbalet (2002); Ahmed

(2004, 2012); Brennan (2004); Clough and Halley (2007). For an excellent review see Wetherell (2015). The work of Skeggs (1997), Reay (2005) and Sayer (2005) has contributed especially to the understanding of social class and affect, as has that of Walkerdine, Lucey and Melody (2001) and Walkerdine (2016).

 7 Wetherell claims that the work of Ahmed (2004), while valuable for understanding the cultural politics of emotion and their affective economies, tends to treat emotions as free-floating; affect is decontextualized, giving it a non-relational, depersonalized representation. Yet affective relations are generated culturally and socially; they are not circulating abstractly in the stratosphere. (Wetherell 2015: 159).

 8 *Current Sociology*, 66 (4). The marketization, transnationalization and governance of care are the main themes of this special issue.

 9 Counting himself among the liberals, Simpson claims that: 'We liberals remain children of our permanent revolutions, both energized and scarred by them' (2019: 348).

10 China is a visible example of this institutionalized intolerance of dissent; access to global internet networks such as Google is prohibited, and the prohibition is enforced through systems of surveillance that are enabled by the very technologies that it disallows.

11 A social group is a collective of people that is distinguishable from at least one other group by cultural forms, norms and practices, and/or ways of life (Young 1990: 43). People inhabit intersecting group-based statuses and identities, some of which may be enabling, others disabling. They are not simply women or men, but women and men of a particular colour, class, age, nationality, dis-ability, culture and so forth (Crenshaw 1991). By virtue of their group affiliations they occupy differential status positions, which, in turn, impact on their economic and political standing.

12 While one can opt for gender reassignment later in life, that is not an option at birth.

13 Research in the US shows that families in the top income quintile (richest 20 per cent) are spending almost seven times as much per child per annum in out-of-school enrichment activities as the poorest 20 per cent (US$9,000 per child compared with US$1,300: Kaushal, Magnuson and Waldfogel 2011). The growing achievement gap by social class is being matched by the persistent achievement gap by race, and all are related to income differentials and economic inequality (Magnuson and Waldfogel 2008; Reardon 2011).

14 When inequalities are deep and extensive, this provokes anxiety and fear about how one is valued. 'Inequality increases the tendency to regard people at the top of society as hugely important and those near the bottom as almost worthless. The result is that we judge each other more by status and become more anxious about where other people think we fit in' (Wilkinson and Pickett 2018: 28).

6 Individualism and Capitalism

1 Individualization refers to those social-structural and cultural-normative processes that enhance and facilitate the pursuit of individualized lifestyles and life situations.

2 While the concept of individualism gained popularity in the nineteenth century, various manifestations of individualization and individualism operated as early as the Middle Ages, in the Renaissance period, within ascetic Protestantism, and in other social movements where people struggled to free themselves from feudal bondage, or simply from the lack of opportunity in rural villages and towns (Beck 1992: 127).

3 Weber claimed that 'The expression individualism includes the most heterogeneous things imaginable' (Weber 1930: 222).

4 The individuality of the person was defined as leading to the individuality of the 'whole', of the nation state. The individualism of the early Romantics became 'transformed into an organic and nationalistic theory of community' that was unique and self-sufficient. Individuality morphed, therefore, from a concept denoting the self-realization of single persons to one denoting a particular community or nation state (Lukes 1973: 54–5).

5 It is arguable that the absence of a socialist tradition in the US is not unrelated to the strong entrepreneurial understanding of individualism that developed in the country from the late nineteenth century onwards.

6 *Caritas* refers to the Christian concept of love of humankind.

7 Luther held that there were two kingdoms: God's kingdom and the kingdom of the world. The kingdom of God and the kingdom of the world were distinct, as the former was spiritual while the latter was temporal. God's kingdom was governed by love and forgiveness rather than by laws. Luther believed that the two kingdoms should work together to make earthly organization successful.

8 Simpson (2019: 248–50) also emphasizes the many differences and conflicts within the Protestant tradition, most especially the fact that Calvinism distrusted institutions and remained in 'a permanent state of revolution' against them.

9 In the context of outlining the mission and purpose of higher education in Ireland, 2011–30, the Irish government regarded the development of human capital as central: 'If Ireland is to achieve its ambitions for recovery and development within an innovation-driven economy, it is essential to create *and enhance human capital* by expanding participation in higher education' (Government of Ireland 2011).

10 While a do-it-yourself biography is normalized, this is not to suggest that people are not also bound by institutional rules and controls; rather, they must work the institutional rules out for themselves: their classed, gendered, raced and related statuses are mediated by their own choices.

11 Whether the 'risk' dimensions of individualism are a defining feature of modernity is open to contention. Risk is not a new phenomenon

for those who have lived in poverty and income insecurity (Breman 2013). Beck and Beck-Gernsheim's (2002) focus on Western and Northern, so-called 'developed' countries ignores the fact that only a tiny proportion of the world's employees work in the Global North: just 3 per cent of the world's total workforce are located in so-called developed countries, including Europe and the US: in contrast, 16 per cent are in Sub-Saharan Africa, 26 per cent in East Asia and almost 33 per cent in South Asia (see ILO's 2013 *Global Employment Trends*). The ILO's (2019) *World Employment Social Outlook* report shows that 61 per cent of the world's workforce (2 billion people) is in informal employment, and many of these have no social protections and have never had any (Breman 2013). Moreover, 'over 25 per cent of workers in low- and middle-income countries were living in extreme or moderate poverty' in 2018 (ILO 2019: 6). And within the 'developed' world, social class, race and gender all impact on choices: there are structural constraints that impact on people's lives, regardless of how dominant the self-reflexive, life-planning and choice narratives may be (Mythen 2005; Atkinson 2007; Brock 2015).

12 In Europe and North America, the number of immigrants has almost doubled since the early 1990s to 141 million from just over 77 million (UN Population Division 2019).

13 Forced displacement, due to war, persecution, famine and economic and environmental hazards, also generates great migrations: in 2018 alone, almost 71 million people were forcibly displaced from their homes, the highest number on record, and more than half of these were children, under eighteen years of age (UNHCR 2020).

14 The Bologna Declaration of 1999 stated that the EU 'must in particular look at the objective of increasing the international competitiveness of the European system of higher education'. *The Official Journal of the European Union* stated in 2011 that there was a 'need to reform further the governance & financing structures of universities allowing for greater autonomy and accountability, so as to facilitate a more diversified revenue stream & more effective collaboration with the business world and to equip universities to participate in the knowledge triangle on a global scale'.

15 A good example of this is the Irish *National Strategy for Higher Education to 2030*, where there are multiple references to the role of higher education as servicing society, particularly the economy (Government of Ireland 2011).

16 Google, Facebook and Apple have been offering egg freezing as an employee benefit since 2014, a year after the US approved it for public consumption ('Why Facebook and Google offer egg freezing as a perk of the job', *The Telegraph*, 3 May 2019).

17 Political and economic rights have been closely aligned for many decades in ways that excluded women and poor people, with the right to vote being confined to property-owning men over the age of thirty until

the late nineteenth or early twentieth century in much of Europe. There were exceptions to this, however: women in Switzerland only gained the right to vote in Federal elections after a referendum in 1971; the right to vote in local council elections was the preserve of property owners in Northern Ireland up to the late 1960s.

18 The Irish Taoiseach (prime minister) Leo Varadkar stated in 2018 that the people who needed to be supported were the people 'who get up early in the morning'. In saying this, he was implying that people who are not employed or are dependent are less valuable.

7 Care-Harming Ideologies of Capitalism

1 Although less is known about psychological violence and its use by the state, it is now recognized as a very serious form of harm to children (Hibbard, Barlow, MacMillan, Committee on Child Abuse and Neglect and American Academy of Child and Adolescent Psychiatry 2012).

2 Wright (2010) lists ten major harms deriving from capitalism, including perpetuating eliminable forms of suffering, violating basic principles of social justice, undermining democracy and good community relations, and promoting environmental destruction.

3 Ideologies are systems of ideas and beliefs that are socially shared (Mannheim 1968). They are ways of thinking and seeing the world, forms of thought behaviour that operate normatively, to prescribe, justify and legitimate action, as well as operatively, directing action in particular ways (Malešević 2006).

4 The study, reported by Rosanvallon (2013), is that of Michel Forsé and Olivier Galland (eds.), *Les Français face aux inégalités et à la justice sociale* (Paris: Armand Colin, 2011).

5 Fourcade and Healy (2017: 14) use the term 'uber' 'to denote 'the meta-generalized or transcendent nature of this capital'. It is partly derived from the traditional forms of capital identified by Bourdieu (economic, cultural, social and symbolic), but also distinct from these. It classifies individuals' capital standing algorithmically, often without their knowledge or consent.

6 See *Irish Times*, 12 March 2020: https://www.irishtimes.com/business/innovation/clearview-from-billionaire-plaything-to-police-surveil-lance-tool-1.4196658.

7 The use of the Clearview app has been challenged by the attorney general of Vermont on privacy and other grounds: https://www.theverge.com/2020/5/7/21251387/clearview-ai-law-enforcement-police-facial-recognition-illinois-privacy-law. The Irish Council of Civil Liberties, ICCL, also initiated a legal challenge in June 2021 to the use of RTB (Real-time Bidding) which broadcasts intimate data gleaned from internet users apps and website usage to advertisers and others without a person's consent. https://www.iccl.ie/rtb-june-2021/.

8 This happens regularly in youth soccer clubs and in amateur dance and

drama competitions. In Ireland, it happens at Gaelic football games (an amateur sport) where scouts from the Australian Professional Football Leagues seek out potential recruits (stars) for the professional sport in Australia with the offer of high pay and other opportunities. Irish dancing mutated from being a cultural artefact with almost no market value to become a major market product with the development of *Riverdance* after the Eurovision Song Contest in 1994: https://www.irishtimes.com/business/retail-and-services/profits-drop-at-riverdance-but-the-shows-go-on-1.3751524.

9 PISA is the OECD's Programme for International Student Assessment. It assesses the educational progress of fifteen-year-olds across nation states on a limited range of educational competencies (reading, mathematics and science).

10 A national survey of mental illness in England in 2007 found that those who were in the 20 per cent lowest-income group were much more likely to experience 'a common mental health disorder' than those in the top 20 per cent. The differences were especially striking for men, with men in the lowest-income group being three times more likely to have a mental health problem than men in the highest group (after taking account of age). Men at the bottom quintile (20 per cent) were thirty-five times more likely to have depression than men in the top quintile (Wilkinson and Pickett 2018: 40).

11 The opposite is also true: data from the European Values study showed that the more equal a given country economically, the more likely people are to show solidarity by being willing to contribute to the welfare of others (Paskov and Dewilde 2012).

12 Due to the circulation of those in powerful positions at senior managerial professional levels, there is much overlapping between the private and the public sector professional/technical elite. This further consolidates their power, as they have insider knowledge of government that they can then deploy in the interests of capital (Sklair 2000). There are numerous examples of people who have served in senior positions in government, or in the civil or public service, moving to work for powerful commercial interests on leaving public service.

13 Although Wilkinson, Lucey and Melody's study applies to young middle-class women, the norms apply equally to young middle-class men.

14 Some of the problems with using algorithms to calculate grades automatically are discussed here: https://blogs.lse.ac.uk/impactofsocialsciences/2020/08/26/fk-the-algorithm-what-the-world-can-learn-from-the-uks-a-level-grading-fiasco.

15 At the individual level, metrics make people up; they invent people with labels and identifiers, which then become part of who they know themselves to be, and by which they are known to others (Hacking 1986). This also happens at the corporate level, as is evident in the rankings of universities, especially since the early 2000s; though rankings are arbitrary in several respects, not least because they do not measure

the entire work of the university, they create their own truth with serious consequences for the universities (Hazelkorn 2011). Even nation states cannot ignore rankings, as eurozone countries found in the financial crisis after 2008: Greece, Ireland, Spain and Portugal had their financial rating lowered by Standard and Poor's rating agency, greatly increasing the cost of borrowing in the financial markets.

16 It was estimated that the cost of the running the Research Assessment Exercise (now the Research Excellence Framework) in the UK was £250,000,000 in 2002 (Muller 2018: 75).

17 Equality of opportunity is a liberal concept. Liberal egalitarians typically define equality in terms of individuals rather than groups. While conservative liberals and left-leaning liberals vary, they all assume that inequality is endemic to society, so equality of opportunity is about equalizing the distribution of educational (and life) chances within an unequal society. For a discussion on the difference between liberal ideas of equality and equality of condition, see Baker, Lynch, Cantillon and Walsh (2004: ch. 2).

18 For Michael Young (1971) this formula was not a principle to be lauded as a fair means of operating social selection; quite the contrary – his book is an ironic critique of the idea, and of the moral judgement that would ensue from its implementation. To fail due to bad luck would be forgivable but to fail because you did not deserve to do well (lacked merit) is to be held accountable for failure and not so easily forgiven.

19 While those with most resources cannot 'buy' superior educational credentials directly, they can protect their likelihood of acquiring these through investment in private (socially exclusive) schooling and tuition (Smyth 2009), and private financial investment is advantaging children in high-income households in terms of educational attainment (Duncan and Murnane 2011).

20 Karabel's (2005) study of how the definitions of merit changed in Harvard, Yale and Princeton over the twentieth century in ways that enabled them to exclude unwanted outsiders, be these non-Whites, Jews, Catholics or women, is proof of the arbitrariness of merit. The inclusion of large numbers of students within contemporary universities who have dyslexia or other disabilities is also proof of how arbitrary exclusions 'on merit' have been historically.

21 A fascinating insight into this meritocratic mindset occurred recently with a colleague. In the context of discussing partners and home life, a recently recruited postdoctoral scholar asked my colleague 'What is it like living with a partner who doesn't have a PhD?' The young woman who asked the question was curious, as she and her partner both had PhDs; she thought it must be difficult to live with a person who did not have one. She knew that the partner of the person to whom she was speaking had both primary and postgraduate degrees, though not a PhD, as it was not relevant for their work. She seemed to think that someone with a PhD was a different kind of person!

22 The derisory term 'bed-blockers' was used widely in the UK and Ireland to refer to older people who were chronically ill in acute hospitals but unable to go home due to lack of care supports. They were framed as 'wasting' beds needed by other (mostly younger) people.

8 The Violation of Non-Human Animals

1 Many thanks to the New Zealand writer Philip McKibbin and to Luciana Lolich, my UCD colleague, for helpful comments on an early draft of this chapter.

2 Like Nibert (2013), I believe that using terms such as *non-human animals* or *other animals* is a way of contesting the false binary between human animals and other animals. For linguistic convenience, I do use *animals* at times in the text.

3 References to non-human animals include birds.

4 There has been an initiative to create a global framework for the protection of animals at the UN level. The UN Convention on Animal Health and Protection (UNCAHP) was drafted in 2018 with the help of GAL, the Global Animal Law Association: https://www.uncahp.org/.

5 'Anthropocentrism' is the belief that humankind is the central or most important element of existence. Eugene Stoermer, a freshwater biologist who studied the Great Lakes of North America, proposed the name 'the Anthropocene' in 2000 to indicate the current geological age of anthropogenic (human-origin) activities and processes that are acidifying the waters and changing the nature of life on Earth. Those processes, emanating from at least the mid-eighteenth century, related to the use of the steam engine and the massive expansion in the use of fossil fuels.

6 https://www.theguardian.com/world/2020/mar/28/is-factory-farming-to-blame-for-coronavirus.

7 There are fewer euphemisms for lamb. The meat of sheep was traditionally known as mutton in Ireland, and 'lamb' was used only for 'spring' (young) lambs among butchers. However, 'mutton' had a negative connotation as 'old and tough', and perhaps this explains the use of 'lamb' rather than 'mutton'; it is a marketing strategy.

8 There are many reasons for the lack of respect for non-human animals. For one, there is a serious lack of education and research on the harms humans do to other animals. By contrast, the advertising and lobbying of the meat industry promoting the eating of meat as morally sustainable, and a health necessity, is systematic and sustained.

9 https://www.independent.ie/business/farming/beef-barons-worth-over-2billion-34475145.html.

10 Young (1990: 37) defines domination as 'the institutional constraint on self-determination', and oppression as 'the institutional constraint on self-development'. Although Young uses these terms with respect to humans, non-human animals are both dominated and oppressed by humans, in Young's terms. Moreover, in human terms alone, the

distributive paradigm fails to recognize fully how procedures and processes of governance and decision-making can be unjust.

11 While the Marxist distributive tradition does recognize the power of structures, especially of social class, it prioritizes economic relations of production (between humans) as the primary site of injustice, and shares liberals' practice of neglecting care relations in families as sites of injustice (Pateman 1988; Okin 1994). The invisibility of care as a justice issue also applies to the care of non-human animals.

12 Kalof's book is wide-ranging, with contributions from over thirty scholars on non-human animals. Contributions are drawn from diverse academic traditions including sociology, ecology, politics, philosophy, animal ethics, anthropology, science, history and zooarchaeology.

13 There are several traditions addressing animals' rights and welfare, including Singer's (1975) utilitarianism, Regan's rights perspective (1983) and Francione's animal ethicist and rights perspective (1995, 2000, 2009), some of which address the role of capitalism in the abuse of animals (Nibert 2013). The ethic-of-care and radical feminists (Donovan and Adams 2007) and ecofeminists (Gaard and Gruen 1993; Gruen 1996, 2014) represent another tradition, as does the work of Haraway (2003, 2007, 2016), who proposes having a dialogical relationship between human and non-human animals and other species.

14 For Singer, rights depend on attributes and interests, and as Singer does not say which interests different species have, it is unclear what unique rights non-human animals have.

15 Cows and bulls eat taller grasses while sheep prefer forbs, smaller grasses and clover; goats eat leaves, twigs, vines and shrubs rather than grazing continually on the ground like sheep, cows, bulls or calves.

16 Francione's perspective (the abolitionist position) is critiqued by Garner because it does not take account of what Garner regards as fundamental moral differences between humans and other animal species. Moreover, Garner (2013) claims that, as we live in a non-ideal world, we need a transitional theory that takes account of how much work there is to do to enhance even basic rights for animals not to endure suffering. His interest-based theory of animal rights focuses on prohibiting suffering rather than addressing the issue of treating animals as property.

17 Nibert suggests that humans' relationships with animals incorporated into human social and economic networks should be referred to not as 'domestication' but as '*domesecration*' because such engagement generally involves non-human animals' effective objectification and enslavement.

18 The use of this term by Francione has caused controversy, as some claim he has stigmatized those who have clinical schizophrenia. Francione has rejected this claim, noting that he is talking about a moral condition, not about mental health. He wants to highlight how human beings are delusional and confused on moral issues: they fail to see that they are party to the abuse of animals by eating them after they are killed by others: https://www.abolitionistapproach.com/a-note-on-moral-schizophrenia.

19 https://www.wired.com/story/why-meatpacking-plants-have-become-covid-19-hot-spots.
20 For Ireland, see https://www.thejournal.ie/meat-processing-plants-covid 19-5102151-May2020. For Germany, see https://www.dw.com/en/germany-meat-industry-statistics/a-53876016.
21 In the sixteenth century the English elite were seeking to extend their control over Ireland, while they were also involved in their own civil wars as well as wars with European neighbours. Ireland became a site where England's civil wars and its European wars were fought out, not least because the Irish earls and chieftains aligned themselves with mainland European adversaries of the British crown to help further their own resistance to English rule in Ireland. There were four major plantations arising from attempts to supress Irish uprisings against the crown: one in Laois/Offaly, beginning *c.*1556 and instigated by Queen Mary; a second in the province of Munster in 1586, instigated by Queen Elizabeth I after the Reformation, where most of the best land was taken by force and granted to English settlers (McCarthy-McMorrow 1986); a third in Ulster (the Northern Province of Ireland), beginning 1609 (Bardon 2011); and a fourth, and arguably the most violent, led by Oliver Cromwell and his new 'Model Army'. The Cromwellian plantation in 1649 involved systematic massacres of entire towns that resisted invasion, notably Drogheda and Wexford, the repression of Irish monasteries, and the extensive confiscation of lands under the Act of Settlement 1652. The aim, as stated in the preamble to the Act, was 'that a total reducement and settlement of that nation may, with God's blessing, be speedily effected'.
22 Not only are more cow, bulls, calves, pigs and sheep being raised in Europe, as elsewhere, but more and more of them are being reared in intensified factory-farming conditions. Almost three quarters of the livestock units (72.2 per cent) in the EU-28 were reared on very large farms in 2013 (Greenpeace 2019). See also Eurostat data 2017: https://ec.europa.eu/eurostat/statistics-explained/index.php?title=Small_and_large_farms_in_the_EU_-_statistics_from_the_farm_structure_survey&oldid=357625.
23 Details of payments made to support farmers directly under the CAP are listed here: https://ec.europa.eu/info/food-farming-fisheries/key-policies/common-agricultural-policy/income-support/income-support-explain ed_en#levelofsupportavailable.
24 Data from the Irish government agriculture and food development authority (Teagasc) shows that in 2018, the subsidy payments comprised 74 per cent of the family farm income of the average farm in Ireland. The figure was much higher for bull/steer, heifer and sheep farmers: https://www.teagasc.ie/publications/2020/cap-provides-important-funds-for-irish-farms.php.
25 While the European Union currently has around 12 million farms, with an average size of 15 hectares (just over 37 acres), the United States only has

2 million farms, with an average size of 180 hectares (444 acres): https://www.farm-europe.eu/travaux/has-the-common-agricultural-policy-realised-its-income-objective/#:~:text=While%20the%20European%20Union%20currently,number%20is%2086.3%25%20in%20Europe.

26 https://www.usda.gov/media/press-releases/2020/05/19/usda-announces-details-direct-assistance-farmers-through.

27 Citing Australia Bureau of Statistics national data on land management, 2013.

28 In Ireland, 'meat' and 'livestock' exports equate to over 30 per cent of total food and drink exports and were valued at €3.9 billion in 2019. Bord Bia's vision for the Irish dairy sector is 'To be the world's most trusted exporter of sustainably driven and technically advanced high-quality dairy products to customers worldwide': https://www.bordbia.ie/industry/irish-sector-profiles/meat-industry/#:~:text=Meat%20and%20Livestock%20Review%20%26%20Outlook,10%25%20reaching%20%E2%82%AC2.1%20billion.

29 See Hilary Rose's definition of caring labour (1983).

30 It is *not* suggested that the genders are naturally or essentially different, merely that they are socialized differently.

31 The global Intergovernmental Panel on Climate Change has been documenting many of these changes: https://www.ipcc.ch.

9 Violence and Capitalism

1 A special edition of *Current Sociology* was devoted to the subject of care in 2018 (Aulenbacher, Lutz and Riegraf 2018). There is also a large literature on the sociology of health care. However, this has a very particular and specialized focus. It does not deal generally with issues of everyday love and care in households, between family, friends, kin and neighbours, except where they relate to health.

2 One woman contributed to this special issue of the *European Journal of Social Theory* (2013) and six men.

3 The gendered division of labour *within* disciplines and fields holds true even in seemingly gender-neutral fields such as demography (Krapf, Kreyenfeld and Wolf 2016).

4 The South Korean satirical film *Parasite* (2020) gives an interesting portrayal of how class polarization under capitalism produces greed and self-interest with different faces. The face of wealth is manifest in all the fine things that the rich can buy: fine housing, clothing, holidays, honed bodies and clear countenances (the Park family). They live off the poor, invisibly, at least to themselves. Those who are without money, education or job opportunities live on the borders of destitution (the Kim family) developing despised attributes of connivance, deceit and dishonesty, just to be able to eat, to survive.

5 The Israeli occupation of Palestinian lands is one of the prime examples of this type of illegal occupation. Despite several UN resolutions, and

the International Court of Justice holding that Israeli settlements in the West Bank, East Jerusalem and the Golan Heights are in violation of international law (Article 49 of the Fourth Geneva Convention), Israel has maintained control over these territories through the use of force.

6 Begging is only an offence in Ireland if it is intimidating people, but poor people can be moved on by police when begging, which can lead to an offence being committed if they refuse to move.

7 Theft is, by definition, taking goods without violence; it is distinct from robbery, which does involve some type of violence. It is the fourth most common reason for imprisonment in England and Wales.

8 At year-end 2018, more than 2.1 million people were in prison in the US; this represents an incarceration rate of 655 persons per 100,000 (Walmsley 2018). By comparison, the median rate of imprisonment in Ireland was 78 and in Western Europe generally 81 per 100,000: https://www.prisonstudies.org/news/icpr-launches-12th-edition-world-prison-population-list.

9 Five of the protesters, all of whom were local residents, farmers and fishermen/women, were also imprisoned for protesting and blocking the entrance to the Shell site: http://www.thepipethefilm.com/main-sect/crew/director-risteard-o-domhnaill.

10 https://www.unhcr.org/en-ie/news/press/2015/7/5592b9b36/mediterranean-crisis-2015-six-months-refugee-migrant-numbers-highest-record.html. In 2019 alone, 1,885 women, men and children lost their lives while trying to cross the Mediterranean to Europe, while 27,200 refugees and asylum seekers remained on the Greek Aegean islands, where there was no clear plan for their future: https://www.unhcr.org/refugeebrief/latest-issues.

11 In 2010, Traveller men's life expectancy was 15 years less than that of settled men while Traveller women's life expectancy was 11.5 years less (UCD 2010). It had not improved much by 2021. https://www.paveepoint.ie/ageing-for-travellers-is-40-years-due-to-low-life-expectancy/.

12 There is virtually no area of life that is not reliant in some way on technology, be it through the use of mobile phones, computers, cars, lorries, heavy machinery, aeroplanes, fridges, cookers, washing machines, cement, tarmacadam, clothes, footwear or the production of food.

13 This is a quote from 'Let them eat pollution', *The Economist*, 8 February 1992. Though Summers subsequently denied this was a policy proposal, claiming that he was merely being ironic, this was not how it was perceived internationally.

14 Marx observed in the *Communist Manifesto* that that which is held through violence can generally only be overthrown through violence: 'the violent overthrow of the bourgeoisie lays the foundation for the sway of the proletariat' (Marx 1969).

15 https://www.army-technology.com/features/arms-exports-by-country.

16 A mechanical engineer by training, Taylor worked closely with the US military, encouraging them to deploy his concept of 'scientific

management' within the army, with considerable success (Petersen 1989).

17 Though men still dominate fields of power in the academy such as science and technology, both numerically and in terms of seniority.

18 A series of studies in Spain shows that women are less likely to be susceptible to partner violence in households where *both* partners are employed. If women alone are working this does not reduce physical violence, as men may try to assert what they feel is their past power and status through violence (Alonso-Borrego and Carrasco 2017).

19 The civil war in Northern Ireland from 1968 to 1998 was driven by complex geopolitical, sectarian and nationalist issues, while the wars in 'Kosovo, Afghanistan and Iraq were initiated and fought much more for ideological and geopolitical reasons than for reasons arising from global economic logic' (Malešević 2010a: 327).

10 Resisting Intellectually, Politically, Culturally and Educationally

1 Numerous studies I was involved in in the field of education showed that people resisted the definition of themselves as simple economic actors. Educators actively resisted the neoliberalization of education in the early 2000s (Lynch, Grummell and Devine 2012); young people sought respect and authority in schools that allowed them to become who they wanted to be; they resisted the imposition of arbitrary power and control (Lynch and Lodge 2002). Luciana Lolich's research showed how students in higher education did not see themselves simply as fodder for a knowledge-based economy; their care relational lives mattered (Lolich and Lynch 2016).

2 Ideal moral theories try to work out what an ideal just society would look like in the abstract, and from there to establish people's moral obligations in realizing that ideal. 'Many global normative theorists, cosmopolitans and social liberals alike, have followed John Rawls in adopting constructivist reasoning as a method of justifying their preferred principles. The constructivist method relies on shared (if often inchoate) notions about justice to guide the theorist's thinking about its specific demands. These notions are modelled into an initial choice situation, or ICS, a purely hypothetical situation characterized so as to lead to a certain conception of justice' (Goodhart 2018: 47).

3 The goal of the Equality Studies Centre was to create a safe and critical intellectual space for activists and scholars to work together for radical egalitarian change (Lynch 1995). It set out to engage in emancipatory and dialogical research *with* rather than *on* groups (Lynch 1999). Consequently, when writing *Equality* (Baker, Lynch, Cantillon and Walsh 2004), we had many dialogues and meetings about the text with working-class community activists, trade unionists, women' groups, people with disabilities, and groups representing Travellers and ethnic minorities. As many of our Masters students in Equality Studies were

drawn from these groups, this was a further fount of education, dialogue and learning for us as academics.

4 A key theme in Boltanski and Chiapello's (2005) work on *The New Spirit of Capitalism*.

5 Wiebers and Feigin (2020) cite the US Centers for Disease Control and Prevention (CDC), who observed that '3 in every 4 new or emerging infectious diseases in people come from animals.' These infections are caused not only by viruses but also by bacteria, fungi, and parasites from a variety of animal sources (Centers for Disease Control and Prevention 2020: https://www.cdc.gov/onehealth/basics/zoonotic-diseases.html). The authors note that 'The alarming increase in frequency of these lethal zoonotic diseases relates in large part to our human-dominated ecosystem with increasingly unnatural human–animal close contact, grossly aberrant crowding of animals for human purposes, destruction of animal habitats, and vast numbers of highly mobile humans to swiftly carry these diseases throughout the world' (Wiebers and Feigin 2020: 2).

6 While recognizing that abstract rules can and do apply, they must be complemented by engaging with the particularities of each person/group and situation.

7 Brian Hayes, a former member of the Irish Dáil (parliament), a former minister of state and a former MEP (Member of the European Parliament), is now working as head of the Banking Federation of Ireland. John Moran, former senior civil servant, secretary general of the Department of Finance, and interim head of the National Land Development Agency, left the latter post to join the board of financial technology company, Revolut.

8 The Freedom Party in Austria, Le Pen and the National Front in France, Golden Dawn in Greece, the Northern League in Italy and Alternative for Germany.

9 Ireland: http://cgireland.org; Vermont: https://vcgn.org; Toronto: http://tcgn.ca.

10 They were part of the Zapatista Army of National Liberation.

11 Seventy thousand women from different parts of the region met in Chaco, Argentina, in 2017 for the thirty-second National Encounter of Women, held every year in the week of 11 October, to discuss what had to be done and what strategies to adopt to change the world (Federici 2019: 135).

12 https://idwfed.org/en.

13 The UN Convention on the Rights of Persons with Disabilities came into force in 2008.

14 https://www.mrci.ie/great-care-co-op.

15 Fifty-five countries are projected to have a population decline by 2050: https://populationmatters.org/news/2019/06/un-report-small-change-family-size-big-change-future-population.

16 Friedman (2013) compared graduates from 1992 and 2012 and found that the number who planned to have children dropped by nearly half

over the twenty-year period. While planning not to have children is not proof that a person will not have them in the future, it does suggest a negative view of that possibility.

17 https://renegadeinc.com/the-politics-of-love-where-to-from-here.

18 https://www.thejournal.ie/childcare-protest-today-4992751-Feb2020.

19 Many thanks to Sara Burke of Trinity College Dublin for bringing this to my attention.

20 There is a need for a resistance model rather than a consensus model of democracy (Medina 2013), not least because consensus often leads to undue pressure or even coercion on dissenting minorities (Anderson 2006).

21 Digitalized communication can help in this as it allows people who are bound to a given place/space, due to non-substitutable care responsibilities, age, disability, mobility impediments and/or remoteness of location, to organize online. Even with all its mining/commercial limitations, and the need for in-presence meetings to mobilize effectively, online communication and mobilization can help initiate action.

Postscript

1 Senior scholars (regardless of discipline) are relatively socially privileged people; they are also disproportionately men, but sometimes women, and are given a 'production pass' out of doing hands-on caring within the household (Tronto 2013: 82).

2 The importance of virtual communication was brought home to me when my mother started to cry with delight on seeing her granddaughter (who was spending one year studying abroad at the time) online via Skype. Born in 1912, my mother saw many of her neighbours and friends emigrate from the West of Ireland, never to be seen again by their friends or families. She thought we were very fortunate to be able to communicate digitally. Emigration was like a death in the family in Ireland in the early to mid-twentieth century. Hence, when someone was leaving for the United States, a party was often held; it was known as an 'American wake' (a wake is a vigil after death).

3 https://blogs.worldbank.org/opendata/impact-covid-19-coronavirus-global-poverty-why-sub-saharan-africa-might-be-region-hardest.

4 See also Fergal Bowers, health correspondent for Radio Telefís Éireann (RTE), 27 2020, based on Department of Health data: https://www.rte.ie/news/coronavirus/2020/0527/1143036-covid-deaths-ireland.

5 As the UK did not count all deaths in care homes in the early stages of the pandemic, some suggest the figures may be much higher (Amnesty International 2020).

6 About two thirds of paid care workers are women, and over 75 per cent of unpaid care workers. Throughout the world, 'there are 215 million care workers in care sectors (in health and social work and in education) and 70.1 million domestic workers ... When workers supporting care

provision are added, the global care workforce reaches 381 million, or 11.5 per cent of total global employment. Women make up 65 per cent of the global care workforce. This proportion is higher among care workers in care occupations (66 per cent) and among domestic workers (70 per cent)' (ILO 2018: 8).

7 What the pandemic showed was that the very old and/or vulnerable, adults with severe intellectual disabilities and children, especially living within institutions, have no mechanisms at their disposal to become an organized political voice. They generally lacked capacity to exert a claim on their rights. While their families or friends could advocate on their behalf, those who were very ill and living in institutions/residential facilities especially did not have a direct way of entering public discourse or debate and claiming and vindicating their rights politically.

8 As Lanoix (2020: 49) observes, 'In the Rawlsian social contract model, persons with advanced dementia and those who are severely cognitively impaired are situated outside the principles of justice' because they are assumed not to be fully rational, and therefore unable to enter into social contract. What this model ignores it that, as people age, they still have needs, interests and relationships that matter to them. They have agency. The citizen must be thought of not as 'this idealised rational being, but as someone who needs care in infancy, may need care later and has varying capacities throughout her life'. There is a need 'to accept age indeterminacy and acknowledge the reality of human variability' (Lanoix 2020: 52).

References

Acker, J. 1990. Hierarchies, jobs, bodies: A theory of gendered organizations. *Gender & Society*, 4: 139–58.

Acker, J. 2006. Inequality regimes: Gender, class, and race in organizations. *Gender & Society*, 20 (4): 441–64.

Acker, K. 2004. Gender, capitalism and globalization. *Critical Sociology*, 30 (1): 17–41.

Adair, V., Brown, P., Clark, N., Perez-Cotrich, R. and Stanfield S. 2007. Poverty and storytelling in higher education: Telling 'the missing story of ourselves'. *Storytelling, Self, Society*, 3: 135–55.

Adam, B. 1995. *Timewatch: The Social Analysis of Time*. Cambridge: Polity.

Adam, B. 2002. The gendered time politics of globalization: Of shadowlands and elusive justice. *Feminist Review*, 70: 3–29.

Adam, B. 2004. *Time*. Cambridge: Polity.

Adams, C. J. 2000. *The Sexual Politics of Meat: A Feminist-Vegetarian Critical Theory*, 2nd edn. New York: Continuum.

Adams, C. J. 2007. The war on compassion. In Donovan, J. and Adams, C. J. (eds.), *The Feminist Care Tradition in Animal Ethics*. New York: Columbia University Press, pp. 21–36.

Adorno, T. W. 1978. *Minima Moralia*, trans. Jephcott, E. F. N. London: Verso.

Adorno, T. W. 2005. *Critical Models: Interventions and Catchwords*, trans. Pickford, H. W. New York: Columbia University Press.

Afsar, R. 2009. *Unravelling the Vicious Cycle of Recruitment: Labour Migration from Bangladesh to the Gulf States*. Geneva: ILO.

Ahmed, S. 2004. *The Politics of Emotions*. Edinburgh: Edinburgh University Press.

Ahmed, S. 2012. *On Being Included: Racism and Diversity in Institutional Life*. Durham, NC: Duke University Press.

Alatas, S. F. 2003. Academic dependency and the global division of labour in the social sciences. *Current Sociology*, 51(6): 599–613.

Albertini, M., Ballarino, G. and De Luca, D. 2020. Social class, work-related incomes, and socio-economic polarization in Europe, 2005–2014. *European Sociological Review*, 1–20. DOI: 10.1093/esr/jcaa005.

Alcock, R. 2020. The unconscious countermovement and the conscious Polanyian movement: A new vocabulary for contemporary Polanyian scholarship. *New Political Economy*, 1–17. DOI: 10.1080/13563467.2020.1721452.

Alexander, S. 2017. *Wild Democracy: Degrowth, Permaculture and the Simpler Way.* Melbourne: Simplicity Institute.

Allen, K. 2007. *The Corporate Takeover of Ireland.* Dublin: Irish Academic Press.

Alonso-Borrego, C. and Carrasco, R. 2017. Employment and the risk of domestic violence: Does the breadwinner's gender matter? *Applied Economics*, 49 (50): 5074–91.

Althusser, L. 1971. *Ideology and Ideological State Apparatuses*, trans. Brewster, B. In *Lenin and Philosophy and Other Essays*. New York: Monthly Review Press.

Alvaredo, F., Chancel, L., Pikettty, T., Saez, E. and Zucman, G. (coords.). 2018. *World Inequality Report 2018*. https://wir2018.wid.world.

Amnesty International. 2020. *As if Expendable: The UK Government's Failure to Protect Older People in Care Homes during the Covid-19 Pandemic.* London: Amnesty.

Andersen, D. and Torbenfeldt Bengtsson, T. 2019. Timely care: Rhythms of bureaucracy and everyday life in cases involving youths with complex needs. *Time & Society*, 28 (4): 1509–31.

Anderson, B. 2000. *Doing the Dirty Work? The Global Politics of Domestic Labour.* London: Zed Books.

Anderson, C. 2016. *White Rage: The Unspoken Truth of Our Racial Divide.* New York: Bloomsbury.

Anderson, E. 2006. The epistemology of democracy. *Episteme*, 3: 8–22.

Apple, M. 1979. *Ideology and Curriculum.* Boston: Routledge and Kegan Paul.

Apple, M. 1982. *Education and Power.* New York: Routledge.

Apple, M. 2013a. *Can Education Change Society?* New York: Routledge.

Apple, M. 2013b. Can education change society? Du Bois, Woodson and the politics of social transformation. *Review of Education*, 1 (1): 32–56.

Apple, M. and Beane, J. (eds.). 2007. *Democratic Schools*, 2nd edn. Portsmouth: Heinemann.

Arcari, P. 2017. Normalised, human-centric discourses of meat and animals in climate change, sustainability, and food security literature. *Agriculture and Human Values*, 34: 69–86.

Archer, M. S. 2000. *Being Human.* Cambridge: Cambridge University Press.

Arnsperger, C. and Varoufakis, Y. 2003. Toward a theory of solidarity. *Eerkenntis*, 59 (2): 157–88.

Asimakopoulos, J. and Gilman-Opalsky, R. (eds.). 2018. *Against Capital in the Twenty-First Century: A Reader of Radical Undercurrents.* Philadelphia: Temple University Press.

Atkinson, W. 2007. Beck, individualization and the death of class: A critique. *British Journal of Sociology*, 58 (3): 349–66.

Aulenbacher, B. and Leiblfinger, M. 2019. The 'fictitious commodity' care and the reciprocity of caring. In Atzmüller, R., Aulenbacher, B., Brand, U., Décieux, F., Fischer, K. et al. (eds.), *Capitalism in Transformation: Movements and Countermovements in the 21st Century*. Cheltenham: Edward Elgar, pp. 245–60.

Aulenbacher, B., Lutz, H. and Riegraf, B. 2018. Introduction: Towards a global sociology of care and care work. *Current Sociology*, 66 (4): 495–502.

Badgett, M. V. L. and Folbre, N. 1999. Assigning care: Gender norms and economic outcomes. *International Labour Review*, 138 (3): 311–26.

Bagilhole, B. and White, K. (eds.). 2011. *Gender, Power and Management: A Cross-Cultural Analysis of Higher Education*. Basingstoke: Palgrave Macmillan.

Baker, J., Lynch, K., Cantillon, S. and Walsh, J. 2004. *Equality: From Theory to Action*. Basingstoke: Palgrave Macmillan.

Balbo, N., Billari, F. and Mills, M. 2013. Fertility in advanced societies: A review of research. *European Journal of Population/Revue Européenne de Démographie*, 29 (1): 1–38.

Baldwin, P. 1990. *The Politics of Social Solidarity: Class Bases of the European Welfare State, 1875–1975*. Cambridge: Cambridge University Press.

Ball, S. J. 2003. *Class Strategies and the Education Market*. London: RoutledgeFalmer.

Ball, S. J. 2012. Performativity, commodification and commitment: An I-Spy guide to the neoliberal university. *British Journal of Educational Studies*, 60: 17–28.

Banerjee, A. and Rewegan, A. 2017. Intensifying relational care: The challenge of dying in long-term residential care. *Journal of Canadian Studies*, 50; 393–421.

Barbalet, J. (ed.). 2002. *Emotions and Sociology*. Oxford: Blackwell.

Barbalet, J. 2010. Citizenship in Max Weber. *Journal of Classical Sociology*, 10 (3): 201–16.

Bardon, J. 2011. *The Plantation of Ulster: The British Colonisation of the North of Ireland in the Seventeenth Century*. Dublin: Gill and Macmillan.

Barnes, C. and Mercer, G. 2005. Disability, work, and welfare: Challenging the social exclusion of disabled people. *Work, Employment and Society*, 19 (3): 527–45.

Barnes, M. 2006. *Caring and Social Justice*. Basingstoke: Palgrave Macmillan.

Bastian, M., Baraitser, L., Flexer, M. J., Hom, A. R. and Salisbury, L. 2020. Introduction: The social life of time. *Time & Society*, 29(2): 289–96.

Bauman, Z. 2001. *The Individualized Society*. Cambridge: Polity.

Bauman, Z. 2003. *Liquid Love: On the Frailty of Human Bonds*. Cambridge: Polity.

Beck, U. 1992. *Risk Society: Towards a New Modernity*. London: Sage.

Beck, U. and Beck-Gernsheim, E. 2002. *Individualization: Institutionalized Individualism and its Social and Political Consequences*. London: Sage.

Becker, G. 1964. *Human Capital: A Theoretical and Empirical Analysis with Special Reference to Education*. Chicago: University of Chicago Press.

Becker, H. 1965. A theory of the allocation of time. *Economic Journal*, 199: 495–517.

Bedaso, A., Ayalew, M., Mekonnen, N. and Duko, B. 2020. Global estimates of the prevalence of depression among prisoners: A systematic review and meta-analysis. *Depression Research and Treatment*, 2020, art. 3695209. DOI: org/10.1155/2020/3695209.

Benhabib, S. 1992. *Situating the Self*. Cambridge: Polity.

Berlant, L. 2007. Slow death: Sovereignty, obesity, lateral agency. *Critical Inquiry*, 33: 754–80.

Berry, D. and Bell, M. P. 2017. Worker cooperatives: Alternative governance for caring and precarious work. *Equality, Diversity and Inclusion: An International Journal*, 37 (4): 376–91.

Bettio, F., Simonazzi, A. and Villa, P. 2006. Change in care regimes and female migration: The 'care drain' in the Mediterranean. *Journal of European Social Policy*, 16 (3): 271–85. DOI: 10.1177/0958928706065598.

Bhopal, K. 2018. *The Experiences of Black and Minority Ethnic Academics: A Comparative Study of the Unequal Academy*. London: Routledge.

Bianchi, S. M., Sayer, L. C., Milkie, M. A. and Robinson, J. P. 2012. Housework: Who did, does or will do it, and how much does it matter? *Social Forces*, 91 (1): 55–63.

Block, F. 2018. *Capitalism: The Future of an Illusion*. Oakland: University of California Press.

Bloom, B. S. (ed.). 1964. *Taxonomy of Educational Objectives: The Classification of Educational Goals. Handbook 1: Cognitive Domain*. London: Longmans.

Boland, E. 1996. *Object Lessons: The Life of the Woman and the Poet in Our Time*. New York: W. W. Norton.

Boland, T. and Griffin, R. 2018. The purgatorial ethic and the spirit of welfare. *Journal of Classical Sociology*, 18 (2): 87–103.

Boltanski, L. and Chiapello, E. 2005. *The New Spirit of Capitalism*. New York: Verso.

Boltanski, L. and Porter, C. 2012. *Love and Justice as Competences: Three Essays on the Sociology of Action*. Cambridge: Polity.

Bolton, S. C. and Laaser, K. 2019. The moral economy: Flexible employment and layers of disconnection. In Gall, G. (ed.), *Handbook of the Politics of Labour, Work and Employment*. Cheltenham: Edward Elgar. pp. 201–13.

Bomert, C. and Leinfellner, S. 2017. Images, ideals, and constraints in times of neoliberal transformations: Reproduction and profession as conflicting or complementary spheres in academia? *European Educational Research Journal*, 16: 106–22.

Bordo, S. 1986. The Cartesian masculinization of thought. *Signs: Journal of Women in Culture and Society*, 11 (3): 439–56.

Borer, V. and Lawn, M. 2013. Governing education systems by shaping data: From the past to the present, from national to international perspectives. *European Educational Research Journal*, 12 (1): 48–52.

Bourdieu, P. 1984. *Distinction: A Social Critique of the Judgement of Taste*. London: Routledge.

Bourdieu, P. 1990. *The Logic of Practice*, trans. Nice, R. Cambridge: Polity.

Bourdieu, P. 1996. *The State Nobility: Elite Schools in the Field of Power*, trans. Clough, L. C. Cambridge: Polity.

Bourdieu, P. and Passeron, J. C. 1977. *Reproduction in Education, Society and Culture*. Beverly Hills: Sage.

Breman, J. 2013. A bogus concept? [Review of G. Standing, *The Precariat*, 2011]. *New Left Review*, 84: 130–8.

Brennan, T. 2004. *The Transmission of Affect*. Ithaca: Cornell University Press.

Bresser-Pereira, L. C. 2012. Five models of capitalism. *Brazilian Journal of Political Economy*, 32 (1): 21–32.

Bridges, T. and Pascoe, C. J. 2014. Hybrid masculinities: New directions in the sociology of men and masculinities. *Sociology Compass*, 8: 246–58.

Britton, D. 2000. The epistemology of the gendered organization. *Gender & Society*, 14 (3): 418–34.

Brock, S. A. M. 2015. The individualization thesis and mothering children with disabilities. *Journal of Family Studies*, 21 (3): 261–81.

Bröckling, U. 2015. *The Entrepreneurial Self: Fabricating a New Type of Subject*. London: Sage.

Brown, P. 2013. Education, opportunity and the prospects for social mobility. *British Journal of Sociology of Education*, 34 (5–6): 678–700.

Brown, P., Lauder, H. and Ashton, F. 2011. *The Global Auction: The Broken Promises of Education, Jobs, and Incomes*. Oxford: Oxford University Press.

Brown, P. and Tannock, S. 2009. Education, meritocracy and the global war for talent. *Journal of Education Policy*, 24 (4): 377–92.

Brown, W. 1995. *States of Injury: Power and Freedom in Late Modernity*. Princeton: Princeton University Press.

Brown, W. 2005. *Edgework: Critical Essays on Knowledge and Politics*. Princeton: Princeton University Press.

Brown, W. 2015. *Undoing the Demos: Neoliberalism's Stealth Revolution*. New York: Zone Books.

Browne, H. 2013. *The Frontman: Bono (In the Name of Power)*. New York: Verso.

Brunkhorst, H. 2009. The transformation of solidarity and the enduring impact of monotheism. *Philosophy and Social Criticism*, 35 (1–2): 93–103.

Brush, B. L. and Vasupuram, R. 2006. Nurses, nannies and caring work: Importation, visibility and marketability. *Nursing Inquiry*, 13: 181–5.

Bryson, V. 2007. *Gender and the Politics of Time*. Bristol: Policy Press.

Bubeck, D. 1995. *Care, Justice and Gender*. Oxford: Oxford University Press.

Budds, K., Hogg, M. and Banister, E. 2017. Parenting agendas: An empirical study of intensive mothering and infant cognitive development. *The Sociological Review*, 65 (2): 336–52.

Burawoy, M. 2016. The neoliberal university: Ascent of the spiralists. *Critical Sociology*, 42: 941–2.

Butler, J. 2004. *Precarious Life: The Power of Mourning and Violence.* New York: Verso.

Butler, J. 2020. *The Force of Non-Violence: An Ethico-Political Bind.* New York: Verso.

Butler, J., Gambetti, Z. and Sabsay, L. (eds.). 2016. *Vulnerability in Resistance.* Durham, NC: Duke University Press.

Bygnes, S. and Bivand Erdal, M. 2017. Liquid migration, grounded lives: Considerations about future mobility and settlement among Polish and Spanish migrants in Norway. *Journal of Ethnic and Migration Studies*, 43 (1): 102–18.

Cacho, L. M. 2012. *Social Death: Racialized Rightlessness and the Criminalization of the Unprotected.* New York: New York University Press,.

Cantillon, S. and Lynch, K. 2017. Affective equality: Love matters. *Hypatia*, 32 (1): 169–86.

Cappellini, B., Harman, V., Marilli, A. and Parsons, E. 2019. Intensive mothering in hard times: Foucauldian ethical self-formation and cruel optimism. *Journal of Consumer Culture*, 19 (4): 469–92.

Cardozo, K. M. 2017. Academic labor: Who cares? *Critical Sociology*, 43 (3): 405–28.

Care Collective (Chatzidakis, A., Hakim, J., Littler, J., Rottenbergh, C. and Segal, L.). 2020. *The Care Manifesto: The Politics of Interdependence.* London: Verso.

Carneiro, R. L. 1970. A theory of the origin of the state. *Science*, 169: 733–58.

Casalini, B. 2017. A materialist analysis of contemporary feminist movements. *Anthropological Theory*, 17 (4): 497–517.

Casalini, B. 2020. Care and injustice. *International Journal of Care and Caring*, 4 (1): 59–73.

Cederström, C. 2019. *State of Nordic Fathers.* Copenhagen: Nordic Council of Ministers.

Champeny, M., Pereira, C., Sweet, L., Khin, M., Ndiaye Coly, A. et al. 2016. Point-of-sale promotion of breastmilk substitutes and commercially produced complementary foods in Cambodia, Nepal, Senegal and Tanzania. *Maternal & Child Nutrition*, 12: 126–39.

Charles, M. and Bradley, K. 2009. Indulging our gendered selves: Sex segregation by field of study in 44 countries. *American Journal of Sociology*, 114: 924–76.

Chatzitheochari, S. and Arber, S. 2012. Class, gender and time poverty: a time-use analysis of British workers' free time resources. *The British Journal of Sociology*, 63 (3): 451–71.

Chou, H. and Edge, N. 2012. 'They are happier and having better lives than I am': The impact of using Facebook on perceptions of others' lives. *Cyberpsychology, Behavior, and Social Networking*, 15: 117–20.

Christopherson, S., Martin, R. and Pollard, J. 2013. Financialisation: Roots and repercussions. *Cambridge Journal of Regions, Economy and Society*, 6 (3): 351–7.

Chubb, J. and Moe, T. 1990. *Politics, Markets and America's Schools.* Washington, DC: Brookings Institute.

Clark, J. T. 2020. The secret of quick thinking: The invention of mental speed in America, 1890–1925. *Time & Society*, 29 (2): 469–93.

Clarke, J. and Newman, J. 1997. *The Managerial State.* London: Sage.

Clough, P. T. and Halley, J. (eds.). 2007. *The Affective Turn.* Durham, NC: Duke University Press.

Coates, T. 2015. *Between the World and Me.* New York: Spiegel and Grau.

Cochrane, A. 2012. *Animal Rights without Liberation: Applied Ethics and Human Obligations.* New York: Columbia University Press.

Colby, L. J. and Punda, I. 2009. *Agribusiness Handbook: Red Meat.* Rome: UN FAO Investment Centre Division.

Coles, R. and Haro, L. 2019. Toward a democratic groove. *Angelaki*, 24 (4): 103–19. DOI: 10.1080/0969725X.2019.1635831.

Collins, P. H. 1990. *Black Feminist Thought: Knowledge, Consciousness, and the Politics of Empowerment.* New York: Routledge.

Collins, R. 1974. Three faces of cruelty: Towards a comparative sociology of violence. *Theory and Society*, 1: 415–40.

Collins, S. 2015. *The Core of Care Ethics.* Basingstoke: Palgrave Macmillan.

Collinson, D. and Hearn, J. (eds.). 1996. *Men as Managers, Managers as Men: Critical Perspectives on Men, Masculinities, and Managements.* London: Sage.

Commission to Inquire into Child Abuse. 2009. *Report of the Commission to Inquire into Child Abuse* [Ryan Report], vols.1–5. http://www.childabuse-commission.ie/rpt/pdfs.

Connell, R. W. 1995. *Masculinities.* Cambridge: Polity.

Connell, R. W. 2000. *The Men and the Boys.* Cambridge: Polity.

Connell, R. W. 2007. *Southern Theory.* Cambridge: Polity.

Connell, R. W. 2016. Masculinities in global perspective: Hegemony, contestation, and changing structures of power. *Theory and Society*, 45 (4): 303–18.

Connell, R. W. and Wood, J. 2005. Globalization and business masculinities. *Men and Masculinities*, 7 (4): 347–64.

Cooke, L. P. and Baxter, J. 2010. 'Families' in international context: Comparing institutional effects across western societies. *Journal of Marriage and Family*, 72 (3): 516–36.

Cooley, C. H. 1992. *Human Nature and the Social Order.* Piscataway: Transaction Books.

Courtois, A. 2018. *Elite Schooling and Social Inequality.* Basingstoke: Palgrave Macmillan.

Coy, M. (ed.). 2012. *Prostitution, Harm and Gender Inequality: Theory, Research and Policy.* Aldershot: Ashgate.

Crean, M. 2018. Affective formations of class consciousness: Care consciousness. *The Sociological Review*, 66 (6): 1177–93.

Crenshaw, K. 1991. Mapping the margins: Intersectionality, identity politics, and violence against women of color. *Stanford Law Review*, 43 (6): 1241–99.

Crouch, C. 2004. *Post-Democracy*. Cambridge: Polity.

Csikszentmihalyi, M. 2002. Time's winged chariot: Reflections on the psychology of time. Paper presented to the Conference on Time Pressure, Work–Family Interface, and Parent–Child Relationships, University of Waterloo, March.

Cudworth, E. 2015. Killing animals: Sociology, species relations and institutionalized violence. *The Sociological Review*, 63: 1–18.

D'Alisa, G., Demaria, F. and Kallis, G. (eds.). 2014. *Degrowth: A Vocabulary for a New Era*. Abingdon: Routledge.

Dalla Costa, M. and James, S. 1972. *The Power of Women and the Subversion of the Community*. Bristol: Falling Wall Press.

Dalrymple, W. 2019. *The Anarchy: The Relentless Rise of the East India Company*. London: Bloomsbury.

Daly, M. 2015. Money-related meanings and practices in low-income and poor families. *Sociology*, 51 (2): 450–65.

Damasio, A. 1994. *Descartes' Error: Emotion, Reason and the Human Brain*. London: Vintage Books.

Darder, A. 2002. *Reinventing Paulo Freire: A Pedagogy of Love*. Boulder: Westview Press.

Da Roit, B., González Ferrer, A. and Moreno-Fuentes, F. J. 2013. The Southern European migrant-based care model. *European Societies*, 15 (4): 577–96.

Davis, G. F. and Kim, S. 2015. Financialization of the economy. *Annual Review of Sociology*, 41: 203–21.

De Beauvoir, S. 1993. *The Second Sex*. London: Penguin.

De Chiro, G. 2008. Living environmentalisms: Coalition politics, social reproduction, and environmental justice. *Environmental Politics*, 17 (2): 276–98.

de Graaff, N. 2020. China Inc. goes global: Transnational and national networks of China's globalizing business elite. *Review of International Political Economy*, 27 (2): 208–33.

della Porta, D. 2017. Political economy and social movements studies: The class basis of anti-austerity protests. *Anthropological Theory*, 17 (4): 453–73.

Delphy, C. and Leonard, D. 1992. *Familiar Exploitation: A New Analysis of Marriage and Family Life*. Cambridge: Polity.

Demetriou, D. 2001. Connell's concept of hegemonic masculinity: A critique. *Theory and Society*, 30 (3): 337–61.

Derrida, J. 2002. The animal that therefore I am (more to follow), trans. Wills, D. *Critical Inquiry*, 28: 369–418.

Descartes, R. 1991. *The Philosophical Writings of Descartes*, vol. 1, ed. Cottingham, J., Murdoch, D., Stoothoff, R. and Kenny, A. Cambridge: Cambridge University Press.

Dillard, J. 2008. A slaughterhouse nightmare: Psychological harm suffered by slaughterhouse employees and the possibility of redress through legal reform. *Georgetown Journal on Poverty Law & Policy*, 15 (391).

Dodson, L. 2010. *The Moral Underground: How Ordinary Americans Subvert an Unfair Economy.* New York: Free Press.

Donaldson, S. and Kymlicka, W. 2011. *Zoopolis: A Political Theory of Animal Rights.* Oxford: Oxford University Press.

Donati, P. 2010. *Relational Sociology: A New Paradigm for the Social Sciences.* London: Routledge.

Donati, P. and Archer, M. 2015. *The Relational Subject.* New York: Cambridge University Press.

Donovan, J. 2007a. Animal rights and feminist theory. In Donovan, J. and Adams, C. J. (eds.), *The Feminist Care Tradition in Animal Ethics.* New York: Columbia University Press, pp. 58–86.

Donovan, J. 2007b. Attention to suffering: Sympathy as a basis for ethical treatment of animals. In Donovan, J. and Adams, C. J. (eds.), *The Feminist Care Tradition in Animal Ethics.* New York: Columbia University Press, pp. 174–97.

Donovan, J. and Adams, C. J. (eds.). 2007. *The Feminist Care Tradition in Animal Ethics.* New York: Columbia University Press.

Douglas, M. 1993. Emotion and culture in theories of justice. *Economy and Society*, 22 (4): 501–15.

Dowling, E. 2021. *The Care Crisis: What Caused It and How Can We End It?* New York: Verso.

Downing, D. 2017. U.S. higher education and the crisis of care. *Humanities*, 6 (2): 1–14.

Du Bois, W. E. B. 2009. *The Souls of Black Folk.* New York: Oxford University Press.

Dubois-Shaik, F. and Fusulier, B. 2017. Understanding gender inequality and the role of the work/family interface in contemporary academia: An introduction. *European Educational Research Journal*, 16: 99–105.

Duffy, M. 2005. Reproducing labor inequalities: Challenges for feminists conceptualizing care at the intersections of gender, race, and class. *Gender & Society*, 19 (1): 66–82.

Duffy, M. 2011. *Making Care Count: A Century of Gender, Race, and Paid Care Work.* New Brunswick: Rutgers University Press.

Duffy, M. 2020. Driven by inequalities: Exploring the resurgence of domestic work in U.S. cities. *Sociological Forum*, 35 (3): 608–27.

Dumutri, S. 2014. From 'brain drain' to 'care drain': Women's labor migration and methodological sexism. *Women's Studies International Forum*, 47: 203–12.

Duncan, G. J. and Murnane, R. J. 2011. *Whither Opportunity? Rising Inequality, Schools, and Children's Life Chances.* New York: Russell Sage Foundation.

Durkheim, E. 1964. *The Division of Labour in Society*, trans. Simpson, G. London: Collier Macmillan.

Dussel, E. and Martinez, A. 2003. *Philosophy of Liberation.* Eugene: Wipf & Stock.

Eagleton-Pierce, M. 2016. Historicizing the neoliberal spirit of capitalism.

In Springer, S., Birch, K. and MacLeavy, J. (eds.), *The Handbook of Neoliberalism*. Abingdon: Routledge, pp. 17–26.

Ehrenreich, B. and Hochschild, A. H. (eds.). 2003. *Global Women: Nannies, Maids and Sex Workers in the New Economy*. London: Granta.

Eisen, D. B. and Yamashita, L. 2019. Borrowing from femininity: The caring man, hybrid masculinities, and maintaining male dominance. *Men and Masculinities*, 22 (5): 801–20.

Elias, J. 2008. Hegemonic masculinities, the multinational corporation, and the developmental state: Constructing gender in 'progressive' firms. *Men and Masculinities*, 10 (4): 405–21.

Elias, N. 1969. *Psychiatry in a Changing Society*. London: Tavistock.

Elias, N. 1978. *What Is Sociology?* London: Hutchinson.

Emond, R. 2016. More than just a bracelet: The use of material symbolism to communicate love. *International Journal of Social Pedagogy*, 5 (1): 34–50.

Engels, F. 1942. *Origins of the Family, Private Property and the State*, trans. West, A. https://www.marxists.org/archive/marx/works/1884/origin-family/index.htm.

England, P. 2005. Separative and soluble selves: Dichotomous thinking in economics. In Fineman, M. A. and Doughterty, T. (eds.), *Feminism Confronts Homo Economicus: Gender, Law and Society*. Ithaca: Cornell University Press, pp. 32–56.

England, P., Budig, M. and Folbre, N. 2002. Wages of virtue: The relative pay of care work. *Gender & Society*, 49 (4): 455–73.

Engster, D. 2005. Rethinking care theory: The practice of caring and the obligation to care. *Hypatia*, 20 (3): 50–74.

Engster, D. 2010. Strategies for building and sustaining a new care movement. *Journal of Women, Politics & Policy*, 3 (14): 289–312.

Engster, D. 2019. Care ethics, dependency, and vulnerability. *Ethics and Social Welfare*, 13 (2): 100–14.

Eriksen, E. O. 2017. Structural injustice: The Eurozone crisis and the duty of solidarity. In Grimmel, A. and My Giang, S. (eds.), *Solidarity in the European Union: A Fundamental Value in Crisis*. Cham: Springer, pp. 97–118.

Escobar, A. 2007. Worlds and knowledges otherwise: The Latin American modernity/coloniality research program. *Cultural Studies*, 21 (2–3): 179–210.

Espeland, W. N. and Sauder, M. 2007. Rankings and reactivity: How public measures recreate social worlds. *American Journal of Sociology*, 113 (1): 1–40.

European Centre for Disease Prevention and Control. 2020. *Surveillance of COVID-19 at Long-Term Care Facilities in the EU/EEA. May 19th, 2020: Technical Report*. Stockholm; European Centre for Disease Prevention and Control.

European Commission. 2013. *SHE Figures 2012*. Brussels: European Commission.

European Commission. 2016. *Study on the Gender Dimension of Trafficking in Human Beings: Summary*. Luxembourg: Publications Office of the European Union.

European Commission. 2018. Report from the Commission to the European Parliament and the Council: *Second Report on the Progress Made in the Fight against Trafficking in Human Beings (2018) as Required under Article 20 of Directive 2011/36/EU on Preventing and Combating Trafficking in Human Beings and Protecting Its Victims*. Brussels: European Commission.

European Commission. 2019. *EU 2019 Report on Gender Equality*. Brussels: European Commission.

European Commission. 2021. *EU 2021 Report on Gender Equality*. Brussels: European Commission.

Fanon, F. 1967. *The Wretched of the Earth*. London: Penguin.

FAO (Food and Agriculture Organization of the United Nations). 2006. Livestock impacts on the environment. *Spotlight: Agriculture and Consumer Protection Department, Food and Agriculture Organization of the United Nations*, November. Paris: OECD. www.gatsby.ucl.ac.uk/~pel/environment/meat_is_evil.htm.

Farris, S. and Marchetti, S. 2017. From the commodification to the corporatization of care: European perspectives and debates. *Social Politics*, 24 (2): 109–31.

Fazio, S., Pace, D., Flinner, J. and Kallmyer, B. 2017. The fundamentals of person-centred care for individuals with dementia. *The Gerontologist*, 58 (1): S10–S19.

Federici, S. 2012. *Revolution at Point Zero: Housework, Reproduction, and Feminist Struggle*. Oakland: PM Press.

Federici, S. 2019. *Re-Enchanting the World: Feminism and the Politics of the Commons*. Oakland: PM Press.

Feeley, M. 2009. Living in care without love: The impact of affective inequalities on learning literacies. In Lynch, K., Baker, J. and Lyons, M. (eds.), *Affective Equality: Love, Care and Injustice*. Basingstoke: Palgrave Macmillan, pp. 199–215.

Feeley, M. 2014. *Learning Care Lessons: Literacy, Love, Care and Solidarity*. London: Tufnell Press.

Fellmeth, G., Rose-Clarke, K., Zhao, C., Busert, L. K., Zheng, Y. et al. 2018. Health impacts of parental migration on left-behind children and adolescents: A systematic review and meta-analysis. *Lancet*, 392: 2567–82.

Ferber, M. A. and Nelson, J. A. (eds.). 1993. *Beyond Economic Man: Feminist Theory and Economics*. Chicago: University of Chicago Press.

Ferguson, A. 2014. Feminist love politics: Romance, care, and solidarity. In Ferguson, A. and Jónasdóttir, A. G. (eds.), *Love: A Question for Feminism in the Twenty-First Century*. New York: Routledge, pp. 250–64.

Ferguson, A. and Jónasdóttir, A. G. (eds.). 2014. *Love: A Question for Feminism in the Twenty-First Century*. New York: Routledge.

Fernandez, B. 2010. Cheap and disposable? The impact of the global economic crisis on the migration of Ethiopian women domestic workers to the Gulf. *Gender & Development*, 18 (2): 249–62.

Ferrarese, E. 2017a. Precarity of work, precarity of moral dispositions: Concern for others in the era of 'emotional' capitalism. *Women's Studies Quarterly*, 45: 176–92.

Ferrarese, E. 2017b. *The Politics of Vulnerability*. London: Routledge.

Fine, M. D. 2007. *A Caring Society? Care and the Dilemmas of Human Service in the Twenty-First Century*. Basingstoke: Palgrave Macmillan.

Fineman, M. 1995. *The Neutered Mother, the Sexual Family and Other Twentieth Century Tragedies*. New York: Routledge.

Fineman, M. 2004. *The Autonomy Myth*. New York: Free Press.

Fineman, M. 2008. The vulnerable subject: Anchoring equality in the human condition. *Yale Journal of Law and Feminism*, 20 (1): 1–24.

Flores, R. 2013. When charity does not begin at home: Exploring the British socioemotional economy of compassion. *Sociological Research Online*, 18 (1). hwww.socresonline.org.uk/18/1/17.html.

Folbre, N. 1994. *Who Pays for the Kids? Gender and the Structures of Constraint*. New York: Routledge.

Folbre, N. 2001. *The Invisible Heart: Economics and Family Values*. New York: New Press.

Folbre, N. 2006. Nursebots to the rescue? Immigration, automation, and care. *Globalizations*, 3 (3): 349–60.

Folbre N. 2008. Reforming care. *Politics & Society*, 36 (3): 373–87.

Folbre, N. 2012. Should women care less? Intrinsic motivation and gender inequality. *British Journal of Industrial Relations*, 50 (4): 597–619.

Folbre, N. 2020. *The Rise and Decline of Patriarchal Systems: An Intersectional Political Economy*. New York: Verso.

Folbre, N. and Bittman, M. (eds.). 2004. *Family Time: The Social Organisation of Care*. New York: Routledge.

Foucault, M. 1977. *Discipline and Punish: The Birth of the Prison*, trans. Sheridan, A. London: Allen Lane.

Foucault, M. 1980. *Power/Knowledge: Selected Interviews and Other Writings*, ed. Gordon, C. New York: Harvester Wheatsheaf.

Foucault, M. 2010. *The Birth of Biopolitics: Lectures at the Collège de France, 1978–1979*, ed. Senellart, M., trans Burchell, G. Basingstoke: Palgrave.

Fourcade, M. 2016. Ordinalization. *Sociological Theory*, 34 (3): 175–95.

Fourcade, M. and Healy, K. 2017. Seeing like a market. *Socio-Economic Review*, 15 (1): 9–29.

Fox, M. F., Fonseca, C. and Bao, J. 2011. Work and family conflict in academic science: Patterns and predictors among women and men in research universities. *Social Studies of Science*, 41 (5): 715–35.

Francione, G. 1995. *Animals, Property and the Law*. Philadelphia: Temple University Press.

Francione, G. 2000. *Introduction to Animal Rights: Your Child or Your Dog?* Philadelphia: Temple University Press.

Francione, G. 2009. *Animals as Persons: Essays on the Abolition of Animal Exploitation*. New York: Columbia University Press.

Fraser, N. 1995. From redistribution to recognition? Dilemmas of justice in a 'post-socialist' age. *New Left Review*, 212: 68–93.

Fraser, N. (ed.). 1997. *Justice Interruptus: Critical Reflections on the 'Postsocialist' Condition*. New York: Routledge:.

Fraser, N. 2005. Mapping the feminist imagination: From redistribution to recognition to representation. *Constellations*, 12 (3): 295–307.

Fraser, N. 2008. *Scales of Justice: Reimagining Political Space in a Globalizing World*. Cambridge: Polity.

Fraser, N. 2010. Injustice at intersecting scales: On 'social exclusion' and the 'global poor'. *European Journal of Social Theory*, 13 (3): 363–71.

Fraser, N. 2016. Contradictions of capital and care. *New Left Review*, 100: 99–117.

Fraser, N. and Gordon, L. 1997. A genealogy of 'dependency'. In Fraser, N. (ed.), *Justice Interruptus: Critical Reflections on the 'Postsocialist' Condition*. New York: Routledge, pp. 121–49.

Freeden, M. 2003. *Ideology: A Very Short Introduction*. Oxford: Oxford University Press.

Freire, P. 1970. *Pedagogy of the Oppressed*. London: Penguin.

Freire, P. 1971. *Cultural Action for Freedom*. London: Penguin.

Frericks, P. 2010. Capitalist welfare societies' trade-off between economic efficiency and social solidarity. *European Societies*, 13 (5): 719–41.

Frericks, P. 2011. Marketising social protection in Europe: Two distinct paths and their impact on social inequalities. *International Journal of Sociology and Social Policy*, 31 (5/6): 319–34.

Frericks, P. 2014. Unifying self-responsibility and solidarity in social security institutions. *European Societies*, 16 (4): 522–42.

Frericks, P., Maier, R. and De Graaf, W. 2009. Toward a neoliberal Europe? Pension reforms and transformed citizenship. *Administration and Society*, 41 (2): 135–57.

Fricker, M. 2007. *Epistemic Injustice: Power and the Ethics of Knowing*. Oxford: Oxford University Press.

Friedman, M. 1948. A monetary and fiscal framework for economic stability. *The American Economic Review*, 38 (3): 245–64.

Friedman, M. 2002. *Capitalism and Freedom*. Chicago: University of Chicago Press.

Friedman, S. D. 2013. *Baby Bust: New Choices for Men and Women in Work and Family*. Philadelphia: Wharton School Press.

Fromm, E. 1976. *To Have or To Be*. New York: Harper and Row.

Fry, D. P. 2007. *Beyond War: The Human Potential for Peace*. New York: Oxford University Press.

Fuchs, S. 2017. Observing facts and values: A brief theory and history. *Canadian Review of Sociology*, 54 (4): 456–67.

Gaard, G. and Gruen, L. 1993. Ecofeminism: Toward global justice and planetary health. *Society and Nature*, 2: 1–35.

Galotti, M. 2015. *Making Decent Work a Reality for Migrant Domestic Workers*. Geneva: ILO. https://www.ilo.org/wcmsp5/groups/

public/---ed_protect/---protrav/---travail/documents/publication/
wcms_436974.pdf.

Gangi, S., Talamo, A. and Ferracuti, S. 2009. The long-term effects of extreme war-related trauma on the second generation of Holocaust survivors. *Violence and Victims*, 24 (5): 687–700.

Gardner, H. 1983. *Frames of Mind: The Theory of Multiple Intelligences*. New York: Paladin.

Garhammer, M. 2002. Pace of life and enjoyment of life. *Journal of Happiness Studies*, 3 (3): 217–56.

Garner, R. 2013. *A Theory of Justice for Animals: Animal Rights in a Nonideal World*. Oxford: Oxford University Press.

Garner, S. L., Conroy, S. F. and Bader, S. G. 2015. Nurse migration from India: A literature review. *International Journal of Nursing Studies*, 52 (12): 1879–90.

Gerth, H. H. and Wright Mills, C. (eds.). 1958. *From Max Weber: Essays in Sociology*. New York: Oxford University Press.

Gheaus, A. 2017. Love and justice: A paradox. *Canadian Journal of Philosophy*, 47 (6): 739–59.

Gibson, J. and McKenzie, D. 2012. The economic consequences of 'brain drain' of the best and brightest: Microeconomic evidence from five countries. *Economic Journal*, 122 (560): 339–75.

Gibson-Graham, J. K. 1996. *The End of Capitalism (As We Knew It): A Feminist Critique of Political Economy*. Oxford: Blackwell.

Gibson-Graham, J. K. 2006. *A Postcapitalist Politics*. Minnesota: University of Minnesota Press.

Gibson-Graham, J. K., Cameron, J. and Healy, S. 2013. *Take Back the Economy: An Ethical Guide for Transforming Our Communities*. Minneapolis: University of Minnesota Press.

Gibson-Graham, J. K., Cameron, J. and Healy, S. 2016. Commoning as a postcapitalist politics. In Amin, A. and Howell, P. (eds.), *Releasing the Commons: Rethinking the Futures of the Commons*. New York: Routledge, pp. 192–212.

Giddens, A. 1984. *The Constitution of Society: Outline of the Theory of Structuration*. Cambridge: Polity.

Giddens, A. 2008. *The Transformation of Intimacy: Sexuality, Love and Eroticism in Modern Societies*. Cambridge: Polity.

Gilbert, P. 2010. *The Compassionate Mind*. London: Constable.

Gill, R. 2009. Breaking the silence: The hidden injuries of neo-liberal academia. In Flood, R. and Gill, R. (eds.), *Secrecy and Silence in the Research Process: Feminist Reflections*. London: Routledge, pp. 228–44.

Gillies, V., Edwards, R. and Horsley, N. 2016. Brave new brains: Sociology, family, and the politics of knowledge. *The Sociological Review*, 64: 219–237.

Gilligan, C. 1982. *In a Different Voice*. Cambridge, MA: Harvard University Press.

Gilligan, C. 1995. Hearing the difference: Theorizing connection. *Hypatia*, 10 (2): 120–7.

Gilligan, C. 2011. *Joining the Resistance*. Cambridge: Polity.

Gilson, E. 2011. Vulnerability, ignorance and oppression. *Hypatia*, 26 (2): 308–32.

Gingrich, J. and Häusermann, S. 2015. The decline of the working-class vote, the reconfiguration of the welfare support coalition and consequences for the welfare state. *Journal of European Social Policy*, 25 (1): 50–75.

Giridharadas, A. 2019. *Winners Take All: The Elite Charade of Changing the World*. New York: Allen Lane.

Giroux, H. 2002. Neo-liberalism, corporate culture and the promise of higher education. *Harvard Educational Review*, 72 (4): 1–31.

Giroux, H. and McLaren, P. (eds.). 1993. *Between Borders: Pedagogy and the Politics of Cultural Studies*. New York: Routledge.

Glenn, E. N. 2000. Creating a caring society. *Contemporary Sociology*, 29: 84–94.

Glenn, E. N. 2010. *Forced to Care: Coercion and Caregiving in America*. Cambridge, MA: Harvard University Press.

Goffman, E. 1963. *Stigma: Notes on the Management of Spoiled Identity*. New York: Simon & Schuster.

Golder, M. 2003. Explaining variation in the success of extreme right parties in Western Europe. *Comparative Political Studies*, 36 (4): 432–66.

Golder, M. 2016. Far right parties in Europe. *Annual Review of Political Science*, 19: 477–97.

Goleman, D. 1995. *Emotional Intelligence*. New York: Bantam Books.

Gomberg, P. 2008. *How to Make Opportunity Equal: Race and Contributive Justice*. Oxford: John Wiley & Sons.

Goodhart, M. 2018. *Injustice: Political Theory for the Real World*. Oxford: Oxford University Press.

Goodley, D., Lawthom, R. and Runswick Cole, K. 2014. Dis/ability and austerity: Beyond work and slow death. *Disability & Society*, 29 (6): 980–4.

Gorski, P. S. 2017. From sinks to webs: Critical social science after the fact–value distinction. *Canadian Review of Sociology*, 54 (4): 423–44.

Gould, S. J. 1997. *The Mismeasure of Man*. London: Penguin.

Gouldner, A. V. 1970. *The Coming Crisis in Western Sociology*. London: Heinemann.

Government of Ireland. 2011. *National Strategy for Higher Education to 2030*. Dublin: Department of Education and Skills, Government Publications Office.

Graeber, D. 2011. *Debt: The First 5,000 Years*. New York: Melville House.

Graham, E., Jordan, L. P. and Yeoh, B. S. 2015. Parental migration and the mental health of those who stay behind to care for children in south-east Asia. *Social Science and Medicine*, 132: 225–35.

Gramsci, A. 1971. *Selections from the Prison Notebooks of Antonio Gramsci*, ed. and trans. Hoare, Q. and Nowell Smith, G. London: Lawrence and Wishart.

Grand View Research. 2020. *Market Analysis Report: Home Healthcare*

Market Size, Share & Trends Analysis Report ... 2020–2027. https://www. grandviewresearch.com/industry-analysis/home-healthcare-industry.

Greenpeace. 2019. *Feeding the Problem: The Dangerous Intensification of Animal Farming in Europe.* Brussels: Greenpeace.

Greger, M. 2009. *Flu Factories: Tracing the Origin of the Swine Flu Pandemic.* DVD. Washington, DC: Humane Society of the United States.

Gruen, L. 1996. On the oppression of women and animals. *Environmental Ethics,* 18 (4): 441–4.

Gruen, L. (ed.). 2014. *The Ethics of Captivity.* Oxford: Oxford University Press.

Grummell, B., Devine, D. and Lynch, K. 2009. The care-less manager: Gender, care and new managerialism in higher education. *Gender and Education,* 21 (2): 191–208.

Gutiérrez-Rodríguez, E. 2010. *Migration, Domestic Work and Affect.* New York: Routledge.

Gutiérrez-Rodríguez, E. 2014. Domestic work – affective labor: On feminization and the coloniality of labor. *Women's Studies International Forum,* 46: 45–53.

Gutmann, A. 1980. *Liberal Equality.* Princeton: Princeton University Press.

Hacking, I. 1986. Making up people. In Heller, T. H., Sosna, M. and Wellbery, D. E. (eds.), *Reconstructing Individualism. Autonomy, Individuality, and the Self in Western Thought.* Stanford: Stanford University Press, pp. 222–36.

Hall, P. A. and Gingerich, D. W. 2009. Varieties of capitalism and institutional complementarities in the political economy: An empirical analysis. *British Journal of Political Science,* 39: 449–82.

Hall, P. A. and Soskice, D. (eds.). 2001. *Varieties of Capitalism.* Oxford: Oxford University Press.

Halldenius, L. 1998. Non-domination and egalitarian welfare politics. *Ethical Theory and Moral Practice,* 1 (3): 335–53.

Hanlon, N. 2012. *Masculinities, Care and Equality: Identity and Nurture in Men's Lives.* London: Palgrave Macmillan.

Hansen, M. E. 2018. *Meat Processing Workers: Occupational Report.* Dublin: Eurofound.

Haraway, D. J. 1991. Situated knowledge: The science question in feminism and the privilege of partial perspective. In Haraway, D. J., *Simians, Cyborgs and Women.* New York: Routledge, pp. 183–201.

Haraway, D. J. 2003. *The Companion Species Manifesto: Dogs, People, and Significant Otherness.* Chicago: Prickly Paradigm Press.

Haraway, D. J. 2007. *When Species Meet.* Minneapolis: University of Minnesota Press.

Haraway, D. J. 2016. *Staying with the Trouble: Making Kin in the Chthulucene.* Durham, NC: Duke University Press.

Harding, S. 1986. *The Science Question in Feminism.* Ithaca: Cornell University Press.

Harding, S. 1991. *Whose Science? Whose Knowledge?* Milton Keynes: Open University Press.

Harding, S. 2008. *Sciences from Below: Feminisms, Postcolonialities, and Modernities*. Durham, NC: Duke University Press.

Harding, S. and Norberg, K. 2005. New feminist approaches to social science methodologies: An introduction. *Signs: Journal of Women in Culture and Society*, 30 (4): 2009–15.

Hardt, M. and Negri, A. 2000. *Empire*. Cambridge, MA: Harvard University Press.

Hardt, M. and Negri, A. 2005. *Multitude: War and Democracy in the Age of Empire*. New York: Penguin.

Hardt, M. and Negri, A. 2009. *Commonwealth*. Cambridge, MA: Harvard University Press.

Harris, D. (ed.). 2004. *The Origins and Spread of Agriculture and Pastoralism in Eurasia*. London: Routledge.

Hartmann, H. I. 1979. The unhappy marriage of Marxism and feminism: Towards a more progressive union. *Capital & Class*, (3) 2: 1–33.

Harvey, B. 2014. *Government Funding and Social Justice Advocacy*. Dublin: Advocacy Initiative, Carmichael House.

Harvey, D. 1990. *The Condition of Postmodernity: An Enquiry into the Origins of Cultural Change*. Oxford: Blackwell.

Harvey, D. 2005. *A Brief History of Neoliberalism*. Oxford: Oxford University Press.

Harvey, D. 2010. *The Enigma of Capital and the Crisis of Capitalism*. London: Profile Books.

Harvey, L., Ringrose, J. and Gill, R. 2013. Swagger, ratings and masculinity: Theorising the circulation of social and cultural value in teenage boys' digital peer networks. *Sociological Research Online*, 18 (4).

Hawkesworth, M. 2006. The gendered ontology of multitude. *Political Theory*, 34 (3): 357–64.

Hay, S. and Kapitzke, C. 2009. 'Smart' state for a knowledge economy: Reconstituting creativity through student subjectivity. *British Journal of Sociology of Education*, 30 (2): 151–64.

Hayek, F. A. 1960. *The Constitution of Liberty*. Chicago: University of Chicago Press.

Hayek, F. A. 1994. *The Road to Serfdom*. Chicago: University of Chicago Press.

Hayry, M. 2020. Causation, responsibility, and harm: How the discursive shift from law and ethics to social justice sealed the plight of nonhuman animals. *Cambridge Quarterly of Healthcare Ethics*, 29: 246–67.

Hays, S. 1996. *The Cultural Contradictions of Motherhood*. New Haven: Yale University Press.

Hazelkorn, E. 2011. *Rankings and the Reshaping of Higher Education: The Battle for World-Class Excellence*. Basingstoke: Palgrave Macmillan.

Healy, K. 2006. *Last Best Gifts: Altruism and the Market for Blood and Organs*. Chicago: University of Chicago Press.

Hearn, J. and Parkin, W. 2001. *Gender, Sexuality and Violence in Organizations*. London: Sage.

Heil, E. C. 2010. The Brazilian landless movement, resistance, and violence. *Critical Criminology*, 18: 77–93.

Held, V. 1993. *Feminist Morality: Transforming Culture, Society and Politics*. Chicago: University of Chicago Press.

Held, V. 2006. *The Ethics of Care: Personal, Political, and Global*. Oxford: Oxford University Press.

Held, V. 2010. Can the ethics of care handle violence? *Ethics and Social Welfare*, 4 (2): 115–29.

Henderson, A. C., Harmon, S. M. and Houser, J. 2010. A new state of surveillance? An application of Michel Foucault to modern motherhood. *Surveillance & Society*, 7 (3–4): 231–47.

Henderson, A. C., Harmon, S. M. and Newman, H. 2016. The price mothers pay, even when they are not buying it: Mental health consequences of idealized motherhood. *Sex Roles*, 74: 512–26.

Henderson, E. F. and Moreau, M.-P. 2019. Carefree conferences? Academics with caring responsibilities performing mobile academic subjectivities. *Gender and Education*, 32 (1): 1–16.

Herring, J. 2020. *Law and the Relational Self*. Cambridge: Cambridge University Press.

Hetzler, A. 2018. Framing work injury/sickness in a changing welfare state: Naming and blaming. In Sowa, F., Staples, R. and Zapfel, S. (eds.), *The Transformation of Work in Welfare State Organizations: New Public Management and the Institutional Diffusion of Ideas*. London: Routledge, pp. 223–41.

Hibbard, R., Barlow, J., MacMillan, H., Committee on Child Abuse and Neglect and American Academy of Child and Adolescent Psychiatry. 2012. Psychological maltreatment. *Pediatrics*, 130 (2): 372–8.

Hicks, G. 1997. *The Comfort Women: Japan's Brutal Regime of Enforced Prostitution in the Second World War*. New York: W. W. Norton.

Hoang, K. K. 2014. Vietnam rising dragon: Contesting Western masculinities in Ho Chi Minh City's global sex industry. *International Journal of Politics, Culture, and Society*, 27: 259–71.

Hobson, B. 2000. *Gender and Citizenship in Transition*. Basingstoke: Macmillan.

Hochschild, A. R. 1983. *The Managed Heart: The Commercialization of Human Feeling*. Oakland: University of California Press.

Hochschild, A. R. 1997. *The Time Bind: When Work Becomes Home and Home Becomes Work*. New York: Henry Holt.

Hochschild, A. R. 2002. Love and gold. In Hochschild, A. R. and Ehrenreich, B. (eds.), *Global Woman: Nannies, Maids and Sex Workers in the New Economy*. New York: Henry Holt, pp. 15–30.

Hochschild, A. R. 2003. *The Commercialization of Intimate Life: Notes from Home and Work*. Oakland: University of California Press.

Hochschild, A. R. 2012. *The Outsourced Self: Intimate Life in Market Times*. New York: Metropolitan Books/Henry Holt.

Hochschild, A. R. 2016. *Strangers in Their Own Land: Anger and Mourning on the American Right*. New York: Free Press.

Hochschild, A. R. and Machung, A. 1989. *The Second Shift: Working Parents and the Revolution at Home*. New York: Viking.

Holmes, S. 2013. *Fresh Fruit, Broken Bodies: Migrant Farmworkers in the United States*. Oakland: University of California Press.

Hondagneu-Sotelo, P. 2001. *Domestica: Immigrant Workers Cleaning and Caring in the Shadows of Affluence*. Berkeley, CA: University of California Press.

Hondagneu-Sotelo, P. and Messner, M. 1994. Gender displays and men's power. In Brod, H. and Kaufman, M. (eds.), *Theorizing Masculinities*. Thousand Oaks: Sage, pp. 200–18.

Honneth, A. 1995. *The Struggle for Recognition: The Moral Grammar of Social Conflicts*, trans. Anderson, J. Cambridge, MA: MIT Press.

Honneth, A. 2003. Redistribution as recognition: A response to Nancy Fraser. In Fraser, A. and Honneth, A. (eds.), *Redistribution or Recognition? A Political-Philosophical Exchange*. London: Verso, pp. 110–97.

Honoré, C. 2004. *In Praise of Slow: How a Worldwide Movement is Challenging the Cult of Speed*. London: Orion.

Honoré, C. 2013. *The Slow Fix: Solve Problems, Work Smarter and Live Better in a World Addicted to Speed*. New York: HarperCollins.

hooks, b. 1994. *Teaching to Transgress: Education as the Practice of Freedom*. New York: Routledge.

hooks, b. 2000. *All about Love*. New York: William Morrow.

Hoppania, H.-K. 2013. Elder care policy in Finland: Remedies for crisis?. In Jónsson, G. and Stefánsson, K. (eds.), *Retrenchment or Renewal? Welfare States in Times of Economic Crisis*. Helsinki: Nordic Centre of Excellence NordWel, pp. 252–69.

Hoppania, H.-K. and Vaittinen, T. 2015. A household full of bodies: Neoliberalism, care and 'the political'. *Global Society*, 29 (1): 70–88.

Hughes, B., McKie, L., Hopkins, D. and Watson, N. 2005. Love's labour lost? Feminism, the disabled people's movement and an ethic of care. *Sociology*, 39 (2): 259–75.

Hutter, S. 2014. *Protesting Culture and Economics in Western Europe: New Cleavages in Left and Right Politics*. Minneapolis: University of Minnesota Press.

Hutton, M. 2015. Consuming stress: Exploring hidden dimensions of consumption-related strain at the intersection of gender and poverty. *Journal of Marketing Management*, 31 (15–16): 1695–1717.

Icaza, R. and Vazquez, R. 2013. Social struggles as epistemic struggles. *Development and Change*, 44 (3): 683–704.

Illouz, E. 2007. *Cold Intimacies: The Making of Emotional Capitalism*. Cambridge: Polity.

Illouz, E. 2012. *Why Love Hurts: A Sociological Explanation*. Cambridge: Polity.

ILO (International Labour Organization). 2013. *Global Employment Trends 2013*. Geneva: ILO.

ILO (International Labour Organization). 2018. *Care Work and Care Jobs for the Future of Decent Work*. Geneva: ILO.

ILO (International Labour Organization). 2019. *World Employment Social Outlook: Trends 2019*. Geneva: ILO.

IOM (International Organization for Migration). 2020. *World Migration Report 2020*. Geneva: IOM.

Ivancheva, M., Lynch, K. and Keating, K. 2019. Precarity, gender and care in the neoliberal academy. *Gender, Work & Organization*, 26: 448–62.

Jeffries, S. 2010. The sex industry and business practice: An obstacle to women's equality. *Women's Studies International Forum*, 33: 274–82.

Jessop, B. 2008. A cultural political economy of competitiveness and its implications for higher education. In Jessop, B., Fairclough, N. and Wodak, R. (eds.), *Education and the Knowledge-Based Economy in Europe*. Rotterdam: Sense, pp. 14–39.

Jessop, B. 2019. Ordoliberalism and neoliberalization: Governing through order or disorder. *Critical Sociology*, 45 (7–8): 967–81.

Jones, R. C. 2015. Animal rights is a social justice issue. *Contemporary Justice Review*, 18 (4): 467–82.

Joseph, E. 2018. Whiteness and racism: Examining the racial order in Ireland. *Irish Journal of Sociology*, 26 (1): 46–70.

Josephson, P. 2020. *Chicken: A History from Farmyard to Factory*. Cambridge: Polity.

Joyce, K. and Loe, M. 2010. A sociological approach to ageing, technology and health. *Sociology of Health & Illness*, 32 (2): 171–80.

Kahl, S. 2005. The religious roots of modern poverty policy: Catholic, Lutheran and Reformed Protestant traditions compared. *European Journal of Sociology*, 46: 91–126.

Kahneman, D. 2003. Maps of bounded rationality: Psychology for behavioral economics. *The American Economic Review*, 93 (5): 1449–75.

Kalaitzake, M. 2017. The political power of finance: The Institute of International Finance in the Greek debt crisis. *Politics & Society*, 45 (3): 389–413.

Kalaitzake, M. 2019a. Central banking and financial political power: An investigation into the European Central Bank. *Competition & Change*, 23 (3): 221–44.

Kalaitzake, M. 2019b. Accounting for success: The Big Four as allies of finance in post crisis regulatory reform. *Business and Politics*, 21 (3): 297–326.

Kalof, L. (ed.). 2017. *The Oxford Handbook of Animal Studies*. Oxford: Oxford University Press.

Kanter, R. M. 1977. *Men and Women of the Corporation*. New York: Basic Books.

Kapeller, J. and Wolkenstein, F. 2013. The grounds of solidarity: From liberty to loyalty. *European Journal of Social Theory*, 16 (4): 476–91.

Kapoor, I. 2013. *Celebrity Humanitarianism: The Ideology of Global Charity.* New York: Routledge.

Karabel, J. 2005. *The Chosen: The Hidden History of Admission and Exclusion at Harvard, Yale, and Princeton.* Boston: Houghton Mifflin Harcourt.

Kaushal, N., Magnuson, K. and Waldfogel, J. 2011. How is family income related to investments in children's learning? In Murnane, R. and Duncan, G. (eds.), *Whither Opportunity? Rising Inequality, Schools, and Children's Life Chance.* New York: Russell Sage Foundation, pp. 187–206.

Kavanagh, E. and Brown, L. 2020. Towards a research agenda for examining online gender-based violence against women academics. *Journal of Further and Higher Education,* 44 (10): 1379–87.

Kearney, R. 2021. *Touch: Recovering Our Most Vital Sense.* New York: Columbia University Press.

Kelly, E. I. 2017. The historical injustice problem for political liberalism. *Ethics,* 128: 75–94.

Kelly, M. C. 2014. *Ireland's Great Famine in Irish-American History: Enshrining a Fateful Memory.* Lanham: Rowman & Littlefield.

Kentikelenis, A. E. and Babb, S. 2019. The making of neoliberal globalization: Norm substitution and the politics of clandestine institutional change. *American Journal of Sociology,* 124 (6): 1720–62.

Kilby, J. 2013. Introduction to special issue: Theorizing violence. *European Journal of Social Theory,* 16 (3): 261–72.

Kilminster, R. 1991. Structuration theory as a world-view. In Bryant, C. and Jary, D. (eds.), *Giddens' Theory of Structuration: A Critical Appreciation.* London: Routledge, pp. 74–115.

Kimmel, M. 2013. *Angry White Men: American Masculinity at the End of an Era.* New York: Nation Books.

Kittay, E. F. 1999. *Love's Labor.* New York: Routledge.

Klein, H. 2015. *Compañeras: Zapatista Women's Stories.* New York: Seven Stories Press.

Klein, N. 2007. *The Shock Doctrine: The Rise of Disaster Capitalism.* New York: Allen Lane.

Klein, N. 2014. *This Changes Everything: Capitalism vs. the Climate.* Toronto: Alfred A. Knopf Canada.

Konings, M. 2015. *The Emotional Logic of Capitalism: What Progressives Have Missed.* Stanford: Stanford University Press.

Konrath, S. H., O'Brien, E. H. and Hsing, C. 2011. Changes in dispositional empathy in American college students over time: A meta-analysis. *Personality and Social Psychology Review,* 15 (2): 180–98.

Korpi, W. 2003. Welfare-state regress in Western Europe: Politics, institutions, globalization, and Europeanization. *Annual Review of Sociology,* 29 (5): 589–609.

Krapf, S., Kreyenfeld, M. and Wolf, K. 2016. Gendered authorship and demographic research: An analysis of 50 years of *Demography. Demography,* 53 (4): 1169–84.

Krathwohl, D. R., Bloom, B. S. and Masia, B. B. 1964. *Taxonomy of Educational Objectives: The Classification of Educational Goals. Handbook 2: Affective Domain.* London: Longmans.

Kross, E., Verduyn, P., Demiralp, E., Park, J., Lee, D. S. et al. 2013. Facebook use predicts declines in subjective well-being in young adults. *PLoS ONE*, 8 (8): e69841. DOI: 10.1371/journal.pone.0069841.

Kubicek, B., Korunka, C. and Ulferts, H. 2012. Acceleration in the care of older adults: New demands as predictors of employee burnout and engagement. *Journal of Advanced Nursing*, 69: 1525–38.

Lakoff, G. 2008. *The Political Mind: Why You Can't Understand 21st-Century American Politics with an 18th-Century Brain.* New York: Viking Press.

Lanoix, M. 2007. The citizen in question. *Hypatia*, (22) 4: 113–29.

Lanoix, M. 2013. Labor as embodied practice: The lessons of care work. *Hypatia*, 28, 85–100.

Lanoix, M. 2020. Re-conceptualizing the political subject: The importance of age for care theory. *International Journal of Care and Caring*, 4 (1): 43–58.

Lareau, A. 2011. *Unequal Childhoods: Class, Race, and Family Life.* Berkeley, CA: University of California Press.

Layard, P. R. G. 2005. *Happiness: Lessons from a New Science.* London: Allen Lane.

Layte, R. 2012. The association between income inequality and mental health: Testing status anxiety, social capital, and neo-materialist explanations. *European Sociological Review*, 28 (4): 498–511.

Leenaert, T. 2017. *How to Create a Vegan World: A Pragmatic Approach.* New York: Lantern Books.

LeGoff, J. 1980. *Time, Work and Culture in the Middle Ages.* Chicago: University of Chicago Press.

Leigh, J. P., Gauthier, H. and Pacholok, S. 2012. Trying to do more with less? Negotiating intensive mothering and financial strain in Canada. *Families, Relationships and Societies*, 1 (3): 361–77.

Leineweber, C., Baltzer, M., Magnusson Hanson, L. L. and Westerlund, H. 2012. Work–family conflict and health in Swedish working women and men. *European Journal of Public Health*, 23: 710–16.

Lemann, N. 1995. The great sorting. *Atlantic Monthly*, September: 84–8.

Leonard, M. 2004. Bonding and bridging social capital: Reflections from Belfast. *Sociology*, 38 (5): 927–44.

Lerner, G. 1986. *The Creation of Patriarchy.* Oxford: Oxford University Press.

Leyva, R. 2019. Towards a cognitive sociological theory of subjectivity and habitus formation in neoliberal societies. *European Journal of Social Theory*, 22 (2): 250–71.

Lichtman, H. 1984. Parental communication of Holocaust experiences and personality characteristics among second-generation survivors. *Journal of Clinical Psychology*, 40: 915–24.

Lieberman, D. M., Schreiber, D. and Ochsner, N. K. 2003. Is political cognition like riding a bicycle? How cognitive neuroscience can inform research on political thinking. *Political Psychology*, 24 (4): 681–704.

Lieberwitz, R. 2005. Confronting the privatization and commercialization of academic research: An analysis of social implications at the local, national, and global levels. *Indiana Journal of Global Legal Studies*, 12 (1): 109–52.

Lingard, B. 2011. Policy as numbers: Ac/counting for educational research. *The Australian Educational Researcher*, 38: 355–82.

Lippel, K. 2016. *Addressing Occupational Violence: An Overview of Conceptual and Policy Considerations Viewed through a Gender Lens*. GED Working Paper No. 5/2016. Geneva: ILO. https://www.ilo.org/gender/Informationresources/Publications/WCMS_535656/lang--en/index.htm.

Lister, R. 2003. *Citizenship: Feminist Perspectives*. Basingstoke: Palgrave Macmillan.

Loewenstein, G. 2010. Insufficient emotion: Soul-searching by a former indicter of strong emotions. *Emotion Review*, 2 (3): 234–9.

Lolich, L. 2011. ... and the market created the student to its image and likening: Neo-liberal governmentality and its effects on higher education in Ireland. *Irish Educational Studies*, 30 (2): 271–84.

Lolich, L. and Lynch, K. 2016. The affective imaginary: Students as affective consumers of risk. *Higher Education Research & Development*, 35 (1): 17–30.

Lolich, L. and Lynch K. 2017. Aligning the market and affective self: Care and student resistance to entrepreneurial subjectivities. *Gender and Education*, 29 (1):115–31.

Lolich, L., Riccò, I., Deusdad, B. and Timonen, V. 2019. Embracing technology? Health and social care professionals' attitudes to the deployment of e-health initiatives in elder care services in Catalonia and Ireland. *Technological Forecasting & Social Change*, 147: 63–71.

Long, S. O. 2012. Bodies, technologies, and aging in Japan: Thinking about old people and their silver products. *Journal of Cross-Cultural Gerontology*, 27: 119–37.

Lorde, A. 2007. The master's tools will never dismantle the master's house. In Lorde, A., *Sister Outsider: Essays and Speeches*. Berkeley, CA: Crossing Press, pp. 110–14.

Lugones, M. 2010. Towards a decolonial feminism. *Hypatia*, 25 (4): 742–59.

Luke, B. 2007. Justice, caring and animal liberation. In Donovan, J. and Adams, C. J. (eds.), *The Feminist Care Tradition in Animal Ethics*. New York: Columbia University Press, pp. 153–73.

Lukes, S. 1973. *Individualism*. Oxford: Blackwell.

Lupton, D. 2020. *Data Selves: More-than-Human Perspectives*. Cambridge: Polity.

Luttrell, W. 2013. Children's counter-narratives of care: Towards educational justice. *Children & Society*, 27: 295–308.

Luttrell, W. 2020. *Children Framing Childhoods: Working-Class Kids' Visions of Care*. Bristol: Policy Press.

Lutz, H. 2016. *Migration and Domestic Work: A European Perspective on a Global Theme.* London: Routledge.

Lutz, H. 2011. *The New Maids: Transnational Women and the Care Economy.* London: Zed Books.

Lynch, K. 1989a. Solidary labour: Its nature and marginalisation. *The Sociological Review*, 37 (1): 1–14.

Lynch, K. 1989b. *The Hidden Curriculum: Reproduction in Education, an Appraisal.* London: Falmer Press.

Lynch, K. 1995. Equality and resistance in higher education. *International Studies in Sociology of Education*, 5 (1): 93–111.

Lynch, K. 1999. Equality studies: The academy and the role of research in emancipatory social change. *Economic and Social Review*, 30 (1): 41–69.

Lynch, K. 2007. Love labour as a distinct and non-commodifiable form of care labour. *The Sociological Review*, 54 (3): 550–70.

Lynch, K. 2010. Carelessness: A hidden doxa of higher education. *Arts and Humanities in Higher Education*, 9 (1): 54–67.

Lynch, K. 2014. Why love, care, and solidarity are political matters: Affective equality and Fraser's model of social justice. In Ferguson, A. and Jónasdóttir, A. G. (eds.), *Love: A Question for Feminism in the Twenty-First Century.* New York: Routledge, pp. 173–89.

Lynch, K. 2015. Control by numbers: New managerialism and ranking in higher education. *Critical Studies in Education*, 56 (2): 190–207.

Lynch, K., Baker, J. and Lyons, M. (eds.). 2009. *Affective Equality: Love, Care and Injustice.* Basingstoke: Palgrave Macmillan.

Lynch, K., Grummell, B. and Devine, D. 2012. *New Managerialism in Education: Commercialization, Carelessness and Gender.* Basingstoke: Palgrave Macmillan.

Lynch, K., Ivancheva, M., Keating, K., O'Flynn, M. and O'Connor, M. 2020. The care ceiling in higher education. *Irish Educational Studies*, 39 (2): 157–74.

Lynch, K. and Kalaitzake, M. 2018. Affective and calculative solidarity: The impact of individualism and neoliberal capitalism. *European Journal of Social Theory*, 17 (3): 343–58.

Lynch, K., Kalaitzake, M. and Crean, M. 2021. Care and affective relations: Social justice and sociology. *The Sociological Review*, 69 (1): 53–71.

Lynch, K. and Lodge, A. 2002. *Equality and Power in Schools.* London: Routledge.

Lynch, K., Lyons, M. and Cantillon, S. 2007. Breaking silence: Educating for love, care and solidarity. *International Studies in Sociology of Education*, 17 (1–2): 1–19.

MacDonald, I. 2011. Cold, cold, warm: Autonomy, intimacy and maturity in Adorno. *Philosophy and Social Criticism*. 37 (6): 669–89.

McCarthy-McMorrow, M. 1986. *The Munster Plantation: English Migration to Southern Ireland, 1583–1641.* Oxford: Clarendon Press.

McDonald, A., Lolich, L., Timonen, V. and Warters, A. 2019. 'Time is more important than anything else': Tensions of time in home care of older adults in Ireland. *International Journal of Care and Caring*, 3 (4).

McDonald, P. 2000. Gender equality, social institutions and the future of fertility. *Journal of Population Research*, 17: 1–16.

McDonnell, P. (2007). *Disability and Society: Ideological and Historical Dimensions*. Dublin: Blackhall.

McGinnity, F. and Calvert, E. 2009. Work–life conflict and social inequality in Western Europe. *Social Indicators Research*, 93: 489–508.

McGuigan, J. 2010. *Cool Capitalism*. London: Pluto Press.

McKibbin, P. 2019. *Love Notes: For a Politics of Love*. New York: Lantern Books.

McKie, L., Gregory, S. and Bowlby, S. 2002. Shadow times: The temporal and spatial frameworks and experiences of caring and working. *Sociology*, 36 (4): 897–924.

MacKinnon, C. A. 1983. Feminism, Marxism, method, and the state: Toward feminist jurisprudence. *Signs: Journal of Women in Culture and Society*, 8 (4): 635–58.

Magnuson, K. and Waldfogel, J. 2008. *Steady Gains and Stalled Progress: Inequality and the Black–White Test Score Gap*. New York: Russell Sage Foundation.

Mahadevan, K. 2020. Cosmopolitanism, care ethics and health care worker migration. In Urban, P. and Ward, L. (eds.), *Care Ethics, Democratic Citizenship and the State*. Cham: Palgrave Macmillan, pp. 199–217.

Maier, F., Meyer, M. and Steinbereithner, M. 2016. Nonprofit organizations becoming business-like: A systematic review. *Nonprofit and Voluntary Sector Quarterly*, 45 (1): 64–86.

Maina, L. W. and Kimani, E. 2019. *Gendered Patterns of Unpaid Care and Domestic Work in the Urban Informal Settlements of Nairobi, Kenya: Findings from a Household Care Survey*. Oxford: Oxfam. http://policy-practice. oxfam.org.uk/publications/gendered-patterns-of-unpaid-care-and-domestic-work-in-the-urban-informal-settle-620910.

Malešević, S. 2006. *Identity as Ideology: Understanding Ethnicity and Nationalism*. New York: Palgrave Macmillan.

Malešević, S. 2010a. *The Sociology of War and Violence*. Cambridge: Cambridge University Press.

Malešević, S. 2010b. How pacifist were the founding fathers? War and violence in classical sociology. *European Journal of Social Theory*, 13 (2): 193–212.

Malešević, S. 2014. Is war becoming obsolete? A sociological analysis. *The Sociological Review*, 62: 65–86.

Mannheim, K. 1968. *Ideology and Utopia*. London: Routledge and Kegan Paul.

Marsh, J. 2011. *Class Dismissed: Why We Cannot Teach or Learn Our Way out of Inequality*. New York: Monthly Review Press.

Marshall, T. H. 1973. Citizenship and social class. In Lipset, S. M. (ed.),

Class, Citizenship and Social Development: Essays by T.H. Marshall. Westport: Greenwood Press, pp. 65–122.

Martin, A., Myers, N. and Viseu, A. 2015. The politics of care in technoscience. *Social Studies of Science*, 45 (5): 625–64.

Marx, K. 1969 [1848]. *Manifesto of the Communist Party*, trans. Moore, S. and Engels, F. https://www.marxists.org/archive/marx/works/1848/communist-manifesto/index.htm.

Marx, K. 1973 [1857–61]. *Grundrisse: Foundations of the Critique of Political Economy*, trans. Nicolaus, M. London: Penguin.

Marx, K. and Engels, F. 1974 [1845–6]. *The German Ideology*, trans. Arthur, C. J. New York: Lawrence and Wishart.

Masschelein, J. and Simons, M. 2002. An adequate education in a globalised world? A note on immunisation against being-together. *Journal of Philosophy of Education*, 36 (4): 589–608.

Mau, S. 2015. *Inequality, Marketization and the Majority Class: Why Did the European Middle Classes Accept Neo-Liberalism?* Basingstoke: Palgrave.

Mau, S. 2019. *The Metric Society.* Cambridge: Polity.

Mauss, M. 1954. *The Gift: The Form and Reason for Exchange in Archaic Societies.* London: Routledge.

Mead, G. H. 1934. *Mind, Self, and Society.* Chicago: Chicago University Press.

Meagher, G., Lundström, T., Sallnäs, M. and Wiklund, S. 2016. Big business in a thin market: Understanding the privatization of residential care for children and youth in Sweden. *Social Policy & Administration*, 50 (7): 805–23.

Medina, J. 2013. *The Epistemology of Resistance.* Oxford: Oxford University Press.

Meijer, E. 2019. *When Animals Speak: Toward an Interspecies Democracy.* New York: New York University Press.

Melamed, J. 2015. Racial capitalism. *Critical Ethnic Studies*, 1 (1): 76–85.

Mellor, M. 1997. *Feminism and Ecology.* New York: New York University Press.

Mercille, J. 2018. Neoliberalism and health care: The case of the Irish nursing home sector. *Critical Public Health*, 28 (5): 546–59.

Mercille, J. and O'Neill, N. 2020. The growth of private home care providers in Europe: The case of Ireland. *Social Policy & Administration*. DOI: 10.1111/spol.12646.

Merton, R. K. 1973. *The Sociology Of Science: Theoretical and Empirical Investigations.* Chicago: University of Chicago Press.

Messerschmidt, J. 2010. *Hegemonic Masculinities and Camouflaged Politics.* Boulder: Paradigm.

Messner, M. 2007. The masculinity of the Governator. *Gender & Society*, 21 (4): 461–80.

Midgley, M. 1983. *Animals and Why They Matter.* Athens: University of Georgia Press.

Midgley, M. 1991. The origin of ethics. In Singer, P. (ed.) *A Companion to Ethics*. Oxford: Blackwell, pp. 3–13.

Mies, M. 2014. *Patriarchy and Accumulation on a World Scale: Women in the International Division of Labour*. London: Zed Books.

Mies, M. and Bennholdt-Thomsen, V. 2000. *The Subsistence Perspective: Beyond the Globalised Economy*, trans. Camiller, P., Mies, M. and Weih, G. London and New York: Zed Books.

Mies, M. and Shiva, V. 1993. *Ecofeminism*. London: Zed Books.

Mignolo, W. D. 2007. Delinking: The rhetoric of modernity, the logic of coloniality and the grammar of decoloniality. *Cultural Studies*, 21 (2–3): 449–514.

Mignolo, W. D. 2009. Epistemic disobedience, independent thought and de-colonial freedom. *Theory, Culture & Society*, 26 (7–8): 1–23.

Mijs, J. J. B. 2016. The unfulfillable promise of meritocracy: Three lessons and their implications for justice in education. *Social Justice Research*, 29 (1): 14–34.

Millett, K. 1977. *Sexual Politics*. London: Virago Press.

Mills, C. W. 2020. The chronopolitics of racial time. *Time & Society*, 29 (2): 297–317.

Misra, J. 2003. Caring about care. *Feminist Studies*, 29: 387–401.

Misra, J., Lundquist, J. H. and Templer, A. 2012. Gender, work, time, and care responsibilities among faculty. *Sociological Forum*, 27 (2): 300–23.

Mitchell, J. 1971. *Women's Estate*. Harmondsworth: Penguin.

Mitchell, K. 2016. Neoliberalism and citizenship. In Springer, S., Birch, K. and MacLeavy, J. (eds.), *The Handbook of Neoliberalism*. Abingdon: Routledge, pp. 118–29.

Mitchell, L. 2011. Moral disengagement and support for nonhuman animal farming. *Society & Animals*, 19: 38–58.

Miyazaki, R. 2019. Migrant care workers and care-migration policies: A comparison between Italy and Japan. *Asia Europe Journal: Studies on Common Policy Challenges*, 17 (2): 161–77.

Moisil, I. 2019. The two faces of healthcare digitalization: Lessons to be learned. *Applied Medical Informatics*, 41 (Suppl. 1): 1.

Mol, A. M. 2008. *The Logic of Care: Health and the Problem of Patient Choice*. London: Routledge.

Monbiot, G. 2000. *The Captive State: The Corporate Takeover of Britain*. Basingstoke; Macmillan.

Montazer, S. and Young, M. 2020. Commuting distance and work-to-family conflict: The moderating role of residential attributes. *Social Currents*, January. DOI: 10.1177/2329496519900491.

Montes López, E. and O'Connor, P. 2019. Micropolitics and meritocracy: Improbable bed fellows? *Educational Management Administration & Leadership*, 47 (5):678–93. DOI:10.1177/1741143218759090.

Mooney, M. 2014. Virtues and human personhood in the social sciences. In Jeffries, V. (ed.), *Palgrave Handbook of Altruism, Morality and Social Solidarity*. Basingstoke: Palgrave, pp. 21–41.

Moore, J. 2015. *Capitalism in the Web of Life*. New York: Verso.

Moore, S. and Hayes, L. J. B. 2017. Taking worker productivity to a new level? Electronic monitoring of home care; the (re)production of unpaid labour. *New Technology, Work and Employment*, 32 (2): 101–14.

Morris, J. 1993. *Independent Lives? Community Care and Disabled People*. London: Macmillan.

Moynihan, D. P. 1973. *The Politics of Guaranteed Income: The Nixon Administration and the Family Assistance Plan*. New York: Random House.

MRCI (Migrant Rights Centre Ireland). 2020. *Special Committee on Covid-19 Response*, Response by Edel McGinley, 17 June. https://data.oireachtas.ie/ ie/oireachtas/committee/dail/33/special_committee_on_covid_19_respon se/submissions/2020/2020-09-30_submission-edel-mcginley-director-migrant-rights-centre-ireland-scc19r-r-0263_en.pdf.

Mudde, C. 2007. *Populist Radical Right Parties*. Cambridge: Cambridge University Press.

Mudde, C. 2014. Fighting the system? Populist radical right parties and party system change. *Party Politics*, 20 (2): 217–26.

Muehlebach, A. 2012. *The Moral Neoliberal: Welfare and Citizenship in Italy*. Chicago: University of Chicago Press.

Muis, J. C. and Immerzeel, T. 2017. Causes and consequences of the rise of populist radical right parties and movements in Europe. *Current Sociology*, 65 (6): 909–30.

Mulkeen, M. 2016. Going to market! An exploration of markets in social care. *Administration*, 64 (2): 33–59.

Mulkeen, M. 2019. *Affective Relations in Children's Residential Care: Challenges of Neoliberalism and Professionalization*. University College Dublin PhD thesis.

Müller, B. 2019. The careless society: Dependency and care work in capitalist societies. *Frontiers in Sociology*, 3: art. 44.

Muller, J. Z. 2018. *The Tyranny of Metrics*. Princeton: Princeton University Press.

Mundy, K., Green, A., Lingard, B. and Verger, A. (eds.). 2016. *The Handbook of Global Education Policy*. Hoboken: Wiley-Blackwell.

Murray, G. 2015. We rule the world: An emerging global class fraction? *Foresight*, 17 (2): 208–25.

Mythen, G. 2005. Employment, individualization and insecurity: Rethinking the risk society perspective. *The Sociological Review*, 53 (1): 129–49.

Nedelsky, J. 1993. Property in potential life: A relational approach to choosing legal categories. *Canadian Journal of Law and Jurisprudence*, 6 (2): 343–65.

Nehring, D. and Kerrigan, D. 2019. *Therapeutic Worlds: Popular Psychology and the Sociocultural Organisation of Intimate Life*. London: Routledge.

Nellemann, C., Verma, R. and Hislop, L. (eds.). 2011. *Women at the Frontline of Climate Change: Gender Risks and Hopes. A Rapid Response Assessment*. Nairobi: United Nations Environment Programme and GRID-Arendal.

Nelson, J. A. 1993. The study of choice or the study of provisioning? Gender and the definition of economics. In Ferber, M. A. and Nelson, J. A. (eds.), *Beyond Economic Man: Feminist Theory and Economics*. Chicago: University of Chicago Press, pp. 23–36.

Nelson, J. A. 1997. Feminism, ecology and the philosophy of economics. *Ecological Economics*, 20 (2): 155–62.

Nelson, J. A. 2013. Ethics and the economist: What climate change demands of us. *Ecological Economics*, 85: 145–54.

Nelson, J. A. 2018. *Economics for Humans*. Chicago: University of Chicago Press.

Newman, J. and Clarke, J. 2009. *Publics, Politics and Power: Remaking the Public in Public Services*. Los Angeles: Sage.

Newman, J. H. 1875. *The Idea of a University*. London: Basil Montagu Pickering.

Neyra, R. 2019. Constructing the people: Left populism and degrowth movements. *The European Legacy*, 24 (5): 563–9.

Ngũgĩ wa Thiong'o. 1986. *Decolonising the Mind: The Politics of Language in African Literature*. Nairobi: EAEP.

Ngũgĩ wa Thiong'o. 1993. *Moving the Centre: The Struggle for Cultural Freedom*. Nairobi: EAEP.

Nguyen, M. T. N., Zavoretti, R. and Tronto, J. 2017. Beyond the global care chain: Boundaries, institutions and ethics of care. *Ethics and Social Welfare*, 11 (3): 199–212.

Ní Aoláin, F., Cahn, N. R., Haynes, D. F. and Valji, N. (eds.). 2018. *The Oxford Handbook of Gender and Conflict*. Oxford University Press.

Nibert, D. 2013. *Animal Oppression and Human Violence: Domesecration, Capitalism, and Global Conflict*. New York: Columbia University Press.

Noddings, N. 1984. *Caring: A Feminine Approach to Ethics and Moral Education* Berkeley, CA: University of California Press.

Noddings, N. 2001. The care tradition: Beyond 'add women and stir'. *Theory into Practice*, 40 (1): 29–34.

Nussbaum, M. C. 1995a. Emotions and women's capabilities. In Nussbaum, M. C. and Glover, J. (eds.), *Women, Culture, and Development: A Study of Human Capabilities*. Oxford: Oxford University Press, pp. 360–95.

Nussbaum, M. C. 1995b. Human capabilities. In Nussbaum, M. C. and Glover, J. (eds.), *Women, Culture, and Development: A Study of Human Capabilities*. Oxford: Oxford University Press, pp. 61–104.

Nussbaum, M. C. 2001. *Upheavals of Thought: The Intelligence of Emotions*. Cambridge: Cambridge University Press.

Nussbaum, M. C. 2013. *Political Emotions: Why Love Matters for Justice*. Cambridge, MA: Harvard University Press.

O'Brien, M. 2007. Mothers' emotional care work in education and its moral imperative. *Gender and Education*, 19 (2): 159–77.

O'Connell Davidson, J. 2013. Troubling freedom: Migration, debt, and modern slavery. *Migration Studies*, 1 (2): 176–95.

O'Connor, M. 2019. *The Sex Economy*. Newcastle: Agenda.

OECD–FAO (Organisation for Economic Co-operation and

Development–Food and Agriculture Organization of the United Nations). 2011. *OECD–FAO Agricultural Outlook 2011–2020*. Paris: OECD. DOI: 10.1787/agr_outlook-2011-en.

OECD–FAO (Organisation for Economic Co-operation and Development–Food and Agriculture Organization of the United Nations). 2020. *OECD–FAO Agricultural Outlook 2020–2029*. Paris: OECD. DOI: 10.1787/1112c23b-en.

O'Flynn, G. and Petersen E. B. 2007. The 'good life' and the 'rich portfolio': Young women, schooling and neoliberal subjectification. *British Journal of Sociology of Education*, 28 (4): 459–72.

O'Hagan, C., O'Connor, P., Myers, E. S., Baisner, L., Apostolov, G. et al. 2019. Perpetuating academic capitalism and maintaining gender orders through career practices in STEM in universities. *Critical Studies in Education*, 60 (2): 205–25.

O'Keefe, T. and Courtois, A. 2019. 'Not one of the family': Gender and precarious work in the neoliberal university. *Gender, Work & Organization*, 26: 463–79.

Okin, S. M. 1989. *Justice, Gender, and the Family*. New York: Basic Books.

Okin, S. M. 1994. Political liberalism, justice, and gender. *Ethics*, 105 (1): 23–43.

Oksala, J. 2016. Affective labor and feminist politics. *Signs: Journal of Women in Culture and Society*, 41 (2): 281–303.

Oleson, J. C. 2016. The new eugenics: Black hyper-incarceration and human abatement. *Social Sciences*, 5 (4): 66-n/a. DOI: http://dx.doi.org.ucd.idm. oclc.org/10.3390/socsci5040066.

Oliver, M. 1990. *The Politics of Disablement*. Basingstoke: Macmillan.

Olivieri, N. 2003. Patients' health or company profits? The commercialisation of academic research. *Science and Engineering Ethics*, 9: 29–41.

O'Neil, C. 2016. *Weapons of Math Destruction: How Big Data Increases Inequality and Threatens Democracy*. New York: Crown.

O'Neill, C. 1992. *Telling It Like It Is*. Dublin: Combat Poverty Agency.

Oxfam. 2020. *Time to Care: Unpaid and Underpaid Care Work and the Global Inequality Crisis*. Oxfam Briefing paper presented to the World Economic Forum, Davos, January. Oxford: Oxfam.

Oxfam. 2021. *The Inequality Virus*. Oxfam Briefing paper presented to the World Economic Forum, Davos, January. Oxford: Oxfam.

Page, J. 2011. Do mothers want professional carers to love their babies? *Journal of Early Childhood Research*, 9 (3): 310–23.

Page, J. 2018. Characterising the principles of professional love in early childhood care and education, *International Journal of Early Years Education*, 26 (2): 125–41.

Palmer, C. and Sandoe, P. 2014. For their own good: Captive cats and routine confinement. In Gruen, L. (ed.), *The Ethics of Captivity*. Oxford: Oxford University Press, pp. 135–55.

Park, L. and Pellow, D. 2011. *The Slums of Aspen*. New York: New York University Press.

Parker Harris, S., Owen, R. and Gould, R. 2012. Parity of participation in liberal welfare states: Human rights, neoliberalism, disability and employment. *Disability & Society*, 27 (6): 823–36.

Parkin, F. 1979. *Marxism and Class Theory: A Bourgeois Critique.* New York: Columbia University Press.

Parreñas, R. S. 2005. *Children of Global Migration: Transnational Families and Gendered Woes.* Stanford: Stanford University Press.

Paskov, P. and Dewilde, C. 2012. Income inequality and solidarity in Europe. *Research in Social Stratification and Mobility*, 30: 415–32.

Patel, R. and Moore, J. W. 2018. *A History of the World in Seven Cheap Things: A Guide to Capitalism, Nature and the Future of the Planet.* New York: Verso.

Pateman, C. 1988. *The Sexual Contract.* Stanford: Stanford University Press.

Patterson, R. 2013. Transnational capitalist class: What's race got to do with it? Everything! *Globalizations*, 10 (5): 673–90.

Pearson, R. 2019. A feminist analysis of neoliberalism and austerity policies in the UK. *Soundings*, 71: 28–39.

Pellow, L. 2007. *Resisting Global Toxics: Transnational Movements for Environmental Justice.* Cambridge, MA: MIT Press.

Pentland, A. 2014. *Social Physics: How Good Ideas Spread – The Lessons from a New Science.* London: Penguin.

Perkins, P. E. 2019. Climate justice, commons, and degrowth. *Ecological Economics*, 160: 183–90.

Peters, M. A. 2005. The new prudentialism in education: Actuarial rationality and the entrepreneurial self. *Educational Theory*, 55 (2): 123–37.

Peters, M. A. 2016. Education, neoliberalism, and human capital. In Springer, S., Birch, K. and MacLeavy, J. (eds.), *The Handbook of Neoliberalism*. Abingdon: Routledge, pp. 297–307.

Petersen, P. B. 1989. The pioneering efforts of Major General William Crozier (1855–1942) in the field of management. *Journal of Management*, 15 (3): 503–16.

Petrakaki, D. and Kornelakis, A. 2016. 'We can only request what's in our protocol': Technology and work autonomy in healthcare. *New Technology, Work and Employment*, 31 (3): 223–7.

Petrovic, Z., Djordjevic, V., Milicevic, D., Nastasijevic, I. and Parunovic, N. 2015. Meat production and consumption: Environmental consequences. *Procedia Food Science*, 5: 235–8.

Pew Commission. 2008. *Putting Meat on the Table: Industrial Farm Animal Production in America.* Baltimore: Pew Charitable Trusts and Johns Hopkins Bloomberg School of Public Health.

Piketty, T. 2014. *Capital in the Twenty-First Century.* Cambridge, MA: Belknap Press of Harvard University Press.

Plumwood, V. 2000. Integrating ethical frameworks for animals, humans, and nature: A critical feminist eco-socialist analysis. *Ethics and the Environment*, 5 (2): 285–322.

Pocock, B. 2005. Work/care regimes: Institutions, culture and behaviour and the Australian case. *Gender, Work & Organization*, 12 (1): 32–49.

Polanyi, K. 1932. *Economy and Democracy*, trans. Polanyi-Levitt, K. http://www.karipolanyilevitt.com/wp-content/uploads/2013/10/5_KP-Economy-andvDemocracy.pdf.

Polanyi, K. 1934. The essence of fascism. In Lewis, J., Polanyi, K. and Kitchin, D. K. (eds.), *Christianity and the Social Revolution*. London: Victor Gollancz, pp. 359–94.

Polanyi, K. 2001. *The Great Transformation: The Political and Economic Origin of Our Time*. Boston: Beacon Press.

Posner, R. A. 1997. Rational choice, behavioral economics, and the law. *Stanford Law Review*, 50: 1551–75.

Poulantzas, N. 1975. *Classes in Contemporary Capitalism*. London: New Left Book.

Puig de la Bellacasa, M. 2011. Matters of care in technoscience: Assembling neglected things. *Social Studies of Science*, 41(1): 85–106.

Puig de la Bellacasa, M. 2012. 'Nothing comes without its world': Thinking with care. *The Sociological Review*, 60 (2): 197–216.

Puig de la Bellacasa, M. 2017. *Matters of Care: Speculative Ethics in More than Human Worlds*. Minneapolis: University of Minnesota Press.

Pulido, L. 2017. Geographies of race and ethnicity II. *Progress in Human Geography*, 41 (4): 524–33.

Quijano, A. 2007. Coloniality and modernity/rationality. *Cultural Studies*, 21 (2–3): 168–78.

Raddon, A. 2002. Mothers in the academy: Positioned and positioning within discourses of the 'successful academic' and the 'good mother'. *Studies in Higher Education*, 27 (4): 387–403.

Raley, S., Bianchi, S. M. and Wang, W. 2012. When do fathers care? Mothers' economic contribution and fathers' involvement in childcare. *American Journal of Sociology*, 117 (5): 1422–59.

Rancière, J. 1999. *Disagreement: Politics and Philosophy*. Minneapolis, MN: University of Minnesota Press.

Rand, A. and Branden, N. 1964. *The Virtue of Selfishness: A New Concept of Egoism*. New York: New American Library.

Rawls, J. 1971. *A Theory of Justice*. Oxford: Oxford University Press.

Rawls, J. 1993. *Political Liberalism*. New York: Columbia University Press.

Reardon, S. 2011. The widening academic achievement gap between the rich and the poor: New evidence and possible explanations. In Murnane, R. and Duncan, G. (eds.), *Whither Opportunity? Rising Inequality, Schools, and Children's Life Chances*. New York: Russell Sage Foundation, pp. 91–116.

Reay, D. 1998. *Class Work: Mothers' Involvement in Their Children's Primary Schooling*. London: UCL Press.

Reay, D. 2005. Beyond consciousness? The psychic landscape of social class. *Sociology*, 39: 911–28.

Redhead, S. (ed.). 2004. *The Paul Virilio Reader*. New York: Columbia University Press.

Regan, T. 1983. *The Case for Animal Rights*. Berkeley, CA: University of California Press.

Reuter, S. Z. 2018. Intersecting ethics of responsibility: Childless academic women and their ambivalence in reproductive decision-making. *Women's Studies International Forum*, 70: 99–108.

Ricoeur, P. 1986. *Lectures on Ideology and Utopia*. New York: Columbia University Press.

Robinson, C. 2000. *Black Marxism: The Making of the Black Radical Tradition*. Chapel Hill: University of North Carolina Press.

Robinson, F. 2011. *The Ethics of Care: A Feminist Approach to Human Security*. Philadelphia: Temple University Press.

Robinson, F. 2015. Care, gender and global social justice: Rethinking 'ethical globalization'. *Journal of Global Ethics*, 2 (1): 5–25.

Robinson, W. I. 2012. Global capitalism theory and the emergence of transnational elites. *Critical Sociology*, 38 (3): 349–63.

Rodríguez-Pose, A. and von Berlepsch, V. 2014. Social capital and individual happiness in Europe. *Journal of Happiness Studies*, 15: 357–86.

Roelants, B., Eum, H., Eşim, S., Novkovic, S., and Katajamäki, W. (eds.). 2019. *Cooperatives and the World of Work*. London: Routledge.

Roex, K., Huijdts, T. and Sieben, I. 2019. Attitudes towards income inequality: 'Winners' versus 'losers' of the perceived meritocracy. *Acta Sociologica*, 62 (1): 47–63.

Rojas, C. 2016. Contesting the colonial logics of the international: Toward a relational politics for the pluriverse. *International Political Sociology*, 10: 369–82.

Rollin, B. E. 2017. The ethics of animal research: Theory and practice. In Kalof, L. (ed.), *The Oxford Handbook of Animal Studies*. Oxford: Oxford University Press, pp. 345–63.

Romagnoli, A. and Wall, G. 2012. 'I know I'm a good mum': Young, low-income mothers' experiences with risk perception, intensive mothering ideology and parenting education programmes. *Health, Risk & Society*, 14: 273–89.

Romero, M. 2018. Reflections on globalized care chains and migrant women workers. *Critical Sociology*, 44 (7–8): 1179–89.

Romero, M. and Perez, N. 2016. Conceptualizing the foundation of inequalities in care work. *American Behavioral Scientist*, 60 (2): 172–88.

Rorty, R. 1989. *Contingency, Irony, and Solidarity*. Cambridge: Cambridge University Press.

Rosa, H. 2013. *Social Acceleration: A New Theory of Modernity*. New York: Columbia University Press.

Rosa, H., Dörre, K. and Lessenich, S. 2017. Appropriation, activation and acceleration: The escalatory logics of capitalist modernity and the crises of dynamic stabilization. *Theory, Culture & Society*, 34 (1): 53–73.

Rosanvallon, P. 2013. *The Society of Equals*, trans. Goldhammer, A. Cambridge, MA: Harvard University Press.

Rose, H. 1983. Hand, brain, and heart: A feminist epistemology for the natural sciences. *Signs: Journal of Women in Culture and Society*, 9 (1): 73–90.

Rose, N. 1999. *Powers of Freedom: Reframing Political Thought*. Cambridge: Cambridge University Press.

Roser, M. and Ortiz-Ospina, E. 2013. Global extreme poverty. *Our World in Data*. https://ourworldindata.org/extreme-poverty.

Roulstone, A. 2015. Personal Independence Payments, welfare reform and the shrinking disability category. *Disability & Society*, 30 (5): 673–88.

Rubery, J., Ward K., Grimshaw D. and Beynon, H. 2005. Working time, industrial relations and the employment relationship. *Time & Society*, 14: 89–111.

Ruby, S. and Scholz, S. 2018. Care, care work and the struggle for a careful world from the perspective of the sociology of masculinities. *Österreichische Zeitschrift für Soziologie*, 43: 73–83.

Ruddick, S. 1989. *Maternal Thinking*. Boston: Beacon Press.

Rudrappa, S. 2015. *Discounted Life: The Price of Global Surrogacy in India*. New York: New York University Press.

Russell, B. 2012. Professional call centres, professional workers, and the paradox of the algorithm: The case of telenursing. *Work, Employment and Society*, 26: 195–210.

Rusu, M. S. 2018. Theorising love in sociological thought: Classical contributions to a sociology of love. *Journal of Classical Sociology*, 18 (1): 3–20.

Said, E. W. 1978. *Orientalism*. New York: Pantheon Books.

Salter, C. 2015. Animals and war: Anthropocentrism and technoscience. *Nanoethics*, 9: 11–21.

Sánchez Bajo, C. and Roelants, B. 2011. *Capital and the Debt Trap: Learning from Cooperatives in the Global Crisis*. Basingstoke: Palgrave Macmillan.

Sandel, M. 2020. *The Tyranny of Merit*. London. Penguin.

Sassen, S. 2001. *The Global City*. Princeton: Princeton University Press.

Sassen, S. 2014. *Expulsions: Brutality and Complexity in the Global Economy*. Cambridge, MA: Harvard University Press.

Sauder, M. and Espeland, W. 2009. The discipline of rankings: Tight coupling and organizational change. *American Sociological Review*, 74 (1): 63–82.

Sayer, A. 2005. Class, moral worth and recognition. *Sociology*, 39: 947–63.

Sayer, A. 2009. The injustice of unequal work. *Soundings*, 43: 102–13.

Sayer, A. 2011. *Why Things Matter to People: Social Science, Values and Ethical Life*. Cambridge: Cambridge University Press.

Sayer, A. 2017. Values within reason. *Canadian Review of Sociology*, 54 (4): 468–75.

Scerri, A., Sammut, R. and Scerri, C. 2021. Formal caregivers' perceptions and experiences of using pet robots for persons living with dementia in long-term care: A meta-ethnography. *Journal of Advanced Nursing*, 77 (1): 83–97.

Schaffner Goldberg, G. (ed.). 2010. *Poor Women in Rich Countries: The Feminization of Poverty over the Life Course*. Oxford: Oxford University Press.

Scheff, T. J. 2000. Shame and the social bond: A sociological theory. *Sociological Theory*, 18 (1): 84–99.

Scheper-Hughes, N. and Bourgois, P. (eds.). 2004. *Violence in War and Peace: An Anthology*. Oxford: Blackwell.

Schinkel, W. 2013. Regimes of violence and the *trias violentiae*. *European Journal of Social Theory*, 16 (3): 310–25.

Schoenhals, M. 2019. *Work, Love and Learning in Utopia: Equality Reimagined*. New York: Routledge.

Scholz, R. 2009. Patriarchy and commodity society: Gender without the body. *Mediations*, 27 (1–2): 123–42. http://www.mediationsjournal.org/articles/patriarchy-and-commodity-society.

Scholz, R. 2011. *Das Geschlecht des Kapitalismus: Feministische Theorien und die postmoderne Metamorphose des Kapitals*. Bad Honnef: Horlemann.

Schöneck, N. 2018. Europeans' work and life: Out of balance? An empirical test of assumptions from the 'acceleration debate'. *Time & Society*, 27 (1): 3–39.

Sennett, R. 1998. *The Corrosion of Character*. New York: W. W. Norton.

Sennett, R. and Cobb, J. 1972. *The Hidden Injuries of Class*. New York: Vintage Books.

Sevenhuijsen, S. 1998. *Citizenship and the Ethics of Care: Feminist Considerations on Justice, Morality and Justice*. London: Routledge.

Shahin, S. and Zheng, P. 2020. Big data and the illusion of choice: Comparing the evolution of India's Aadhaar and China's Social Credit System as technosocial discourses. *Social Science Computer Review*, 38 (1): 25–41.

Shakespeare, T. 2000. *Help*. Birmingham: British Association of Social Workers.

Shapiro, K. 2007. The caring sleuth: Portrait of an animal rights activist. In Donovan, J. and Adams, C. J. (eds.), *The Feminist Care Tradition in Animal Ethics*. New York: Columbia University Press, pp. 153–73.

Shefer, G., Henderson, C., Frost-Gaskin, M. and Pacitti, R. 2016. Only making things worse: A qualitative study of the impact of wrongly removing disability benefits from people with mental illness. *Community Mental Health Journal*, 52 (7): 834–41.

Shore, C. and Wright, S. 2015. Audit culture revisited: Rankings, ratings and the reassembling of society. *Current Anthropology*, 56 (3): 421–39.

Shukin, N. 2009. *Animal Capital: Rendering Life in Biopolitical Times*. Minneapolis: University of Minnesota Press.

Simpson, J. 2019. *Permanent Revolution: The Reformation and the Illiberal Roots of Liberalism*. Cambridge, MA: Harvard University Press.

Singer, P. 1975. *Animal Liberation: A New Ethics for Our Treatment of Animals*. New York: New York Review.

Singer, P. 1993. *Practical Ethics*, 2nd edn. Cambridge: Cambridge University Press.

Skeggs, B. 1997. *Formations of Class and Gender: Becoming Respectable.* London: Sage.

Skeggs, B. 2004. *Class, Self, Culture.* London: Routledge.

Sklair, L. 2000. *The Transnational Capitalist Class.* Oxford: Blackwell.

Slaughter, S. and Leslie, L. 2001. Expanding and elaborating the concept of academic capitalism. *Organization*, 8 (2): 154–61.

Slicer, D. 2007. Your daughter or your dog? A feminist assessment of the animal research issue. In Donovan, J. and Adams, C. J. (eds.), *The Feminist Care Tradition in Animal Ethics.* New York: Columbia University Press, pp. 105–24.

Smith, D. E. 1987. *The Everyday World as Problematic: A Feminist Sociology.* Boston: Northeastern University Press.

Smith, D. E. 1990. *The Conceptual Practices of Power: A Feminist Sociology of Knowledge.* Boston: Northeastern University Press.

Smyth, E. 2009. Buying your way into college? Private tuition and the transition to higher education in Ireland. *Oxford Review of Education*, 35 (1): 1–22.

Snowden, E. 2013. Open letter to the people of Brazil. *Washington Post*, 17 December.

Soederberg, S. 2014. *Debtfare States and the Poverty Industry.* Abingdon: Routledge.

Sorokin, P. A. 2002 [1954]. *The Ways and Power of Love: Types, Factors, and Techniques of Moral Transformation.* Boston: Beacon Press.

Sowa, F., Staples, R. and Zapfel, S. (eds.). 2018. *The Transformation of Work in Welfare State Organizations: New Public Management and the Institutional Diffusion of Ideas.* London: Routledge.

Spivak, G. 1988. Can the subaltern speak? In Nelson, C. and Grossberg, L. (eds.), *Marxism and the Interpretation of Culture.* London: Macmillan, pp. 271–313.

Springer, S. 2016. The violence of neoliberalism. In Springer, S., Birch, K. and MacLeavy, J. (eds.), *The Handbook of Neoliberalism.* Abingdon: Routledge, pp. 153–63.

Standing, G. 2011. *The Precariat: The New Dangerous Class.* London: Bloomsbury.

Stanley, L. and Wise, S. 1993. *Breaking Out Again: Feminist Ontology and Epistemology.* London: Routledge.

Stets, J. and McCaffree, K. 2014. Linking morality, altruism and social solidarity using identity theory. In Jeffries, V. (ed.), *The Palgrave Handbook of Altruism, Morality and Social Solidarity.* Basingstoke: Palgrave, 333–51.

Stjernø, S. 2004. *Solidarity in Europe: The History of an Idea.* Cambridge: Cambridge University Press.

Stjernø, S. 2011. The idea of solidarity in Europe. *European Journal of Social Law*, 3: 156–76.

Storey, A. 2019. Authoritarian neoliberalism in Europe: The red herring of ordoliberalism. *Critical Sociology*, 45 (7–8): 1035–45.

Strazdins, L. and Broom, D. H. 2004. Acts of love (and work): Gender imbalances in emotional work and women's psychological distress. *Journal of Family Issues*, 25 (3): 356–78.

Streeck, W. 2016. *How Will Capitalism End?* London: Verso.

Sturge, G. 2019. *UK Prison Population Statistics*. Briefing Paper no. CBP-04334, 23 July. London: House of Commons Library.

Sullivan, S. and Tuana, N. (eds.). 2007. *Race and Epistemologies of Ignorance*. Albany: SUNY Press.

Szebehely, M. and Meagher, G. 2018. Nordic eldercare: Weak universalism becoming weaker? *Journal of European Social Policy*, 28 (3): 294–308.

Taibbi, M. 2014. *The Divide: American Injustice in the Age of the Wealth Gap*. New York: Spiegel and Grau.

Tawney, R. H. 1964. *Equality*. London: Allen and Unwin.

Tawney, R. H. 1972. *Religion and the Rise of Capitalism: A Historical Study*. Harmondsworth: Penguin.

Taylor, F. 1911. *Principles of Scientific Management*. New York: Harper and Brothers.

Taylor-Gooby, P. (ed.). 2005. *Ideas and Welfare State Reform in Western Europe*. Basingstoke: Palgrave Macmillan.

Taylor-Gooby, P. 2011. Opportunity and solidarity, *Journal of Social Policy*, 40 (3): 453–70.

Tett, L. and Hamilton, M. (eds.). 2021. *Resisting Neoliberalism in Education: Local, National and Transnational Perspectives*. Bristol: Policy Press.

Thompson, J. B. 1984. *Studies in the Theory of Ideology*. Cambridge: Polity.

Thornton, M. 2013. The mirage of merit. *Australian Feminist Studies*, 28 (76): 127–43.

Thrift, N. 2005. *Knowing Capitalism*. London: Sage.

Tilly, C. 1999. *Durable Inequality*. Berkeley, CA: University of California Press.

Tironi, M. and Rodríguez-Giralt, I. 2017. Healing, knowing, enduring: Care and politics in damaged worlds. *The Sociological Review*, 65 (2): 89–109.

Toffoletti, K. and Starr, K. 2016. Women academics and work–life balance: Gendered discourses of work and care. *Gender, Work & Organization*, 23 (5): 489–504.

Tooze, A. 2018. *Crashed: How a Decade of Financial Crises Changed the World*. New York: Allen Lane.

Torres, B. 2007. *Making a Killing: The Political Economy of Animal Rights*. Oakland: AK Press.

Traustadóttir, R. 2000. Disability reform and women's caring work. In Harrington Meyer, M. (ed.), *Care Work: Gender, Class and the Welfare State*. London: Routledge, pp. 249–69.

Tresson, C. 2018. Managerial control of public sector IT professionals via IT systems. In Sowa, F., Staples, R. and Zapfel, S. (eds.), *The Transformation of Work in Welfare State Organizations: New Public Management and the Institutional Diffusion of Ideas.* London: Routledge, pp.13–34.

Tronto, J. C. 1993. *Moral Boundaries: A Political Argument for an Ethic of Care.* New York: Routledge.

Tronto, J. C. 2013. *Caring Democracy: Markets, Equality, and Justice.* New York: New York University Press.

Tronto, J. C. 2017. There is an alternative: *Homines curans* and the limits of neoliberalism. *International Journal of Care and Caring,* 1 (1): 27–43.

Tsri, K. 2016. *Africans are Not Black: The Case for Conceptual Liberation.* London: Routledge.

Tuhiwai Smith, L. 1999. *Decolonizing Methodologies: Research and Indigenous Peoples.* London: Zed Books and University of Otago.

Twigg, J. 2000. Carework as a form of bodywork. *Ageing and Society,* 20: 389–411.

Twine, R. 2012. Revealing the 'animal-industrial complex': A concept and method for critical animal studies. *Journal for Critical Animal Studies,* 10 (1): 12–39.

Tyler, I. 2009. Against abjection. *Feminist Theory,* 10 (1): 77–98.

Tyner, J. 2016. *Violence in Capitalism: Devaluing Life in an Age of Responsibility.* Lincoln, NB: University of Nebraska Press.

UCD (University College Dublin) School of Public Health. 2010. *All Ireland Traveller Health Study: Our Geels.* Dublin: University College Dublin.

Uhls, Y. and Greenfield, P. 2011. The value of fame: Preadolescent perceptions of popular media and their relationship to future aspirations. *Developmental Psychology,* 48 (2): 315–26.

UN Population Division (United Nations Population Division). 2019. *International Migration.* https://www.un.org/en/development/desa/population/migration/data/estimates2/estimates19.asp.

UNHCR (United Nations High Commission for Refugees). 2020. *Figures at a Glance.* https://www.unhcr.org/figures-at-a-glance.html.

Vahabi, M. and Wong, J. P. 2017. Caught between a rock and a hard place: Mental health of migrant live-in caregivers in Canada. *BMC Public Health,* 17 (498). DOI: 10.1186/s12889-017-4431-4.

Vahter, P. and Masso, J. 2019. The contribution of multinationals to wage inequality: Foreign ownership and the gender pay gap. *Review of World Economics,* 155: 105–48.

Vaittinen, T. 2015. The power of the vulnerable body: A new political understanding of care. *International Feminist Journal of Politics,* 17 (1): 100–18.

Van Aswegen, J. 2020. Disabling discourses and charitable model of disability: Labour market activation for people with disabilities, Ireland – a critical policy analysis. *Disability & Society,* 35 (3): 435–59.

Vandenberghe, F. 2017. Sociology as moral philosophy (and vice versa). *Canadian Review of Sociology/La Société Canadienne de Sociologie,* 54 (4): 405–22.

Vandenberghe, F. 2018. Sociology as practical philosophy and moral science. *Theory, Culture & Society,* 35 (3): 77–97.

Van Gervan, M. and Ossewaarde, M. 2012. The welfare state's making of cosmopolitan Europe. *European Societies*, 14 (1): 35–55.

Veltmeyer, H. 2019. Resistance, class struggle and social movements in Latin America: Contemporary dynamics. *The Journal of Peasant Studies*, 46 (6): 1264–85.

Verma, R. and Apple, M. (eds.). 2020. *Disrupting Hate in Education: Teacher Activists, Democracy, and Global Pedagogies of Interruption*. New York: Routledge.

Vincent, C. and Maxwell, C. 2016. Parenting priorities and pressures: Furthering understanding of 'concerted cultivation'. *Discourse: Studies in the Cultural Politics of Education*, 37 (2): 269–81.

Voght, K. 2021. Planes, trains, and working women. *Mother Jones*, 16 April. https://www.motherjones.com/politics/2021/04/caregiving-is-infrastructure-joe-biden.

Wacquant, L. 2009. *Punishing the Poor: The Neoliberal Government of Social Insecurity*. Durham, NC: Duke University Press.

Walby, S. 2009. *Globalization and Inequalities: Complexity and Contested Modernities*. London: Sage.

Walby, S., Towers, J. and Francis, B. 2014. Mainstreaming domestic and gender-based violence into sociology and the criminology of violence. *The Sociological Review*, 62 (S2): 187–214.

Walker, U. M. 2007. *Moral Understandings: A Feminist Study in Ethics*. New York: Oxford University Press.

Walkerdine, V. 2016. Affective history, working-class communities and self-determination. *The Sociological Review*, 64: 699–714.

Walkerdine, V., Lucey, H. and Melody, J. 2001. *Growing Up Girl: Psychosocial Explorations of Gender and Class*. Basingstoke: Palgrave Macmillan.

Walmsley, R. 2018. *World Prison Population List*, 12th edn. London: Institute for Criminal Policy Research. https://www.prisonstudies.org/news/icpr-launches-12th-edition-world-prison-population-list.

Waring, M. 2004. *Counting for Nothing: What Men Value and What Women Are Worth*. Toronto: University of Toronto Press.

Watson, D. 2019. Fordism: A review essay. *Labor History*, 60 (2): 144–59.

Weber, M. 1930. *The Protestant Ethic and the Spirit of Capitalism*, trans. Parsons, T. Boston: Unwin Hyman.

Weber, M. 1978. *Economy and Society: An Outline of Interpretive Sociology*, vol. 2. London: University of California Press.

Weber, M. 1994. Suffrage and democracy in Germany. In Lassman, P. and Speirs, R. (eds.), *Weber: Political Writings*. Cambridge: Cambridge University Press, pp. 80–129.

Weicht, B. 2019. The commodification of informal care: Joining and resisting marketization processes. In Atzmüller, R., Aulenbacher, B., Brand, U., Décieux, F., Fischer, K. et al. (eds.), *Capitalism in Transformation: Movements and Countermovements in the 21st Century*. Cheltenham: Edward Elgar, pp. 261–73.

Weiner, R. R. and López, I. 2017. *Los Indignados: Tides of Social Insertion in Spain*. Winchester/Washington, DC: Zero Books.

Weis, T. 2014. *The Ecological Hoofprint: The Global Burden of Industrial Livestock*. London: Zed Books.

Wetherell, M. 2015. Trends in the turn to affect: A social psychological critique. *Body & Society*, 21 (2): 139–66.

WHO (World Health Organization). 2018. *Global Health Workforce Statistics: The 2018 Update*. Geneva: WHO.

WHO (World Health Organization). 2019. *Health in Prison: Factsheets for 38 European Countries*. Geneva: WHO.

Wiebers, D. O. and Feigin, V. L. 2020. What the COVID-19 crisis is telling humanity. *Neuroepidemiology*, 54 (4): 1–4.

Wilkinson, E. 2014. Love in the multitude? A feminist critique of love as a political concept. In Ferguson, A. and Jónasdóttir, A. G. (eds.), *Love: A Question for Feminism in the Twenty-First Century*. New York: Routledge, pp. 237–49.

Wilkinson, R. G. and Pickett, K. 2009. *The Spirit Level: Why More Equal Societies Almost Always Do Better*. London: Penguin.

Wilkinson, R. G. and Pickett, K. 2018. *The Inner Level: How More Equal Societies Reduce Stress, Restore Sanity and Improve Everybody's Wellbeing*. London: Allen Lane.

Williams, F. 2010. Migration and care: Themes, concepts and challenges. *Social Policy and Society*, 9 (3): 390–2.

Williams, F. 2018. Care: Intersections of scales, inequalities, and crises. *Current Sociology*, 66 (4): 547–61.

Williams, R. 1973. Base and superstructure in Marxist cultural theory. *New Left Review*, 82: 3–16.

Williams, R. 1977. *Marxism and Literature*. Oxford: Oxford University Press.

Winters, J. A. 2011. *Oligarchy*. New York: Cambridge University Press.

Witz, A. and Savage, M. 1991. The gender of organizations. *The Sociological Review*, 39 (Suppl. 1): 3–62.

Wright, E. O. 2010. *Envisioning Real Utopias*. London, Verso.

Wright, J. 2019. Robots vs migrants? Reconfiguring the future of Japanese institutional eldercare. *Critical Asian Studies*, 51 (3): 331–54.

Wright, S. and Shore, C. (eds.). 2017. *Death of the Public University? Uncertain Futures for Higher Education in the Knowledge Economy*. New York: Berghahn.

Yeates, N. 2009. *Globalizing Care Economies and Migrant Workers: Explorations in Global Care Chains*. Basingstoke: Palgrave Macmillan.

Young, I. M. 1990. *Justice and the Politics of Difference*. Princeton: Princeton University Press.

Young, M. 1971. *The Rise of the Meritocracy, 1870–2033*. London: Thames and Hudson.

Yuill, C. and Mueller-Hirth, N. 2019. Paperwork, compassion and temporal conflicts in British social work. *Time & Society*, 28 (4): 1532–51.

Yuval-Davis, N. 2006. Intersectionality and feminist politics. *European Journal of Women's Studies*, 13 (3): 193–209.

Žižek, S. 2008. *Violence*. New York: Picador.

Zuboff, S. 2019. *The Age of Surveillance Capitalism*. New York: Verso.

Index